WHAT MAKES A DIFFERENCE: EARLY HEAD START EVALUATION FINDINGS IN A DEVELOPMENTAL CONTEXT

EDITED BY

John M. Love, Rachel Chazan-Cohen,

Helen Raikes, and Jeanne Brooks-Gunn

Patricia J. Bauer
Series Editor*

MONOGRAPHS OF THE SOCIETY FOR RESEARCH IN CHILD DEVELOPMENT

Serial No. 306, Vol. 78, No. 1, 2013

*This monograph was accepted under the editorship of W. Andrew Collins.

WILEY   *Boston, Massachusetts   Oxford, United Kingdom*

EDITOR
PATRICIA J. BAUER
Emory University

MANAGING EDITOR
ADAM MARTIN
Society for Research in Child Development

EDITORIAL ASSISTANT
LAURA KOZMINSKI
Society for Research in Child Development

WHAT MAKES A DIFFERENCE: EARLY HEAD START EVALUATION FINDINGS IN A DEVELOPMENTAL CONTEXT

CONTENTS

ABSTRACT*

The federal Early Head Start (EHS) program began in 1995, and a randomized trial was conducted to evaluate the efficacy of 17 EHS programs. In all, 3,001 low-income families (35% African American, 24% Hispanic, and 37% White) with a pregnant women or an infant under the age of 12 months were randomly assigned to a treatment or control group (with 91% of the treatment group receiving some services). Data were collected when the children were about 1, 2, and 3 years of age, and at age 5 (2 years after leaving EHS). Research questions examined (1) impacts of EHS at ages 2 and 3 (when services were being offered) and at age 5, and (2) contributions of early education experiences across children's first 5 years of life. Child outcomes included cognition, language, attention, behavior problems, and health; maternal outcomes included parenting, mental health, and employment.

Overall impact analyses at ages 2 and 3 indicated that EHS benefited children and families: impacts were seen in all domains, with effect sizes of significant impacts ranging from .10 to .20. At age 5, EHS children had better attention and approaches toward learning as well as fewer behavior problems than the control group, although they did not differ on early school achievement. Subgroup analyses indicated that cognitive impacts were sustained 2 years after the program ended for African American children and language impacts for Hispanic children who spoke Spanish. Some significant family benefits were seen at age 5. Mediated analyses identified which child and family impacts at ages 2 and 3 contributed to the child impacts at age 5 (most relevant were earlier treatment effects on child cognition and on engagement with the parent). Growth curve analyses were also conducted.

Although fewer than half the children enrolled in center-based preschool programs between ages 3 and 4, almost 90% participated in the year preceding kindergarten. A higher percentage of EHS than control children were enrolled. Nonexperimental analyses suggested that formal program participation enhanced children's readiness for school while also increasing parent-reported aggression. At age 5, those children and families who experienced EHS followed by formal programs fared best overall. However,

---

*This monograph was accepted under the editorship of W. Andrew Collins.

the benefits of the two experiences were associated with outcomes in different ways. Benefits in language, behavior, and parenting were associated primarily with EHS; benefits in early school achievement were associated primarily with preschool attendance.

I. BACKGROUND LITERATURE REVIEW PERTAINING TO THE EARLY HEAD START STUDY

Helen H. Raikes, Jeanne Brooks-Gunn, and John M. Love

Although considerable information exists about the effects of early interventions for at-risk children, we know more about intervention effects and results of investments in programs for children of specific ages, for example, 3- to 5-year-olds, than about when to invest or for whom specific investments are most advantageous across the age span from birth to 5. Outside of a few program evaluations that span the period from birth to age 5 (Garber & Heber, 1981; Ramey & Campbell, 1984; St. Pierre, Goodson, Layzer, & Bernstein, 1994), little is known about cumulative intervention experiences during the period from birth until formal schooling begins. Moreover, variations in program models and timing of services have not been examined. Investigation of the variability in quantity and timing of services over the years from birth to age 5, the focus of this monograph, is likely to be useful to programs for fine-tuning the timing and intensity of interventions, to policy makers for optimizing early childhood investments, and to developmental scientists for better understanding trajectories of development especially of poor children in the context of environmental influences.

This monograph reports on a program evaluation of 3,001 children in 17 sites from poor families, half of whom were randomized to receive Early Head Start (EHS) services in the first 3 years of life (for some families in some sites EHS services began prenatally; ACF, 2002a; Love et al., 2005), and half of whom were not. Children's outcomes were examined at ages 2 and 3 when concurrent impacts of the EHS programs could be examined, and at age 5, 2 years after EHS ended and when formal program experiences subsequent to EHS could be examined. Analysis of program impacts for families and children in the first 5 years of life are based on an experimental evaluation. However, looking at the services that families obtained for their children in

Corresponding author: Helen Raikes, Child, Youth and Family Studies, 257 Mabel Lee Hall, University of Nebraska-Lincoln, Lincoln, Nebraska 68588-0236, email: hraikes2@unl.edu

the preschool years allows for a description of how combinations of infant and toddler (for children from birth to age 3) and preschool (for 3- to 5-year-old children) services may influence school readiness in low-income children.[1] Thus, the monograph addresses both longitudinal treatment impacts, as well as longitudinal variations in experience and associated outcomes.

The advantages of early intervention programs for vulnerable children prior to school entry are generally acknowledged (Barnett, 2011; Camilli et al., 2010; Duncan & Magnuson, 2006). Although programs may have multiple purposes, most ultimately aim to reduce gaps in school readiness between low-income and more advantaged children. Low-income children typically enter school from half to a full standard deviation below more advantaged children in academic-related domains such as vocabulary, cognition, and specific literacy-related skills, and often demonstrate challenges in social–emotional and regulatory functioning (Brooks-Gunn & Duncan, 1997; Duncan & Magnuson, 2005; Hart & Risley, 1995; Reardon & Galindo, 2009; Rouse, Brooks-Gunn, & McLanahan, 2005; Stipek & Ryan, 1997). Moreover, many of these gaps are observable much before school entry, as early as age 3 (Klebanov, Brooks-Gunn, McCarton, & McCormick, 1998) and possibly in the toddler years. Differences in children's environments during the earliest years have been linked to school-age outcomes, typically operating through links with early outcomes (Duncan, Brooks-Gunn, & Klebanov, 1994; Hart & Risley, 1995). Several notable studies document that low-income children receive less cognitive and linguistic stimulation than do children in higher-income families (Bradley et al., 1989; Brooks-Gunn & Markman, 2005; Klebanov et al., 1998; Zill, 1999). For example, low-income children receive about a fifth of the language inputs from parents that more-advantaged children receive (Hart & Risley, 1995).

Children who receive high-quality intervention services, compared to children who do not receive these services, enter school with greater skills in school-success domains (Barnett, 2011; Karoly, Kilburn & Cannon, 2005; Ramey & Ramey, 2006; Schweinhart, 2006), and continue on relatively higher success trajectories at least through elementary school (Camilli, Vargas, Ryan, & Barnett, 2010; Heckman, 2006). As a consequence, many states now invest in prekindergarten programs and/or services for younger children (Barnett, et al., 2006). Policy makers agree that high-quality early childhood services for low-income children are valuable (Brooks-Gunn, 2011; Gormley, 2011). However, most evaluations have examined effects of a single program (Olds et al., 1997; Ramey & Ramey, 2006) or for a discrete portion of the preschool years (e.g., Schweinhart, 2006). Investigations of relative and cumulative contributions of combinations of program services from birth to age 5 have been limited, although it has been recommended that comprehensive and systematic assessment of early childhood experiences over time would be

2

more productive than relying on investigations of brief or one-time programs (e.g., Reynolds, Wang, & Walberg, 2003).

In this monograph, we present findings from multiple analyses from the Early Head Start Research and Evaluation Project (EHSREP) that tell a story about when and how intervention experiences throughout the period birth to age 5 may have contributed to the outcomes for poor children at school entry. Outcomes are examined for children who were randomly assigned before age 1 into EHS or a control group and followed through age 5 (shortly before they began kindergarten). Specifically, in this monograph, we (1) examine the patterns of impacts of EHS on children ages 2, 3, and 5, emphasizing age 5 impacts measured 2 years after the program ended; (2) report on children's formal program experiences after EHS and examine the impact of EHS on the probability of children receiving follow-up program experiences; (3) report on the influences of formal preschool programs on age 5 outcomes above and beyond the effects of EHS; and (4) consider how various patterns of early experiences from birth to age 5 are associated with the observed prekindergarten outcomes. A formal preschool program is defined as a center-based program that may include child care, prekindergarten, or Head Start.[2] We present each of the findings for selected subgroups of children and families, examining variations according to race/ethnicity (African American, Hispanic, or White), and level of cumulative family demographic risk (summing across whether mother was a teenager at the time child's birth, unemployed or not in school, unmarried, receiving TANF/AFDC, and not a high school graduate at the time the study began). We also examine three EHS program models (comparing infant and toddler experiences that were initially center-based, home-based/home-visiting, or a combination of these). The monograph addresses these questions using several design and analytic approaches including experimental and nonexperimental regressions as well as more exploratory, descriptive approaches. Although confidence in inferring conclusions varies as a result of these different approaches, the several questions, linked by an overarching conceptual framework, provide fertile ground for more comprehensive ways of thinking about children's early development in the context of poverty and early childhood intervention programs than has been typical in the literature to date.

This literature review begins the monograph by laying out the theoretical foundation for the work, and it surveys what is known about the prevalence of formal program participation prior to school entry and the effects of intervention programs. We also provide an overview of the EHS program. Next, we provide an overview of the service context for low-income children birth to age 5; examine outcomes from programs for children targeting infants and toddlers, preschoolers, or children from birth to age 5; and examine extant research that pertains to subgroups of children of interest in this monograph. These subgroups are defined by race/ethnicity and level of

3

cumulative demographic risk factors. We also examine the impacts for families enrolled in different program models.

THEORETICAL FRAMEWORK

Our work is informed by a developmental perspective that suggests interventions are likely to change the slope of developmental trajectories and that differential experiences of children during various periods may influence different aspects of child well-being ("principle of developmental timing" proposed by Ramey & Ramey, 1998). This principle leads us to expect (1) that parents will be most affected by parenting services during the infant and toddler years when they are forming their expectations of the child and for their own parenting; (2) that intervention effects for the parent-child relationship and social–emotional development will be greatest during the period of relationship and attachment formation; and (3) that intervention effects for children will be greatest during periods of most rapid learning in specific developmental areas. For example, language will be most affected during periods of rapid language learning; and school-like tasks will be most affected by periods close to school entry. Our thinking has been guided by a perspective suggesting that concurrent intervention effects are most likely to influence readiness in the first 5 years. However, we have been further informed by alternative views about timing of intervention effects. Few research teams have considered the additive or interactive effects of intervention and time. We acknowledge the relative newness and potentially post hoc nature of this way of thinking currently; however, we also note the soundness of the basic principles, the importance of questions about the most effective timing of intervention for different forms of development, and challenge the field to further develop time by intervention hypotheses to guide studies in the future.

The NICHD Early Child Care Research Network (NICHD ECCRN, 2001) has proposed four alternative explanations or hypotheses for how the timing of experiences may influence development: (1) The hypothesis of Experiences at Specific Points in Development posits that interventions will have more value when timed to coincide with sensitive periods in children's development, for example, we might expect that providing responsive parenting during the first year of life might be most important for subsequent relationships; (2) the Early Experiences hypothesis suggests that early experiences will outweigh later ones; consistent with this hypothesis, we would expect some effects from EHS to outweigh those of later prekindergarten experiences because of the former's primacy in setting trajectories, as might be the case for social and emotional development; (3) the Contemporaneous Experiences hypothesis posits that current experiences may be more important than earlier ones; here, we might expect prekindergarten education to matter more than earlier services vis-à-vis school readiness; (4) the hypothesis of Incremental or Augmented Experiences suggests that early experiences produce effects that are maintained by later experiences. We might expect children who received EHS together with preschool education to be better prepared for school than children who did not receive it.

Certainly, developmental processes are amplified by transactional processes (Sameroff & Fiese, 2000), by which children's development and experiences at one point in time contribute to experiences that children receive subsequently. This way of thinking is consistent with that of Heckman and Masterov (2004), who suggest that "more begets more." Children who have more skills attract more experiences subsequently. However, little is known about the relative contributions of "early" (e.g., 0–3) and "later" (e.g., 3–5) experiences to later development.

In their conceptual approach to early childhood intervention, Ramey and Ramey (1998) postulate that intensity, directness, breadth, and flexibility of program experiences maximize opportunities for children at risk. However, precisely *when* to target intervention within the first 5 years of life, which is generally a time of rapid development, and *how* to vary intensity and breadth and for different subgroups has yet to be explicated. Moreover, as stated by the Rameys' "principle of environmental maintenance of development" (p. 117), adequate supports must be in place to maintain children's positive gains after programs end. The current study investigates variability in timing and type of intervention for children with differing characteristics. Particularly, our study investigates variability in supportive early childhood experiences in the two years following the 3 years of EHS intervention.

Heckman's (2006) analyses of early childhood provide continued support for the notion that early learning influences later learning. One set of analyses (Cunha, Heckman, Lochner, & Masterov, 2006) suggests that cognitive processes not only relate to later school success but are particularly amenable to early intervention whereas social and emotional processes seem to respond to later intervention. However, these researchers did not have the opportunity to examine social and emotional processes as early in life as we did (i.e., before 3 years of age), an investigation worth making given the importance of this early period for attachment and self-regulation. The current study provides an opportunity to investigate whether specific aspects of development are more amenable to early (0–3) invention and whether other aspects of development may be more amenable to later (3–5) intervention.

THE EARLY HEAD START PROGRAM

We begin by providing background on the EHS program, on the EHSREP, and on general findings when the program ended; this monograph emphasizes children's experiences after EHS, during the period when children were 3–5, and child and parent outcomes just prior to children's entry into kindergarten as well as describing earlier treatment impacts (at ages 2 and 3) to illustrate *patterns* of program impacts over time. The 3,001 children and families in the EHSREP enrolled in one of the 17 EHS programs chosen to participate in the study (the first 68 EHS programs were funded in fall 1995). These 17 communities were reflective of all EHS sites at the time in geographic and family diversity.

The EHS program was created through the reauthorization of the Head Start Act in 1994 and was expanded in 1998. EHS is a Head Start (HS) program and, as is true for all HS programs, must serve at least 90% families at the federal poverty level or below, must implement additional criteria so that children in families with greatest needs in communities are served, and must recruit at least 10% children with disabilities. EHS programs can begin services during pregnancy and continue to serve children and families until children reach age 3. All HS programs are two-generation, providing services for both children and parents, although many parent services may be referred to community organizations. At the time of the evaluation, up to 10% of the national HS budget could be allocated for EHS services. In 2009, the program served about 70,000 families in 65 communities. However, EHS received $1.1 billion under the American Recovery and Reinvestment Act of 2009, and in 2010 began to serve an additional 55,000 children.

EHS programs conduct community needs assessments to determine the most appropriate of four specific service delivery models for families: center-based, home-based, combination, or locally designed options. For purposes of the research, sites were classified as to whether they were offering home-based, center-based, or mixed services (a combination of home-based and center-based services). Program protocols for services to families were established by the Head Start Program Performance Standards (U.S. Department of Health and Human Services [DHHS], 1996). Requirements for each program model are specified (e.g., curriculum, educational requirements for teachers, group sizes, frequency and length of home visits, health and developmental screening) and programs are monitored every 3 years for their adherence to the Program Performance Standards. The Program Performance Standards are undergirded by the Report of the Advisory Committee on Services for Infants and Toddlers (US DHHS, 1994), the committee that designed EHS.

The authorizing Head Start Act required evaluation of EHS and, therefore, an evaluation was launched at the same time the program began. Because the program was new, an extensive implementation study was conducted as well. A national contractor was selected (Mathematica Policy Research, Princeton, NJ, together with Columbia University's National Center on Children and Families), and local researchers in 15 universities partnered with sites to collect data and to pursue specific local questions. They formed a research consortium with the contractors and ACF. Using the experimental design, analyses compared program and control groups when children were 2 years old and when they were 3 years old and their enrollment in the program had ended. EHS services end when children reach age 3. What expectations were there for children's education experiences from the time they left EHS until they entered kindergarten? As noted, the Advisory Committee on Services to Families with Infants and Toddlers (U.S. DHHS, 1994) specified that EHS programs "transition" their 3-year-old children into community formal care and education when the EHS program services ended. The Advisory Committee did not expect impacts to be maintained if children did not have subsequent early childhood education experiences. In the next section of this literature review, we first examine the prevalence of formal programs for children 3–5 (and the likelihood that the vision of the Advisory Committee for post-EHS experiences could be achieved) and then report on child and parent outcomes from various combinations of program experiences for children from 0 to 3, 3 to 5, and 0 to 5.

PREVALENCE OF PARTICIPATION IN FORMAL CARE AND EDUCATION

Although we tracked children's experiences after EHS into formal programs when they were 3–5 years of age, it is important to know what would have been available to them. What was the prevalence of the types of follow-up experiences the Advisory Committee sought for EHS children? Low-income children may be served in multiple community settings, with services that vary in intensity, breadth, and scope. Of particular interest were formal preschool programs as emphasized by the Advisory Committee (primarily center-based services that included a structured early childhood program). National prevalence statistics provide a context for the types of care and education that could have been available for children starting at age 3. Next we present data on the prevalence of formal programs for 3- to 5-year-olds, and for specific types of formal programs (e.g., HS, child care, prekindergarten) during the period (early 2000s) when follow-up data were collected.

Data from the Early Childhood Longitudinal Study-Kindergarten Cohort (ECLS-K), which studied a nationally representative sample of children who attended kindergarten in the fall of 1998, showed that 68% of children attended structured early childhood education programs (prekindergarten, Head Start, or center-based child care) during the year before kindergarten (Rosenthal, Rathbun, & West, 2005). Attendance figures were about 10% lower for disadvantaged children (58%; Reynolds, Magnuson, & Ou, 2006). Similarly, data from the National Household Survey of Education Programs show that 66% of 4-year-olds and 43% of 3-year-olds were in center-based care and educational settings in 2001 (Mulligan, Brimhall, & West, 2005), and in 2005, 55% of 3- to 5-year-olds were in a center-based program (basically the average of 3- and 4-year-olds since most 5-year-olds are in kindergarten; Iruka & Carver, 2006). These included three common forms of formal care and education—prekindergarten, Head Start, and center-based child care.

Prekindergarten programs provide increasing opportunities particularly for 4-year-olds. State funding for prekindergarten has grown in the past 10–15 years although the rate of growth has recently slowed. In 2001–2002, about the time EHSREP sample children were in or completing preschool, 40 states served about 700,000 children, mostly 3- and 4-year-olds, including both general and special education, with state spending of about $2.4 billion. Nine years later these figures about doubled: in 2010–2011, 39 states served 1.3 million children, at a total cost of $5.5 billion. (Barnett, Robin, Hustedt, & Schulman, 2003; Barnett, Carolan, Fitzgerald, & Squires, 2011). Many state programs target low-income children, but in some states preschool services are nearly universally available, typically for 4-year-olds. Most prekindergarten programs do not serve children under age 3, although there are exceptions.

HS provides services primarily to 3- and 4-year-old children from the lowest-income families, those living at or below the federal poverty line, particularly. With a federal budget of $7.6 billion in 2011, HS served 942,354 children in 2011 and 912,345 in 2001–2002 (Schmit, 2012b), 90% of whom were at the federal poverty level or below. Of these, the vast majority, 90%, were age 3 and older. EHS, serving children under age 3, drew 17.6% of the federal HS appropriation and served an additional 165,522 children and pregnant women nationally (Schmit, 2012a). (EHS services were recently expanded to these numbers by a one-time funding increase through the American Recovery and Reinvestment Act of 2009.) HS is believed to serve between 40% and 50% of the eligible children living in poverty in the United States; however, state-sponsored prekindergarten programs (in some states HS and state prekindergarten programs may be combined) also serve children eligible for HS. The smaller EHS program, even with expansion, serves only a small proportion of eligible infants and toddlers, approximately 3%.

Child care programs (including center-based and home-based programs) serve large numbers of children beginning when children are infants. In 2002, data from the nationally representative National Survey of America's Families (NSAF) showed that more than 68% of children younger than 5 with low-income, employed mothers were in some form of nonparental care (Capizzano & Adams, 2003). The authors reported that 25% of these children were in center-based child care, an option more commonly used for 3- and 4-year-olds than for younger children. Other prevalent forms of out-of-home care were relative care (30%), family child care homes (11%), and nonrelative in-home care (4%). Federal contributions to child care in 2005, mostly for low-income children, were approximately $5.3 billion (Child Care

Bureau, 2006a); states added at least \$2.2 billion in maintenance of effort funds (Child Care Bureau, 2006b) and TANF transfers and other funds further contributed. About 1.8 million children were served by federal/state subsidy child care programs (Child Care Bureau, 2006a).

The foregoing are the common forms of formal programs. In this monograph, formal program settings (i.e., preschool education) for children aged 3–5 years were the focus.[3] Altogether, several million children living in low-income families are served in various combinations of formal programs when children are 3–5 years of age (HS, prekindergarten, and child care). Yet, as is clear from this brief review, more formal program services tend to be available for 4-year-olds than for 3-year-olds. EHS programs were charged with placing children in quality formal care and education through their remaining preschool years. It is important to determine if services were available and whether it was possible to meet that goal.

Moreover, early childhood educational services represent billions of dollars in state and federal investments and time spent in these programs constitutes substantial proportions of children's early years. As we will demonstrate later, many of these programs intend to influence children's development and, in the case of those serving poor children, to help reduce the gaps in school readiness skills.

Children's access to preschool education programs could vary by community context (e.g., whether communities are in rural or urban areas and whether there are good quality formal programs available in a community for low-income children aged 3–5), family race/ethnicity, family risk factors, and EHS program model. Anecdotally, it is well known that variability exits in access to quality early childhood programs across communities. The striking differences in access to prekindergarten programs for 4-year-olds versus for 3-year-olds (Barnett, Hustedt, Hawkinson, & Robin, 2006), and the greater number of 4-year-olds than 3-year olds served in HS—in 2002–2003, 53% of HS children were 4 years old and 34% were 3; the rest were 5 or under 3 years of age (Early Childhood Learning and Knowledge Center, 2004)—suggest that some communities might not have services to carry out the EHS vision of quality preschool follow-up services. For example, studies also show that children are more likely to have been in center-based care during the year prior to kindergarten in urban areas than in rural areas. Among African American children entering kindergarten (in most U.S. states when children enter kindergarten they must be age 5, although some may be as old as 6), those in urban areas were more likely to have been in center-based care the year prior to kindergarten (37%) than those in rural areas (14%); 55% of urban White children had been in center care the year before kindergarten as compared to 35.3% of rural White children (Grace et al., 2006). On the other hand, the same study showed that children were more likely to have been in HS if they were rural (17% of all rural children in the kindergarten sample)

9

versus urban (8.7%). Additionally, 37% of rural African American children attended HS the year before kindergarten versus 20% of urban African American children.

Not only are disparities seen *within* racial groups according to urbanicity; they are seen *between* racial/ethnic groups. Low-income African American children tend to be more likely to use center-based care than are other low-income children, and Hispanic children tend to be least likely to use this form of care (Capizzano, Adams, & Ost, 2007; Magnusson & Waldfogel, 2005). Though studies examining formal program use by cumulating family demographic risk factors do not exist, prekindergarten programs serve children across a wider socio-economic range than does Head Start. However, one of the variables that comprises the risk index used in the current monograph—mother's education—is known to be associated with program participation. In one study, children were more likely to enroll in preschool if their mothers had a graduate or professional degree (66% in at least one weekly care arrangement) than if they had a high school diploma or GED (55%) or had not completed high school (35%; Iruka & Carver, 2006).[4] We found no studies examining availability of programs for children ages 3–5 related to types of program services children had received during the preceding three years, a matter we will pursue in the current study. In general, the variability in differential supply and access is an issue for the field of early childhood education (Burchinal, Nelson, Carlson, & Brooks-Gunn, 2008).

IMPACTS OF INTERVENTION PROGRAMS OFFERING SERVICES PRENATAL TO AGE 3

Since the 1960s, a number of programs have provided intervention services for children from birth (or prior to birth), during infancy, and in some cases up to age 3. The programs we consider first do not provide follow-up services after age 3. During the infant and toddler years, the programs frequently offer two-generation services to both children and parents. Here, we review outcomes for children and parents from the Infant Health and Development Program (Brooks-Gunn, Klebanov, Liaw, & Spiker, 1993; Infant Health and Development Program [IHDP], 1990; McCarton et al., 1997; McCormick et al., 2006); the Parent Child Development Centers (PCDCs; Johnson & Blumenthal, 1985); the Yale Child Welfare program (Seitz, Rosenbaum, & Apfel, 1985); Healthy Families America (HFA; Daro & Harding, 1999); Nurse Family Partnership (NFP; Olds et al., 1997; Olds, Henderson, Kitzman, & Cole, 1995), UCLA Home Visiting/Mother Infant Group Intervention (Heinicke, Fineman, Rodning, Recchia, & Guthrie, 2001), and Parents as Teachers (PAT: Wagner & Clayton, 1999). Services these programs offered during the infant and toddler years were home-based, center-based, or a combination (Howard & Brooks-Gunn, 2009; Sweet & Appelbaum, 2004). For example, IHDP offered home visits early after infants' discharge from the hospital; at age 1, children began center-based care as well.

Intervention effects have been reported at age 2 or 3 (when the programs ended) from participation in intensive infant/toddler programs. Favorable effects of intervention were found (1) for children's cognitive development in the IHDP (IHDP, 1990; Brooks-Gunn et al., 1993) and the Houston PCDC (Johnson & Blumenthal, 1985); (2) on language development in the IHDP (Brooks-Gunn et al., 1993) and Yale Child Welfare participants (Seitz & Provence, 1990); and (3) on social and emotional development among treatment groups in the IHDP (Brooks-Gunn et al., 1993; IHDP, 1990). Overall effect sizes in these studies ranged from small to large. Few home visiting programs studied using rigorous experimental design have demonstrated positive impacts on child outcomes at or before age 3 across their entire sample (Howard & Brooks-Gunn, 2009; Sweet & Appelbaum, 2004).

Many infant and toddler programs offer parenting support; most of these are home visiting programs and a number of them have reported positive effects for parents (see Howard & Brooks-Gunn, 2009, for a recent review). Home visiting programs have reported improvements in maternal mental health and reduced subsequent pregnancies (Kitzman, Cole, Yoos, & Olds, 1997), increased parental reading to children (Johnson, Howell, & Molloy, 1993), greater reliance on nonviolent discipline (Heinicke et al., 2001), increased sensitivity in interactions (Olds et al., 2002), reduced depressive symptoms (Gelfand, Teti, Seiner, & Jameson, 1996), and less child maltreatment (Daro & Harding, 1999; Olds et al., 1997; Olds et al., 1995; Wagner & Clayton, 1999). Programs that affect parenting have been criticized because these changes in parents have not been consistently linked to changes in children's development (Duncan & Magnuson, 2006, Howard & Brooks-Gunn, 2009). However, Olds and colleagues have demonstrated longer term favorable child outcomes following early gains in parent-related behaviors (Olds, 2006) using impact analyses at multiple points in time.

Of particular relevance is that some of these evaluations have followed their children through the elementary school years and, in some cases, even longer. Positive effects attributable to services received during the infant and toddler years were found on vocabulary test scores in the Yale Child Welfare Study (Seitz & Provence, 1990), on standardized Iowa Basic Skills test scores among boys in the Houston PCDC (Johnson & Blumenthal, 1985), and on IQ, reading, and math achievement in heavier low-birth-weight infants in IHDP (McCarton et al., 1997) at age 8. Achievement scores were higher at age 18 in the IHDP-treated group (McCormick et al., 2006). Long-term effects of the Yale Child Welfare study also included reduced behavior problems for boys at age 8 (Seitz et al., 1985) and reduced need for remedial and support services (Zigler, Taussig, & Black, 1992). The Nurse Family Partnership study found

11

fewer arrests, convictions, and probation violations among intervention participants during adolescence (Olds, 2006). Effect sizes from these evaluations range from small to moderate, although Hill, Brooks-Gunn, and Waldfogel (2003) report a dosage effect with large effect sizes on cognitive development at age 8 among children who experienced more than 350 days of center-based care in the IHDP study over 2 years.

IMPACTS OF PROGRAMS SERVING PREKINDERGARTEN CHILDREN, AGES 3–5

Programs focused specifically on the prekindergarten period (ages 3 and 4, but most typically for 4-year-olds), have an extensive history. These programs typically include center-based experiences for young children, and some include comprehensive services for parents, although the parent component tends to be less prevalent than in programs serving children under age 3. Fewer programs exclusively target parents of children 3–5 years of age but rather most tend to focus more directly on children.

Some notable evaluations of preschool programs include those of the Perry Preschool Program (Schweinhart, 2006); Chicago Child-Parent Program (Reynolds & Temple, 2006); Tulsa Prekindergarten Program (Gormley, Gayer, Phillips, & Dawson, 2005); five state-sponsored prekindergarten programs in Michigan, New Jersey, Oklahoma, South Carolina, and West Virginia (Barnett, Lamy, & Jung, 2005), and Head Start (US DHHS, 2005).

A recent meta-analysis identifies 123 experimental or quasi-experimental evaluations (Camilli et al., 2010). Early childhood programs have short-term effects on children's cognitive development and on specific school readiness measures such as reading. Effect sizes have often been notable, ranging from 0.2 (US DHHS, 2005) to 0.6 (ACF, 2006; Camilli et al., 2010; Reynolds & Temple, 2006). Short-term school-related achievement gains are possible, with some evidence pointing to the importance of direct instruction (Barnett, 2011).

Those evaluations that have followed children into later years suggest that children receiving early childhood education are less likely to be held back in school or to receive special education services (Camilli et al., 2010). Notable too are findings showing that treatment children are more likely to finish high school, less likely to engage in crime, and more likely to be productively engaged throughout adulthood (Reynolds & Temple, 2006; Schweinhart, 2006). Larger, publically funded programs also have shown evidence of success, most notably the evaluations of prekindergarten programs (Barnett et al., 2005; Gormley et al., 2005).

With regard to HS, the HS Impact Study found few lasting effects through 1st grade, although effects were maintained for some subgroups, most notably

African American children (ACF, 2010). Other nonexperimental research designs have been used to examine effects of HS. Using a sibling design, Garces, Thomas, and Currie (2002) found that White children who had attended HS showed a significantly greater likelihood of completing high school and attending college, as well as some evidence of higher earnings in early adulthood. African Americans who were former HS participants were significantly less likely to have been charged or convicted of a crime. Ludwig and Miller (2006), using a regression discontinuity design, also found evidence of increased high school graduation rates and postsecondary participation, irrespective of race/ethnicity, in poor counties with enhanced HS participation. And, using propensity score matching procedures, preschool children who attended HS have been compared to those receiving prekindergarten, other center-based care, noncenter-based care, and parental care, with school readiness scores being higher for children attending HS compared to parental or noncenter-based care, but being similar or lower for children attending prekindergarten programs (Zhai, Brooks-Gunn, & Waldfogel, 2011; Zhai, Brooks-Gunn, & Waldfogel, 2011). The largest effects for IHDP were found when comparing children who received the treatment with those in parental or noncenter-based care (Hill, Waldfogel, & Brooks-Gunn, 2002). Using nonexperimental data from FACES, 2 years of HS was shown to confer more benefits than 1 year (Wen, Leow, Hahs-Vaughn, Korfmacher, & Mancus, 2011).

IMPACTS OF PROGRAMS BIRTH TO SCHOOL ENTRY

Studies that focus on services from birth to age 5 are more limited. These programs are likely to be quite expensive to implement and so it is perhaps not surprising that their prevalence is not widespread and that research comes largely from single-site demonstrations. Studies focused on children's early care and education experiences from birth to age 5 include the Abecedarian Project (Ramey & Ramey, 2006); the Milwaukee Project (Garber & Heber, 1981), the Brookline Early Education Project (BEEP; Bronson, Pierson, & Tivnan, 1984; Pierson, Bronson, Dromey, Swartz, Tivnan, & Walker, 1983; Pierson, Walker, & Tivnan, 1984), and the federal Comprehensive Child Development Program (CCDP; St. Pierre et al., 1994). Most of the studies employed a treatment versus control group experimental design. BEEP used a within-treatment experimental design, randomly assigning participants to varying levels of program services.

The Abecedarian Project (Ramey & Ramey, 2006) provided continuous services for children in center-based settings from 4 months to the start of kindergarten. Of the 111 children, half were randomly assigned to receive the center-based program and half to a control group that received no program (both groups received health and social support services); children's mothers were primarily primiparous, African American, and single. Similarly, the Milwaukee Project provided intensive, continuous, center-based and family support services to a special population: an extremely small sample of 20 African American mothers with very low IQs (75 or below; Garber & Heber, 1981). The BEEP study randomly assigned parents and children to three levels of intensity— (1) monthly home visits, meetings, and center-based child care; (2) similar but less frequent services; or (3) information and support at the center and by phone from birth to kindergarten. The CCDP provided intensive family support services in 21 locations. CCDP emphasized case management with family services and to a much lesser extent child development services (St. Pierre et al., 1994).

Two of these evaluations reported very large effects on children's cognitive development (effect sizes of 1.0) at the time the program ended and/or when children entered school (Garber & Heber, 1981; Ramey & Ramey, 2006). The BEEP study observed social and emotional benefits among treatment children (Pierson et al., 1983). The CCDP program did not demonstrate cross-site positive outcomes, leading researchers to conclude that family support programs not providing child development services were not sufficient to affect child development (St. Pierre et al., 1994).

Birth to 5 programs have also been found to have positive impacts beyond the intervention period. Most notably, the Abecedarian Project reported that treatment children were less likely to be retained in grade or require special education and were more likely to graduate from high school and attend college (Ramey & Ramey, 2006). The treatment group had higher IQ, math, and reading scores from age 8 to 21 (McLaughlin, Campbell, Pungello, & Skinner, 2007; Ramey & Ramey, 2006). Milwaukee Project children at age 10 demonstrated an average IQ that was 20 points higher than that for the control group (105 vs. 85; Garber & Heber, 1981). BEEP children were observed in the spring of second grade, 3 years after the program ended, with significant differences favoring the most intensive BEEP intervention children found for reading and teacher-reported "learning skills" (Pierson et al., 1984).

In summary, these evaluations provide evidence that early childhood services, especially those that are educational, can influence child development. However, these evaluations tell us little about how timing and duration affect children's development and parenting either directly or through mediation effects. The infant and toddler programs may affect emotional as well as cognitive development (especially if the program includes a center-based component) and may influence parenting (especially if the program includes a home-based or parent focus). Programs for 3- to 5-year olds (that tend to be center-based) seem to have their strongest impacts on school-related cognitive skills. Few evaluations of programs starting in the first year of

14

life and continuing until kindergarten have been conducted. One—the Abecedarian Project with a strong center-based focus—had strong, lasting child development impacts whereas another—CCDP with no center-based focus—had few impacts, perhaps because its focus was on family support rather than child development. We speculate that an optimal package of services might include parent and child services in order to enhance child social-emotional, language and cognitive outcomes and parenting in the infant and toddler years, followed by formal care and education that is child focused in the preschool years. However, except for some preliminary findings pertaining to school readiness skills (e.g., preliteracy or math skills), we know little about how broader domains (e.g., language, broad cognitive development, or social-emotional development) might be differentially affected by program timing, duration, or two-generation versus child-only services, and we know little about how these effects might differ across subgroups determined by family or program characteristics.

EFFECTS OF EARLY CHILDHOOD PROGRAMS ON CHILD OUTCOMES WITHIN SUBGROUPS

It is somewhat challenging to determine whether programs are differentially effective for subgroups, which is a question we would like to address ultimately. In this monograph, three types of subgroups are examined, based on program model of EHS service delivery, family race/ethnicity, and family level of demographic risk.

Because infant and toddler early childhood programs are sometimes home-based, sometimes center-based, and sometimes a combination of the two, we cluster sites by the type of model employed. Effects may to be larger and broader among programs offering a combination of home visiting and center-based services (ACF, 2002a; Gomby, 2005), although direct tests of this premise do not exist as programs were not randomly assigned to program approach. For primarily home-based services, positive child outcomes have been detected in areas related to health and safety (Johnson et al., 1993; Kitzman et al., 1997) and, to a lesser extent children's emotional functioning (ACF, 2002a; Jacobson & Frye, 1991), whereas center-based programs tend more frequently to report cognitive outcomes for children (e.g., Field, Widmayer, Stringer, & Ignatoff, 1980; Ramey, Bryant, Sparling, & Wasik, 1985). Home-based programs often report positive effects on parents (Howard & Brooks-Gunn, 2009).

We are interested in whether early childhood program opportunities and effects vary for low-income children depending on race/ethnicity. For example, many early childhood intervention studies have focused on at-risk African American children (Olds et al., 2004; Ramey & Ramey, 2006; Reynolds

& Temple, 2006; Schweinhart, 2006). With some exceptions (Gormley et al., 2005), fewer studies have demonstrated effects for Hispanic children. The IHDP (Brooks-Gunn et al., 1993) reported that children of African American mothers were more influenced by the intervention than children of White mothers at 2 years, possibly, as the authors note, because the former were less educated and more poor.

Programs may differentially affect children and families with different levels of risk. Previous evaluations have examined this premise. For example, IHDP had the greatest impact on children's cognitive development in families where mothers had a high school education or less (Brooks-Gunn et al., 1992; Liaw & Brooks-Gunn, 1993). Using a cumulative risk index rather than just maternal education, effect sizes were largest for children whose families had a moderate number of risks (Liaw & Brooks-Gunn, 1994). The NFP often reports the most positive benefits for mothers with psychological and emotional risk factors (Olds et al., 1994). Most intervention programs are targeted at children at risk but there has been little standardization of the variables used to define risk factors. In addition, intervention programs serve different populations, both in terms of central tendency and distribution. Moreover, who is at greatest risk in one cohort may differ from who is at greatest risk in another cohort, even under the same definition. Thus, it is difficult to compare whether the "highest risk" in one study is comparable to "highest risk" in other studies. To distinguish EHS families with different levels of risk, we counted up to five demographic risk factors that families had when they enrolled: (1) being a single parent; (2) receiving public assistance; (3) being neither employed nor in school or job training; (4) being a teenage parent; and (5) lacking a high school diploma or GED. To form groups of reasonable size, families were divided into three subgroups based on the number of risk factors they had when they enrolled: (1) lower risk families who had zero, one, or two risk factors; (2) moderate-risk families who had three risk factors; and (3) highest risk families who had four or five risk factors. Because the current study quantifies levels of risk, the findings reported here should be helpful in beginning to clarify who benefits from what combinations of services.

RESEARCH QUESTIONS AND HYPOTHESES

Despite over 40 years of research on effects of early childhood programs on children's development, surprisingly little is known about the timing of intervention mechanisms by which programs affect development. We offered theoretical perspectives earlier on how early and later experiences might influence children's development. These perspectives lead to the research questions this monograph addresses in Chapters III–VI.

1. **What were the impacts of EHS on children and parents when the children were 2 and 3 years of age (age 3 being the end of the program) and 2 years after the end of the program when the children were age 5 (Chapter III)?**

We expected that impacts would be seen across a range of outcomes when the children were 2 and 3 years of age. Sustained impacts were expected at age 5, although effect sizes would be smaller than at ages 2 and 3, given that effects in previous programs diminished several years after the intervention. Such findings would be consistent with early experiences influencing development, since the intervention experience, occurring in the first years of life, would influence development later. We expect such effects, if found, to be most pronounced for social and emotional outcomes. Consistent with the hypotheses that pertain to intervention being particularly effective if offered during specific periods of development, and that programs focused on improving mother–child relationships, we expected that parental impacts would be seen at age 2 on parenting measures that would mediate impacts of social and emotional functioning in the children later on. We also expected some impacts on parents to be sustained to age 5 as well (Howard & Brooks-Gunn, 2009). Moreover, we expected that age 3 EHS impacts on children's language, cognitive, social, and emotional development would mediate age 5 impacts in similar domains. Furthermore, based on the expectation that EHS would provide transition experiences for children (US DHHS, 1994), we hypothesized that EHS would increase the probability that children would participate in formal programs at ages 3 and 4. We further hypothesized that EHS would increase the probability that children would enter HS.

2. **What were the impacts of EHS on children and parents within prespecified subgroups at ages 2, 3, and 5 (that is during, at the end of, and following the intervention) (Chapter IV)?**

It is important to know whether effects of EHS vary depending on family and child characteristics. Differential treatment effects are examined for the three racial/ethnic groups and for three groups of families defined by number of risk factors. Some (but not all) evidence suggests that African American children, and perhaps Hispanic children, show larger benefits of early intervention than White children, although these links may be due, in part, to the fact that even within low-income families, the former two groups are less educated and poorer than the later group (Bassok, 2010; Brooks-Gunn, et al., 1993).

3. **What were the impacts of EHS across ages 2, 3, and 5 in the three clusters of programs—those that offered home-based, center-based, or a combination of the two? (Chapter V).**

We expected that children and families in mixed-approach programs would experience more positive age 3 outcomes than their counterparts, given that they would have had the advantages of participating in programs with the capacity to provide either or both home-based and center-based services to individual families in a flexible way designed to meet their specific goals and needs. We expected more child impacts for center-based programs and more parent-related impacts among participants in home-based programs.

4. What were the effects of out-of-home, formal preschool program participation during the age 3–5 period and how did effects of children's experiences across the age 0–5 period accumulate (Chapter VI)?

This question asks whether some conditions post-EHS enhance or detract from outcomes at age 5. Controlling for EHS use during the children's years from birth to age 3, we hypothesized that effects for preschool services would be similar to what has been found in other studies in which school achievement-related outcomes tend to be associated with formal care and education experiences, if the care settings are of good quality (Gormley et al., 2005; Magnuson & Waldfogel, 2005; NICHD ECCRN, 2005a). We also expected that emotional outcomes would be related to program experience in a negative way, consistent with the previous nonexperimental analyses (Magnussun, Ruhm, & Waldfogel, 2007; NICHD ECCERN, 2005a).

We hypothesized that children who had both EHS (infant and toddler) and preschool formal programs (ages 3–5) would fare the best at age 5, consistent with the original theory of change for EHS that emphasized early gains would be sustained and augmented by assisting EHS families find preschool programs (US DHHS, 1994). As an overarching hypothesis we hypothesized that experiences are incremental and augmented (NICHD ECCRN, 2001), whereby later experiences during the preschool years would build on early EHS impacts. At the same time, EHS impacts might act as a buffer such that if preschool program attendance was associated with aggressive behavior as others have found, EHS might offset this association (NICHD ECCRN, 2003a; Magnusson et al., 2007). For cognitive, school achievement-related outcomes, we predicted, as has been found in other studies (Gormley et al., 2005; Magnusson et al., 2007; NICHD ECCRN, 2000), that contemporaneous experiences from formal preschool education would be linked to age 5 outcomes as would EHS intervention. As for school-related outcomes, we predicted that EHS language impacts would be strengthened among children who had attended formal programs. We also hypothesized that parents in EHS would engage in more cognitive stimulation and support for children's development and that preschool attendance would not be an influence, given that preschool education programs, in general, spend less time working with parents than infant and toddler programs do.

NOTES

1. It has been the practice of Head Start to refer to the eligible population of "low-income" families as those with annual incomes below the federal poverty level. In many research

contexts, however, "low income" refers to families whose incomes are below 200% of the poverty threshold. However, to be consistent with usage within most Head Start and EHS research, in this monograph we refer to the enrolled families as low income.

2. We have more than one reason for limiting our focus during the years 3–5 to formal early care and education programs. First, drawing on an extensive literature pertaining to the importance of center-based care for children during the prekindergarten years, the Advisory Committee on Services to Families with Infants and Toddlers, the committee appointed by then Secretary Donna Shalala to design what would become EHS, recommended that children receive formal program services following EHS (U.S. Department of Health and Human Services, 1994). Arguably, family support and home visiting services could be recommended for children in families following EHS but this was not the specific recommendation of the committee for all children and it is not the question addressed in this monograph. Second, few children/families in the EHS sample, in either the program or control group, were enrolled in exclusively home visiting services during the years 3–5, although families with children in HS would have received at least two home visits a year, whereas formal care and education experience for children was relatively common as will be shown.

3. Home visiting programs reach many children, most but not all of whom are served during the years 0–3 and many but not all are considered low income or are otherwise at risk. As of the early 2000s, as many as 400,000 children are served annually in home visiting programs, at a cost of approximately $750 million to $1 billion and these numbers will expand under current administration proposals (Gomby, 2005).

4. Children are *less* likely to enroll in HS or EHS, however, the higher their parents' level of education attainment, as would be expected given the income requirements and the relationship between income and educational attainment (Iruka & Carver, 2006).

II. DESIGN AND METHODS IN THE EARLY HEAD START STUDY

Richard A. Faldowski, Rachel Chazan-Cohen, John M. Love, and Cheri Vogel

The EHSREP followed 3,001 low-income families who applied to receive Early Head Start (EHS) services between July 1996 and September 1998 at 17 program sites around the country. Upon application, families were randomly assigned to receive either EHS plus local community services or usual community services alone (i.e., all services, except EHS, available in local communities) through the child's third birthday (Administration for Children and Families [ACF], 2002a; Love et al., 2005).

In March 1996, ACF, the federal agency responsible for the evaluation, selected 15 programs that were able to recruit twice as many families as they could serve and had a strong local research partner. ACF also ensured that, in aggregate, the sites would be nationally distributed and would include the major programmatic approaches, settings, and family demographics that were characteristic of the 68 programs then funded. When these criteria resulted in too-few center-based programs, ACF added two more sites. Although the 17 programs cannot be considered a nationally representative sample of all EHS programs, analyses of key program features demonstrated that the program and family characteristics of the 17 reflected EHS programs operating at that time (ACF, 2002a; Love et al., 2005).

The EHS study was designed to document the consequences of receiving either EHS services or other community services up until age 3 combined with subsequent Head Start or other formal early care and education programs on children's school readiness and parent functioning in the preschool years (ACF, 2007a). This chapter focuses on key design issues and methods relevant for understanding the substantive analyses reported in this monograph.

Corresponding author: John M. Love, 1016 Canyon Park Drive, Ashland, OR 97520, email: jlove@mind.net

EHS DESIGN (UP TO AGE 3)

During the sample intake period, which extended over 26 months, 3,001 families were randomly assigned to the program and control groups, roughly in equal numbers. About a quarter of the research sample enrolled during pregnancy, but all families had to have a child under the age of 1 year. For more information on the randomization process, please refer to the project's technical impact reports (ACF, 2002a; Administration on Children, Youth, and Families [ACYF], 2001). At the time of enrollment, parents completed *Head Start Family Information System (HSFIS) Program Application and Enrollment Forms* for the programs. Demographic information was extracted from these forms for use in the research. We used this information to create subgroups defined by family characteristics at baseline, and to adjust for differences in the characteristics of program and control group members when estimating program impacts (i.e., to gain precision in our estimates). We also used data from the forms to compare the characteristics of interview respondents with nonrespondents, and to construct weights to adjust for potential nonresponse bias.

Data collection included both time in program assessments as well as child age-based assessments. The time-in-program assessments were all parent interviews and included the following:

Parent Services Follow-Up Interviews (PSI) Targeted for Collection 6, 15, and 26 Months After Random Assignment. These interviews collected information on (1) the use of services provided both by EHS and other providers, such as home visits, case management, parenting education, health care, employment assistance, and child care; (2) progress toward economic self-sufficiency, such as employment status, welfare receipt, and participation in education and training programs); (3) family health; and (4) children's health. Most PSIs were conducted by telephone with the focus child's primary caregiver, although some interviews were conducted in person for those not reachable by phone.

Exit Interviews When Children Reached 3 Years of Age. These interviews were conducted only with EHS parents (not the control group) when children were 3 years old and had to transition out of Early Head Start. The exit interviews obtained retrospective information on the use of EHS services. Whenever possible, the interviews were conducted in conjunction with the age 3 parent interviews (see below), but in some cases were conducted in conjunction with the 26-month PSIs.

The child age-based data collections included:

Parent Interviews (PI) Targeted for Collection When Children Were 14, 24, and 36 Months Old. These interviews obtained a large amount of information from the primary caregivers about their child's development and family functioning. These data usually were collected in person, but some PIs or portions of them were conducted by telephone when necessary.

Child and Family Assessments Targeted for Collection When Children Were 14, 24, and 36 Months Old. Field interviewers provided data on their observations of children's behavior and home environments. Interviewers conducted direct child assessments (such as Bayley assessments) and videotaped semistructured parent–child interactions. Quality of center-based care was also observed at this time.

This monograph reports results for assessments at ages 2 and 3 (some of these data have been reported elsewhere—CF, 2002; ACYF, 2001; Love et al., 2005). We did not analyze impacts at 14 months because some families had been in the program only a short time.

DESIGN OF THE PREKINDERGARTEN FOLLOW-UP (AGE 5)

The prekindergarten follow-up study was designed to follow former EHS and control group children and families from the time children turned 3 years old until the summer preceding their scheduled kindergarten entry. Two types of data collection were conducted. First, families participated in a telephone tracking interview. These tracking interviews helped researchers maintain contact with sample members and collected information on children's enrollment in formal early care and education programs, along with parents' education and employment status. Second, during the spring or summer preceding each child's scheduled kindergarten entry, families participated in a parent interview, direct child assessments, videotaped parent–child interactions, and early care and education provider observations and interviews. Twelve percent of the parent interviews were conducted in Spanish.

DESCRIPTIONS OF MEASURES

Measures were chosen to capture multiple aspects of child and family functioning. The selection of measures for the prekindergarten phase of the study was guided by two major goals. First, there was the need to maintain continuity with the birth to 3 phase of the project. Second, when new or substitute measures were selected, measures that had been employed in Head Start FACES (ACF, 2003, 2006, 2007a, b) or other national surveys (e.g., Early Childhood Longitudinal Study, Birth Cohort [ECLS-B]; National Center for Education Statistics, n.d.; National Institute of Child Health and Human Development Study of Early Child Care [NICHD SECC], n.d) were given priority (Brooks-Gunn, Fuligni, & Berlin, 2003). Table 1 documents the measures within each of the major outcome domains that are included in the analyses reported in this monograph. We do not report on all measures

TABLE 1

Comprehensive List of Outcomes Analyzed in Subsequent Chapters

Domain	Outcome	Source	Possible Range	Mean (SD)	Interpretation
Child Negative Social-Emotional & Positive Approaches to Learning Outcomes					
	CBCL Aggressive Behavior (ages 2, 3, 5)	Parent Report	0–38	Age 2: 12.6 (6.76) Age 3: 11.1 (6.47) Age 5: 10.9 (6.73)	Higher scores: More aggressive behavior
	FACES Social Behavior Problems (age 5)	Parent Report	0–24	Age 5: 5.6 (3.58)	Higher scores: More behavior problems
	Child Negativity Toward Parent During Play (ages 2, 3, 5)	Observer Rating/ Parent–Child Play Video	1–7	Age 2: 1.7 (0.98) Age 3: 1.3 (0.57) Age 5: 1.2 (0.56)	Higher scores: Higher rates at which the child shows anger, hostility, or dislike toward the parent during play
	Child Engagement During Play (ages 2, 3, 5)	Observer Rating/ Parent–Child Play Video	1–7	Age 2: 4.3 (1.14) Age 3: 4.7 (1.01) Age 5: 4.7 (0.95)	Higher scores: Higher rates at which the child shows, initiates, and/or maintains interaction with the parent; and communicates positive regard and/or positive affect to the parent during play
	Sustained Attention With Objects During Play (ages 2, 3)	Observer Rating/ Parent–Child Play Video	1–7	Age 2: 5.0 (0.94) Age 3: 4.9 (0.95)	Higher scores: More sustained attention with objects during play
	FACES Positive Approaches to Learning (age 5)	Parent Report	0–14	Age 5: 12.0 (1.88)	Higher scores: More positive approach to learning
	Observed Bayley Emotion Regulation (ages 2, 3)	Observer Rating	1–5	Age 2: 3.6 (0.80) Age 3: 3.9 (0.76)	Higher ratings: better emotion regulation and ability to shift tasks, less frustration and negativity
	Observed Leiter Emotion Regulation (Leiter-R Examiner Rating Scales) (age 5)	Interviewer Rating/ Child Assessment	Raw Scores: 0–66 Scaled Scores: 46–113	Age 5: 91.1 (9.80)	Higher scores: Greater levels of energy, positive emotion, and lack of anxiety; as well as appropriate levels of self-regulation and indistractibility
	Observed Attention (age 5) (Leiter-R Examiner Rating Scales)	Interviewer Rating/ Child Assessment	Raw Scores: 0–30 Scaled Scores: 1–10	Age 5: 8.6 (1.97)	Higher scores: Greater levels of attention, concentration, focus, and indistractibility while performing challenging tasks
Child Language/Cognitive/Academic Skills					
	MacArthur CDI Vocabulary (age 2)	Parent report	0–100	Age 2: 54.8 (22.95)	Higher scores: Larger vocabulary
	English Receptive Vocabulary (Peabody Picture Vocabulary Test III) (ages 3, 5)	Child Assessment	Raw Scores: 0–204 Scaled Scores: 40–160	Age 3 SS: 83.0 (15.56) Age 5 SS: 91.5 (15.16)	Higher scores: Greater English receptive vocabulary

(*Continued*)

23

24

TABLE 1. (*Continued*)

Domain	Outcome	Source	Possible Range	Mean (SD)	Interpretation
	Spanish Receptive Vocabulary (Test de Vocabulario en Imagenes Peabody) (ages 3, 5)	Child Assessment	Raw Scores: 0–125 Scaled Scores: 40–160	Age 3 SS: 95.1 (8.16) SS: 84.4 (23.1)	Higher scores: Greater Spanish receptive vocabulary
	Bayley MDI (ages 2, 3)	Child Assessment	49–134	Age 2: 89.1 (13.68) Age 3: 90.6 (12.63)	Higher scores: higher developmental functioning
	Bayley MDI < 85 (ages 2, 3)	Child Assessment	0–1	Age 2: 0.37 (0.48) Age 3: 0.30 (0.46)	1 = Child has an MDI < 85
	Woodcock-Johnson-Revised Letter-Word Identification (age 5)	Child Assessment	Raw Scores: 0–57 Scaled Scores: 40–160	Age 5 SS: 89.3 (13.66)	Higher scores: Greater English letter/word knowledge preliteracy skills
	Spanish Woodcock-Muñoz-Revisada Identificación de Letras y Palabras (age 5)	Child Assessment	Raw Scores: 0–58 Scaled Scores: 40–160	Age 5: 86.9 (16.9)	Higher scores: Greater Spanish letter/word knowledge preliteracy skills
	Woodcock-Johnson-Revised Applied Problems (age 5)	Child Assessment	Raw Scores: 1–60 Scaled Scores: 40–160	Age 5 SS: 88.3 (20.08)	Higher scores: Greater representation, counting, and simple addition/subtraction emerging numeracy skills
	Woodcock-Muñoz-Revisada Problemas Aplicados (age 5)	Child Assessment	Raw Scores: 0–59 Scaled Scores: 40–160	Age 5: 88.7 (17.15)	Higher scores: Greater representation, counting, and simple addition/subtraction emerging numeracy skills
	Leiter-R Attention Sustained	Child Assessment	Raw Scores: 74–74 Scaled Scores: 1–19	Age 5 SS: 11.0 (3.18)	Higher scores indicate greater number of correct answers with few errors, suggesting greater vigilance and focused attention during a repetitive task: negative raw scores occur when more errors than correct answers are given
	Leiter-R Attention Sustained Total Correct	Child Assessment	Raw Scores: 0–74 Scaled Scores: 1–19	Age 5 SS: 10.9 (3.11)	Higher scores: Greater number of correct answers
	Leiter-R Attention Sustained Total Errors	Child Assessment	Raw Scores: 0–74 Scaled Scores: 1–19	Age 5 SS: 10.7 (2.75)	Higher error scaled scores correspond to lower raw error scores; therefore, higher error scaled scores indicate fewer number of incorrect answers
Child Health	ER Visit Due to Accident or Injury (ages 2, 3)	Parent Report	0–1	Age 2: 0.08 (0.27) Age 3: 0.11 (0.31)	1 = ER visit due to accident or injury
	Any Immunizations (ages 2, 3)	Parent Report	0–1	Age 2: 0.97 (0.16) Age 3: 0.98 (0.13)	1 = Immunized

(*Continued*)

24

TABLE 1. (*Continued*)

Domain	Outcome	Source	Possible Range	Mean (SD)	Interpretation
	Child Has Individualized Education Plan (ages 2, 3, 5)	Parent Report	0–1	Age 2: 0.04 (0.19) Age 3: 0.07 (0.25) Age 5: 0.8 (0.27)	1 = Child has individualized education plan
	Speech Problems (age 5)	Parent Report	1–3	Age 5: 0.22 (0.41)	Lower scores: Child has fewer/less serious speech problems
Parenting and the Home Environment					
	HOME Language & Literacy (ages 2, 3, 5)	Parent Report + Interviewer Observation	0–12	Age 2: 10.2 (1.71) Age 3: 10.5 (2.02) Age 5: 10.7 (3.12)	Higher scores: Home environment is more supportive of child's language and literacy
	Reads to Child Daily (ages 2, 3, 5)	Parent Report	0–1	Age 2: 0.55 (0.50) Age 3: 0.54 (0.50) Age 5: 0.32 (0.47)	1 = Someone at home reads to child daily
	Child Spanked Within Past Week (ages 2, 3, 5)	Parent Report	0–1	Age 2: 0.50 (0.50) Age 3: 0.50 (0.50) Age 5: 0.36 (0.48)	1 = Child spanked within past week
	Parent Supportiveness During Play (ages 2, 3, 5)	Observer Rating/ Parent–Child Play Video	1–7	Age 2: 4.0 (1.10) Age 3: 3.9 (0.93) Age 5: 4.0 (1.01)	Higher scores: Greater degree to which the parent is emotionally available and physically and affectively present to the child during play
	Parent Detachment During Play (ages 2, 3, 5)	Observer Rating/ Parent–Child Play Video	1–7	Age 2: 1.4 (0.86) Age 3: 1.23 (0.60) Age 5: 1.35 (0.77)	Higher scores: Greater degree to which the parent was unaware, inattentive, and/or indifferent to the child during play
	Child Has Regular Bedtime (ages 2, 3)	Parent Report	0–1	Age 2: 0.59 (0.49) Age 3: 0.59 (0.49)	1 = Child has regular bedtime
	8 Teaching Activities (ages 2, 3, 5)	Parent Report	0–16	Age 2: 4.51 (0.84) Age 3: 4.4 (0.85) Age 5: 11.1 (3.93)	Higher scores: Greater engagement in more types of or more frequent teaching activities with the child
	Children's Books (26 or more) (age 5)	Parent Report	0–1	Age 5: 0.62 (0.49)	1 = Has 26 or more children's books
	Parent Attends Meetings/Open Houses (age 5)	Teacher Interview	0–1	Age 5: 0.8 (0.38)	1 = Parent attended meetings/open houses this year
Family Well-Being and Mental Health					
	Depression: Composite International Diagnostic Interview, Depression Module (age 2)	Parent Interview	0–100	Age 2: 15.9 (32.59)	Probability of depression

(*Continued*)

25

TABLE 1. (Continued)

Domain	Outcome	Source	Possible Range	Mean (SD)	Interpretation
	Depression: Center for Epidemiologic Studies—Depression Scale—Short Form (ages 3, 5)	Parent Interview	0–36	Age 3: 7.7 (7.00) Age 5: 8.0 (7.15)	Higher scores: Greater number/frequency of depressive symptoms
	Parenting Distress (ages 2, 3)	Parent Interview	12–60	Age 2: 25.4 (9.30) Age 3: 25.2 (9.59)	Higher scores: more distress associated with parenting
	Family Conflict (ages 2, 3)	Parent Interview	1–4	Age 2: 1.7 (0.54) Age 3: 1.7 (0.53)	Higher scores: more conflict
	Someone in Household Had Alcohol/Drug Problem During Past Year (age 5)	Parent Interview	0–1	Age 5: 0.1 (0.29)	1 = Exposure to household drug or alcohol problems within the past year
	Child Witnessed Violence (age 5)	Parent Interview	0–1	Age 5: 0.11 (0.32)	1 = Child exposed to violence
	Parent Was Abused in Past Year (age 5)	Parent Interview	0–1	Age 5: 0.09 (0.28)	1 = Parent abused in past year
Parent Self-Sufficiency	Parent Employed (ages 2, 3)	Parent Interview	0–1	Age 2: 0.72 (0.45) Age 3: 0.85 (0.36)	1 = Employed since enrollment or since last interview
	Time Parent Employed in Past 6 Months (age 5)	Parent Interview	1–5	Age 5: 3.5 (1.73)	Lower values: Greater fraction of time employed during past 6 months (1 = all, 2 = most of the time, 3 = about half the time, 4 = less than half the time, 5 = never)
	Parent in School or Job Training (ages 2, 3)	Parent Interview	0–1	Age 2: 0.43 (0.50) Age 3: 0.54 (0.50)	1 = Parent in school or job training since enrollment or time since last interview
	Income (annual at ages 2, 3; monthly at age, 5)	Parent Interview	n.a.	Age 2: $14,415 ($12,168) Age 3: $16,809 ($12,865) Age 5: $2.287 ($1,808)	Higher numbers: Higher income
Formal Program Experience Ages 3–5	Formal Program Experience Ages 3 and 4	Parent Interview	0–1	Age 5: 0.42 (0.49)	1 = Child in formal educational program at ages 3 and 4
	Ever in Head Start	Parent Interview	0–1	Age 5: 0.51 (0.50)	1 = Child attended Head Start at some point between ages 3 and 4

26

collected, yet we selected those that reflect all key domains of outcomes studied. Where multiple measures were used to assess a domain, the following rules were used to choose what to report: priority was given to (1) measures that we used at more than one time point; (2) psychometric strength; and (3) the measures' total scores rather than individual scales, unless there was a compelling reason why an individual scale would be of particular interest. Information on psychometrics of the measures is included elsewhere for the 0–3 phase of the study (ACF, 2002a, ACYF, 2001) so we summarize here only measures reported for the prekindergarten phase (unless a measure was also used at ages 2 or 3).

Child Social, Emotional, and Approaches to Learning Outcomes

The *Child Behavior Checklist (CBCL)—Aggressive Behavior Problems* subscale was used at all three ages (2, 3, and 5), to capture children's aggressive behavior. The CBCL for ages 1.5–5 (Achenbach & Rescorla, 2000) is a widely used standardized assessment of child behavioral, emotional, and social functioning. Items yield scores of 0, 1, and 2 (whether the statement is "not true," "somewhat or sometimes true," or "very true or often true" of the child). The aggressive behavior subscale includes 19 items, including items indicating defiance, poor impulse control, antisocial behavior, and maladaptive attention seeking. Total scores on the subscale could range from 0 to 38. The observed internal consistency at age 5 was $\alpha = .89$ ($n = 2{,}014$).

FACES Social Behavior Problems is a summary of 12 negative behaviors reported by mothers. For each item, parents rated their children on a 3-point scale—"not true," "somewhat or sometimes true," and "very true or often true." The scale combines 12 problem behavior items into a total problem behaviors score that represents the overall degree to which a child has problems with aggressive or disruptive behavior, hyperactivity, and withdrawn types of behavior. The FACES total problem behaviors score ranges from 0 to 24, with higher scores representing more frequent or severe behavior problems. In the FACES study, the internal consistency of the total problem behavior scores for Head Start children was .76 in 2002 (ACF, 2006, p. A-32). At age 5 in the EHSREP sample, the internal consistency was the same: $\alpha = .76$ ($n = 2{,}029$).

Child Behavior During Parent–Child Semistructured Play. We collected similar data across the three waves of data collection, although the situation changed somewhat. In the age 2- and 3-year assessments, the parent and child were given three bags of interesting toys and asked to play with the toys in sequence. At the prekindergarten assessment, the dyad was given two cans of Play-Doh, a rolling pin, and a cookie cutter. At all ages, the task was videotaped, and child behaviors were coded by child development researchers on a scale adapted for this evaluation from the Three Box coding scales used in the NICHD Study of

27

Early Child Care (Owen, Barefoot, Vaughn, Dominguez, & Ware, 1996). Three aspects of children's behavior with the parent were rated on a 7-point scale: *Negativity Toward Parent*, the degree to which the child shows anger, hostility, or dislike toward the parent; *Engagement*, the extent to which the child shows, initiates, or maintains interaction with the parent; and *Sustained Attention With Objects*, the degree to which the child is involved with the toys presented. These were coded only at 2 and 3 years of age.

Coding methods and reliability on 2- and 3-year data are reported elsewhere (Brady-Smith et al., 2013; Fuligni & Brooks-Gunn, 2013; Fuligni et al., 2013), so we focus on the prekindergarten data collection here. Coders were required to attain at least 85% agreement to within 1 point of a "gold standard" rater before independently coding interactions. Thereafter, a random 9% of all tapes assigned were used to check coders' ongoing reliabilities. Intercoder reliability was assessed on ratings of 157 tapes. Intercoder agreement was high for both the child variables (96% for child engagement of parent and 99% for negativity toward parent). Intraclass correlations (ICCs), which can be considered a generalization of kappa coefficients for multiple raters (Fleiss & Cohen, 1973; Rae, 1988; Shrout & Fleiss, 1979), ranged between .64 and .70 as they are based on the substantially more stringent criterion of exact agreement (see Fuligni & Brooks-Gunn, 2013, for information on all observational coding in EHS).

The *FACES Social Skills and Positive Approaches to Learning* scale assesses children's positive social interaction skills as well as their behavioral dispositions toward learning. Comprising seven items, it assesses the degree to which children exhibit skills in making friends and accepting their ideas, enjoying learning and trying new things, showing imagination, comforting/helping others, and wanting to hear positive feedback. Like the FACES problem behavior scales, for each item, parents rated their children on a 3-point scale—"not true," "somewhat or sometimes true," and "very true or often true." The social skills and positive approaches to learning scale score ranges from 0 to 14, with higher scores indicating higher levels of social skills and more positive approaches to learning (ACF, 2006, p. A-31–A-32). In the FACES study, the internal consistency of this scale was .66 (ACF, 2006, p. A-32). At age 5 in EHSREP, the internal consistency was similar: $\alpha = .64$ ($n = 2,048$).

Leiter-R Examiner Rating Scales (Roid & Miller, 1997) were used to rate emotion regulation at the prekindergarten assessment (the Bayley Behavioral Rating Scale [BRS; Bayley, 1993] was used at the earlier ages). At the conclusion of the child assessment, assessors completed a set of ratings about the child's behavior observed throughout the testing session. The Leiter-R Examiner Rating Scales evaluate children's behavior in eight domains: (1) attention, (2) organization and impulse control, (3) activity level,

(4) sociability, (5) energy and feelings, (6) mood and regulation, (7) anxiety, and (8) sensory reactivity. Each item in the domains is rated on a 4-point scale anchored to the rate at which a child exhibited a behavior during the testing session: (0) "Rarely/never occurred" (i.e., less than roughly 10% of the time), (1) "Sometimes occurred" (i.e., around 10–50% of the time), (2) "Often occurred" (i.e., approximately 50–90% of the time), or (3) "Usually/always occurred" (i.e., more than 90% of the time). We report on the *Attention* domain given the salience to school functioning, as well as one composite scale, *Emotion Regulation* (comprising energy and feelings, mood and regulation, anxiety, and sensory reactivity subscales). Raw scores on the subscales and composites were converted to scaled scores by application of age-appropriate norms. In the EHS prekindergarten child assessment, internal consistencies of the subscales and composites of the Leiter-R examiner ratings ranged from .81 (sociability subscale) to .96 (cognitive/social composite). The internal consistencies of the attention rating and the emotion regulation composite, were $\alpha = .93$ ($n = 1,821$) and $\alpha = .93$ ($n = 1,796$).

Child Language, Cognitive, and Academic Skills Outcomes

At ages 3 and 5, the *PPVT-III* and *TVIP* were used to assess language, because the MacArthur Communicative Development Inventories (Fenson et al., 2000) used at age 2 were no longer appropriate. The PPVT-III measures listening comprehension of spoken words in standard English for children and adults age 2½ and over (Dunn & Dunn, 1997; Williams & Wang, 1997). The child is presented with four pictures and is asked to point to the picture that matches the word spoken by the interviewer. The PPVT-III was normed on a nationally representative sample of children and adults of various ages so that raw scores can be converted to age-adjusted, standardized scores with a mean of 100 and a standard deviation of 15. At age 5, its internal consistency was .96 ($n = 1,691$). Similarly, the *Test de Vocabulario en Imagenes Peabody* (*TVIP*) measures the listening comprehension of spoken words in Spanish for Spanish-speaking and bilingual children from age 2½ to 18 (Dunn, Padilla, Lugo, & Dunn, 1986). The TVIP was normed on a sample of Mexican and Puerto Rican children of various ages so that raw scores can be converted to age-adjusted, standardized scores with a mean of 100 and a standard deviation of 15. In the EHS sample of Spanish-speaking children, the alpha was .96 ($n = 174$).

Two subscales of the *Woodcock-Johnson Tests of Achievement—Revised* (Woodcock & Johnson, 1990) were used to assess children's preacademic skills: Letter Word Identification, ability to identify decontextualized individual letters and words; and Applied Problems, skills in analyzing and solving practical problems in mathematics. The only analogous measure at ages 2 and 3 was the Bayley Mental Development Index (MDI; Bayley, 1993). The internal consistency of the Letter-Word Identification test with preschool children averages .92 (Woodcock & Johnson, 1990, p. 100), whereas in this sample α was .84 ($n = 1,757$). The Spanish version of the test, the *Batería Woodcock-Muñoz-R Identificación de Letras y Palabras* (Woodcock & Muñoz-Sandoval, 1996), was used for children whose primary language was Spanish. The internal consistencies of the Identifcación de Letras y Palabras test with Spanish-speaking FACES study children was .83 in 2002 (ACF, 2006, pp. A-16–A-17). In the EHS prekindergarten evaluation α was .96 ($n = 115$). The Spanish version of Applied Problems, the *Woodcock-Muñoz-R Problemas Aplicados* (Woodcock & Muñoz-Sandoval, 1996) was used for children whose primary language was Spanish. Since the Woodcock-Muñoz-R Problemas Aplicados was developed as a parallel measure to the Woodcock-Johnson-R Applied Problems test; scores on the two versions are directly comparable and they were combined in analyses. The internal consistency of the Applied Problems test with preschool children averages .91 (Woodcock & Johnson, 1990, p. 100), and the internal consistency in FACES was also .91 in 2002 (ACF, 2006, pp. A-16–A-17). In EHS, the internal consistency was $\alpha = .85$ ($n = 1,870$).

Leiter International Performance Scale-Revised—Attention Sustained (Leiter-R; Roid & Miller, 1997) was developed as a set of cross-culturally appropriate intellectual functioning assessments for individuals with limited verbal abilities. The Attention Sustained subtest for 4- to 5-year-olds is a timed cancellation task. Children are presented with a target figure ("flower," "butterfly," "funny guy," or "goat") and are asked to find and cross out as many of the target figures on the page as possible and to work as fast as they can within the allotted time (which varies by target figure from 30 to 60 seconds). Poor performance in the absence of a diagnosable motor impairment is typically attributed to difficulty in sustaining attention to a detailed task (Roid & Miller, 1997, p. 118). The Attention Sustained test results in three raw scores: a total correct score, a total errors score, and a total correct adjusted-for-errors score. Each set of scores is converted to scaled scores by application of age-appropriate norms. Because of the wide range of children's ages at the prekindergarten assessment, only scaled scores are used in analyses in this monograph. The Leiter-R manual reports an Attention Sustained internal consistency for 4- to 5-year-olds of .83 (p. 157), and test–retest reliability for 6- to 18-year-olds of .85 (Roid & Miller, 1997, p. 162). In FACES, the internal consistency of the attention sustained test scores among 4- to 5-year-old Head Start children was $\alpha = .80$ ($n = 920$) in 2002 (ACF, 2006, pp. A-17–A-18). The internal consistency in the EHS study was $\alpha = .75$ ($n = 1,782$).

Child Health

At ages 2 and 3 years, parents were asked if the child had visited the *emergency room because of accident or injury*. At the same time, parents were asked about the child's *immunization status*, i.e., whether they were up to date on immunizations. At 2, 3, and 5 age points, parents were asked if their child had an identified disability and an *Individualized Education Plan* (*IEP*). At age 5, parents were also asked about the presence and severity of a *speech problem*.

Parenting and the Home Environment

At all three ages we used the *HOME Support for Language and Literacy* subscale of the *Home Observation for Measurement of the Environment* (*HOME*), one of the most widely used measures designed to assess characteristics of a child's home environment important for stimulating optimal child development (Bradley, 1994; Bradley & Caldwell, 1988; Caldwell & Bradley, 1984). A shortened form was used in the EHS Study (Mott, 2004). The *Support of Language and Literacy* subscale measures the breadth and quality of the mother's speech and verbal responses to the child during the home visit, as rated by the interviewer; whether the parent encourages the child to learn shapes, colors, numbers, and the alphabet; the presence of books, toys, and games accessible to the child; and whether the parent reads to the child several times per week. Items are obtained by a combination of parent report and interviewer observation (Fuligni, Han, & Brooks-Gunn, 2004).

Parent Behavior During Parent–Child Semistructured Play measures parent behavior during a semistructured play task. (See details above in child outcomes.) Several aspects of parents' behavior with their child were rated on a 7-point scale (Fuligni, Brooks-Gunn, & Brady-Smith, 2008). Here we report two aspects, one negative and one positive: *Supportiveness*, an average of parental sensitivity, cognitive stimulation, and positive regard during play with the child; and *Detachment*, the extent to which the parent is inattentive to the child, inconsistently attentive, or interacts with the child in an indifferent manner (Fuligni & Brooks-Gunn, 2013; Fuligni et al., 2013; Brady-Smith et al., in press). Intercoder reliability of the child and parent variables was assessed on ratings of 157 tapes. Intercoder agreement was high for both the parent variables (94% for supportiveness and 92% for detachment). ICCs, which can be considered a generalization of kappa coefficients for multiple raters (Fleiss & Cohen, 1973; Rae, 1988; Shrout & Fleiss, 1979), ranged between .64 and .70 as they are based on the substantially more stringent criterion of exact agreement.

Specific parent interview questions analyzed as parenting outcomes included frequencies of engagement in *teaching and play activities*,[5] whether someone *reads to the child daily*, the *number of children's books* in the household, and whether the child had been *spanked within the past week*. At age 2, parents were asked about whether they had a *regular bedtime* for their child. The parent had to name the time and report that the child went to bed at that time at least 4 of the past 5 weekdays.

Family Well-Being and Mental Health

The *Parental Distress* subscale of the short form of the Parenting Stress Index was used at 2 and 3 years.

The *Center for Epidemiological Studies Depression Scale.* Short Form (CESD-SF) was used to measure symptoms of depression at all three ages (Ross, Mirowsky, & Huber, 1983). The scale includes 12 items taken from the full, 20-item CESD scale (Radloff, 1977). Respondents were asked the number of days in the past week they had a particular symptom. Symptoms include poor appetite, restless sleep, loneliness, sadness, and lack of energy. In the EHS prekindergarten sample, the estimated internal consistency of caregiver CES-D scores was $\alpha = .88$ ($n = 2,033$).

The *Family Conflict* subscale of the Family Environment Scale was used at 2 and 3. Parents respond to items on a 4-point scale, where 4 indicates higher levels of agreement with statements such as, "We fight a lot," and "We hardly ever lose our tempers." Items were recoded and averaged so that 4 indicated high level of conflict (Moos & Moos, 1976).

The prekindergarten parent interview included a number of items related to family risk factors. Specific parent interview health and well-being questions included whether anyone in the household had *drug or alcohol problems*, whether the child had *witnessed violence*, and whether *the parent had been abused*.

Parent Self-Sufficiency

In the Parent Services Interviews (corresponding with the 2- and 3-year-old data) and in the 5-year-old interview, parents were asked about self-sufficiency, including *Education* (parents were asked about education and job training programs that they had participated in during the follow-up period); *Employment* (parents were asked about jobs that they had held during the follow-up period); and *Family Income* (for the first two waves, parents were asked about their family income during the past year). At the age 5 interview, parents were asked about monthly household income.

ANALYSIS OF RESPONSE RATES AND RESPONSE BIAS

Response Rates

High response rates, maximizing preservation of the original randomized EHS sample, are a key requirement for ensuring the validity of follow-up study

32

results. In calculating response rates, nonrespondents are defined as any sample member for whom a designated data element was not collected. They include sample members whose children died (and who were not, by design, followed up), withdrew from the study, could not be located, or refused an interview/assessment/observation. At least one element of tracking or prekindergarten data was collected for 78% of the original 3,001 sample members (see Figure 1). Prekindergarten data were collected on 2,142 (71%) of the sample. Figure 1 shows the sample disposition from the original 3,001 sample members randomized to the number with complete parent interview data.

Response Bias Analysis[6]

Effects that sample attrition exerts on the composition of the follow-up sample—expressed as response bias—are as important as response rates. Internal validity of findings is maximized when there are few differences in baseline characteristics between treatment and control respondents (Cook &

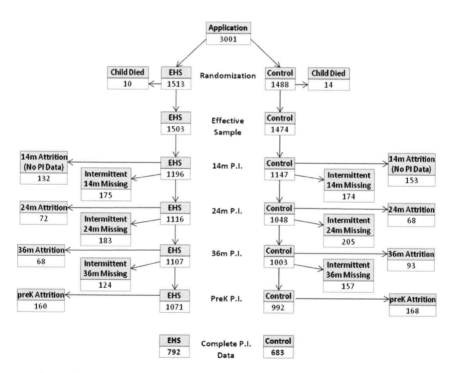

FIGURE 1.—Sample retention and attrition at each data collection point in the EHSREP
Note: Overall sample disposition for 14 months through prekindergarten parent interviews.

Campbell, 1979; Shadish, Cook, & Campbell, 2002). Attrition bias, an especially important threat to internal validity in longitudinal studies, is minimized when the follow-up sample still resembles, on baseline characteristics, the original sample that was randomized. Attrition bias is tested by comparing treatment group respondents to nonrespondents and comparison group respondents to nonrespondents.

Overall, analysis indicates that the treatment and control groups are comparable at the prekindergarten follow-up point, thereby maintaining internal validity of the results. Among prekindergarten respondents, only two of the differences between program and control groups are statistically significant, even at the liberal significance level of .10 (analyses available upon request). This is fewer than half of the five differences that would be expected by chance. Therefore, we conclude that the impact analyses reported in Chapters III and IV represent valid assessments of the effects of the EHS treatment.

Furthermore, despite some statistical differences between respondents and nonrespondents on many important characteristics, the prekindergarten sample remains comparable to the baseline sample and the magnitude of attrition bias may be modest (analyses available upon request). Specifically, the baseline and prekindergarten samples are similar on such key characteristics as age of mother at birth of focus child, mother's educational attainment, whether employed or in school/training, number of children in the household, income, age of focus child at enrollment, focus child with preterm birth or low birthweight, or having established biological or environmental risks. The EHS sample at prekindergarten overrepresents center-based programs (22.7% of respondents were in center-based programs vs. 13.4% of nonrespondents) and programs that were later implementers of the Head Start Program Performance Standards; while under-representing home-based and incomplete implementers (see ACF, 2002a, for definitions of levels of program implementation). The sample at prekindergarten is somewhat less disadvantaged than the baseline sample: Respondents were more likely to own their own home, less likely to be receiving TANF or Food Stamps, more likely to be low risk, and more likely to be living with a spouse or other adults.

These differences suggest that some attrition bias may be manifest in a number of characteristics and some caution is warranted when drawing inferences from the prekindergarten analyses and applying them to the original EHS sample. The magnitudes of the statistically significant differences, however, are not large and values of the characteristics remain well with the ranges of variability observed among low-income families eligible for EHS services nationally, suggesting that practical implications of the potential bias may be small. Furthermore, the program and control groups remain comparable on baseline characteristics. We conclude, therefore, that findings from the prekindergarten sample in the EHS continue to have internal validity for assessing the impacts of EHS.

CONCLUSIONS

The next several chapters focus on questions about the enduring effects of EHS program participation as well as the contributions of formal program experiences ages 3–5. Although the specific questions considered in each chapter differ and the methods employed to address them vary, all are set in the context of the research design, methods, and instrumentation described here. The age 5 response rates were consistent with patterns and variations by data collection component observed in the age 3 data collection wave (see ACF, 2002a, chapter II). Importantly, the respondents in the program and control groups were virtually indistinguishable on a host of baseline characteristics at the age 5 assessment point. Finally, although a number of differences between baseline and follow-up samples (respondents vs. nonrespondents) on baseline characteristics were present, the magnitudes of the differences were generally modest and the values well within ranges typically observed among EHS families.

NOTES

5. The teaching activities, which are also listed in Table 1, include (1) Told child a story; (2) Taught child letters, words, or numbers; (3) Taught child songs or music; (4) Worked on arts and crafts together; (5) Played with indoors toys or games; (6) Played a game, sport, or exercised together; (7) Took child along while doing errands; and (8) Involved child in household chores.

6. Results available from authors upon request.

III. IMPACTS OF EARLY HEAD START PARTICIPATION ON CHILD AND PARENT OUTCOMES AT AGES 2, 3, AND 5

Cheri Vogel, Jeanne Brooks-Gunn, Anne Martin, and Mary M. Klute

In this chapter, we describe the impacts that EHS participation had on children's participation in formal center-based programs after leaving EHS and follow this with a presentation of the impacts of the EHS program for the total sample at three time points—when the children were 2, 3, and 5 years old. We conducted three different analyses, the first estimating impacts at each age, the second using growth curve analyses to estimate impacts across all three ages, and the third examining possible age 3 mediators of impacts seen at age 5. Subgroup analyses are presented in later chapters (child and family characteristics in Chapter IV and program service delivery characteristics in Chapter V).

Impacts at age 2 provide a picture of the progress of the EHS group (compared to the control group) at a mid-point during the receipt of EHS services. Impacts at age 3 compare the two groups at the end of the intervention, and impacts at age 5 compare the groups 2 years after the intervention ended. The first set of impacts (at age 2) might be labeled "intermediate" effects, the second (at age 3) "end-of-program" effects, and the third (at age 5) "postintervention" effects.

As a comprehensive program, EHS services target a wide range of areas intended to benefit children, their parents, and their families (ACF, 2002b; Berlin, Brooks-Gunn, & Aber, 2001; Connell & Kubisch, 2001). Consequently, we collected a rich array of measures, including the following domains: child social, emotional, and attention outcomes; child language, cognitiveg, and academic skills; child health; parenting and the home environment; family well-being and mental health; and parent self-sufficiency. In total, the EHS evaluation assessed 9 child outcomes at ages 2 and 3, and 10 at age 5. There were 13 family outcomes at all three ages. See Chapter II for details on study design and measures.

Corresponding author: Jeanne Brooks-Gunn, Teachers College and the College of Physicians and Surgeons, Columbia University, 525 West 120th Street, New York, New York 10027, email: brooks-gunn@columbia.edu

In creating Head Start's new program serving low-income pregnant women and families with children from birth (or prenatally) to age 3, the Advisory Committee on Services for Families with Infants and Toddlers recommended that programs seek to place children leaving EHS in high-quality, formal early childhood programs in which the children could receive services between the age of 3 and entry into kindergarten (U.S. Department of Health and Human Services [USDHHS], 1994).

After leaving their EHS program, the EHS sample, as a group, no longer had consistent access to the kinds of support they received while enrolled. In addition, a substantial percentage of families left EHS before their child turned 3, perhaps even before the program had developed a transition plan. Thus, we could examine the impacts on program participation between the ages of 3 and 5 when (1) parents largely had to find programs and care arrangements on their own; (2) many Head Start and other prekindergarten programs (where they existed) did not enroll children until they were age 4, potentially creating a gap in services between leaving EHS and entering Head Start; (3) some families received help in finding child care and other program arrangements from an EHS, Head Start, or similar program; and (4) a wider variety of programmatic experiences was possible.

At age 5, we asked parents about children's formal program experiences from ages 3 to 5. Formal program experiences included center-based child care, prekindergarten programs, and Head Start. Former EHS children were more likely to attend a formal program at both ages 3–4 and 4–5 than non-EHS children ($p < .05$), although fewer than half of EHS children (47%) attended a formal program at both ages. Former EHS children were also more likely to have attended Head Start during this period ($p < .01$): 55% of former EHS children attended Head Start (Table 2). This exposure to formal center-based programs by both the EHS and control group children is important context for our analysis of EHS program impacts at age 5.

IMPACTS ON CHILD AND PARENT OUTCOMES AT AGES 2, 3, AND 5

Research Questions

The overall analyses presented in this chapter focus on the impacts of EHS across all 17 sites. The sites differed in the mix of services offered to families (in Chapter V, we present findings by the three different approaches that sites used—home-based only, primarily center-based, and a mix of home-based and center-based services). In formulating our hypotheses, we considered results from previous early childhood education (ECE) evaluations that included children up to age 3, both those that were home visiting programs and those that were a combination of home visiting and center

TABLE 2

OVERALL IMPACTS OF EARLY HEAD START ON PROGRAM PARTICIPATION AFTER EARLY HEAD START

Outcome (Percentages)	Program Group	Control Group	Estimated Impact	Effect Size[a]
Any Formal Program Participation				
Ages 3–4	49.0	43.6	5.4*	.11
Ages 4–5	81.7	82.3	−0.5	−.01
Ever 3–5	89.6	88.2	1.3	.04
Both Ages	46.6	41.9	4.7*	.10
Head Start Participation				
Ages 4–5	47.2	42.8	4.4*	.09
Ever 3–5	54.9	48.8	6.0**	.12
Other Formal Program Participation				
Ages 4–5	50.2	55.3	−5.1*	−.10
Ever 3–5	59.4	62.9	−3.5	−.07
Other				
Total Time in All Formal Programs (Months)	13.5	13.1	0.4	.06
Ever in Informal Care (Percentage)	56.1	51.9	4.2*	.08
Sample Size[b]	**934–1,071**	**856–991**		

Source. Parent interviews, interviewer observations, and assessments of semistructured parent–child interactions conducted when children were in their prekindergarten year.
Note. All impact estimates were calculated using regression models, in which each site was weighted equally.
$^+p < .10.$ $^*p < .05.$ $^{**}p < .01.$
[a]The effect size was calculated by dividing the estimated impact by the standard deviation of the outcome measure for the control group.
[b]Sample varied slightly depending on the outcome variable.

based (none of the previous intervention programs for young children were only center based).

We had several expectations for the overall impact analyses. First, we expected that impacts would be more likely during the program than 2 years after it concluded (i.e., at ages 2 and 3 vs. age 5). Other program evaluations targeting young children and families have reported stronger effects at the end of a program than years later (e.g., Barnett, 1995; Brooks-Gunn, 2011; Brooks-Gunn et al., 1994; Camilli et al., 2010; Karoly et al., 2005). Effect sizes are often smaller than those seen earlier 2 or more years after the treatment ends. The timing of EHS effects at age 2 versus 3 was difficult to predict. On the one hand, one might expect effects to appear by age 2, given that the families entered the program during a mother's pregnancy or during a child's first year of life (median age of entry about 6 months). On the other hand, if more intervention services are needed to alter a particular behavior, or if emerging behaviors at age 3 are more influenced by the intervention than by precursors at age 2, then effects might be stronger at the later age. It is important to note that by age 2, families had between 14 and 27 months of intervention services (depending on when they entered EHS); given the variation in service length, which was allowed by the research design, many families had not had 2 years of intervention when the age 2 assessment was conducted. Similarly, at the time of the age 3 assessment, the duration of family program participation averaged 22 months. This design feature is different from previous ECE evaluation in which families were recruited in a much narrower developmental frame.

Second, we expected that the strongest effects would be seen for parenting behavior and the home environment, given the emphasis that EHS programs placed on this aspect of family life and the comprehensive services provided by the program (ACF, 2002b). Additionally, well-evaluated home visiting programs for young children and their families are most likely to exhibit effects in this domain, compared to other domains (Brooks-Gunn, Berlin, & Fuligni, 2000; Howard & Brooks-Gunn, 2009; Sweet & Appelbaum, 2004). Although EHS programs varied by program approach in the amount of home visiting offered and the extent to which they offered center-based care, virtually all children and families did receive home visits, although the number of visits was much smaller in center-based programs than in home-based and mixed-approach programs (see Chapter V).

Third, whereas parenting distress and mental health are usually targeted by home visiting programs, past literature is mixed as to the benefits in this domain (see Table 2 in Howard & Brooks-Gunn, 2009). The EHS program is not a mental health program. Thus it seemed more likely that EHS would reduce parenting distress and possibly family conflict than maternal depression.

Fourth, we expected EHS to affect child outcomes in the language, cognitive, social, emotional, and approaches to learning domains. Previous ECE program evaluations have reported such findings, although past evaluations have not included the rich array of measures used in the EHS study. The EHS evaluation assessed not only behavior problems, as have most past evaluations, but also social behavior problems, attention, engagement with the mother, and emotion regulation. Given the emphasis EHS program staff placed on these aspects of development, we expected to find effects across these measures. We expected that children's language would be enhanced by the EHS program; however, we expected that the overall impacts would be smaller than those seen in previous evaluations of center-based programs for infants and toddlers (such as the Abecedarian Project and IHDP). In general, rigorous evaluations of home visiting programs have found either small or no effects on young children's language and cognitive development (Gomby, 2005; Howard & Brooks-Gunn, 2009; Sweet & Appelbaum, 2004). Given the moderate intensity of center-based services, and the likelihood that home-based services might not affect language/

cognition, we expected effects to be small when averaged across the entire sample.

Analytic Approach

We present the impacts of participation in EHS on child and family outcomes as differences in mean outcomes between the program and control groups. To increase the precision of our estimates, we estimated regression-adjusted means for each group. Each site was weighted equally because EHS services are administered at the site level and differ across programs. The impacts are presented as two-tailed tests. They are not corrected for multiple comparisons. Historically, evaluations of early childhood interventions, including meta-analyses that have been conducted, do not correct for multiple comparisons. Social science disciplines differ on their criteria for assessing significance, although most scholars look at patterns within findings, an approach that we have adopted.

We defined an EHS participant as a program group member who received more than one EHS home visit, met with an EHS case manager more than once, received at least 2 weeks of EHS center-based care, or participated in a group activity. Because 91% of those families assigned to EHS participated by this definition, we found very few differences between impact estimates based on two-stage least squares regression (treatment on the treated or TOT) and those based on ordinary least squares regression (intent to treat or ITT). Both estimates are shown in the tables reporting impacts in this chapter and in Chapters IV and V; in the text, however, we focus on the TOT impacts. The control group mean is based on the control group members who would have participated in EHS if they had been assigned to the program group instead. This unobserved mean was estimated as the difference between the program group mean for participants and the impact per participant. The estimated impact per participant is measured as the estimated impact per eligible applicant divided by the proportion of program group members who participated in EHS services (which varied slightly by site; see ACF, 2002a for more details). Psychometric information on specific outcomes and descriptive statistics are in Chapter II.

Table 3 presents the findings for the child, parent, and family outcomes at ages 2, 3, and 5. The effect size (ES) was calculated by dividing the estimated impact per participant by the standard deviation of the outcome measure for the control group (Cohen's d; Cohen, 1988). We report significant impacts when $p < .05$ or $< .01$; we report impact estimates with $p < .10$ as approaching significance or as trends when they contribute to a conceptually consistent pattern of impacts across multiple outcomes. We estimated separate models for each outcome measure and discuss results for each of the child, parent, and family domains outlined previously.

TABLE 3

IMPACTS ON SELECTED CHILD AND FAMILY OUTCOMES AT AGES 2, 3, AND 5: FULL SAMPLE

Program-Control Differences, Full Sample

Outcome	Age 2					Age 3					Age 5				
	Program Group Participants[a]	Control Group[b]	Impact Estimate[c]	Effect Size (TOT)[d]	Effect Size (ITT)[d]	Program Group Participants[a]	Control Group[b]	Impact Estimate[c]	Effect Size (TOT)[d]	Effect Size (ITT)[d]	Program Group Participants[a]	Control Group[b]	Impact Estimate[c]	Effect Size (TOT)[d]	Effect Size (ITT)[d]
Child Social–Emotional and Approaches to Learning Outcomes															
CBCL Aggressive Behavior	12.2	13.0	−0.8	−0.12*	−0.11*	10.6	11.3	−0.7	−0.11+	−0.09+	10.6	11.0	−0.4	−0.05	−0.04
FACES Social Behavior Problems											5.3	5.7	−0.4	−0.12*	−0.10*
Negativity Toward Parent During Play	1.7	1.8	−0.1	−0.07	−0.07	1.2	1.3	−0.1	−0.14*	−0.12*	1.2	1.3	−0.0	−0.02	−0.03
Engagement During Play	4.3	4.2	0.1	0.09+	0.08+	4.8	4.6	0.2	0.20**	0.18**	4.7	4.7	−0.0	−0.01	−0.01
Sustained Attention with Objects During Play	5.0	5.0	0.1	0.07	0.07	5.0	4.8	0.2	0.16**	0.14**					
FACES Positive Approaches to Learning[e]											12.2	11.9	0.3	0.14**	0.12**
Observed Bayley Emotion Regulation[e]	3.6	3.7	−0.0	−0.01	−0.01	4.0	4.0	0.0	0.01	0.00					
Observed Leiter Emotion Regulation											91.2	90.9	0.3	0.03	0.02
Observed Attention											8.6	8.4	0.2	0.09+	0.08+
Leiter Attention Sustained											10.9	10.9	0.1	0.02	0.01
Child Language/Cognitive/Academic Skills															
MacArthur CDI Vocabulary	56.5	53.8	2.7	0.12*	0.11*										
English Receptive Vocabulary (PPVT)						83.3	81.1	2.1	0.13*	0.11*	92.0	90.7	1.3	0.09+	0.07
Spanish Receptive Vocabulary (TVIP)						97.2	94.9	2.3	0.27	0.25	90.0	83.0	7.0	0.29*	0.26*
Average Bayley MDI	90.0	88.0	2.1	0.15**	0.14**	91.4	89.9	1.6	0.12*	0.11*					
Percentage Bayley MDI <85	34.1	40.9	−6.8	−0.14**	−0.12**	27.3	32.0	−4.7	−0.10*	−0.08+					
Woodcock Johnson Letter-Word Identification (English)											89.6	90.4	−0.9	−0.06	−0.06
Woodcock Johnson Applied Problems											89.8	88.4	1.4	0.07	0.05
Child Health															
ER Visit Due to Accident or Injury	7.0	8.8	−1.9	−0.07	−0.06	10.2	10.9	−0.8	−0.02	−0.02					
Any Immunizations[f]	98.3	96.5	1.8	0.10*	0.09*	99.0	97.7	1.2	0.09+	0.07+					

(Continued)

41

TABLE 3. (Continued)

Program-Control Differences, Full Sample

	Age 2					Age 3					Age 5				
Outcome	Program Group Participants[a]	Control Group[b]	Impact Estimate[c]	Effect Size (TOT)[c]	Effect Size (ITT)[d]	Program Group Participants[a]	Control Group[b]	Impact Estimate[c]	Effect Size (TOT)[c]	Effect Size (ITT)[d]	Program Group Participants[a]	Control Group[b]	Impact Estimate[c]	Effect Size (TOT)[c]	Effect Size (ITT)[d]
Child Has Individualized Education Plan[g]	3.6	3.9	-0.3	-0.02	-0.02	7.7	5.7	2.0	0.09+	0.08	7.9	7.6	0.3	0.01	0.02
Speech Problems (low score = fewer)											18.8	22.7	-3.9	-0.09+	-0.07+
Parenting and the Home Environment															
HOME Language and Literacy	10.3	10.1	0.2	0.13**	0.12**	10.6	10.4	0.2	0.10*	0.09*	10.4	10.3	0.1	0.03	0.02
Percent Reading Daily	57.9	52.1	5.8	0.12*	0.10*	56.8	52.0	4.9	0.10*	0.09*	34.0	29.3	4.8	0.10*	0.09*
Percent Spanked Last Week	47.2	52.9	-5.7	-0.11*	-0.11*	46.7	53.8	-7.1	-0.14**	-0.13**	35.4	36.6	-1.2	-0.03	-0.02
Parent Supportiveness During Play	4.1	4.0	0.1	0.08+	0.09+	4.0	3.9	0.1	0.15**	0.13**	4.0	3.9	0.1	0.06	0.05
Parent Detachment During Play	1.4	1.5	-0.1	-0.10*	-0.10*	1.2	1.3	-0.1	-0.09+	-0.09+					
Percent Regular Bedtime	61.1	55.4	5.7	0.11*	0.10*	59.4	58.2	1.3	0.03	0.03	11.3	11.0	0.3	0.11*	0.09*
Teaching Activities	4.6	4.5	0.1	0.10*	0.09*	4.4	4.3	0.1	0.09+	0.07	64.1	59.9	4.1	0.08+	0.07+
Children's Books (26 or more)											87.5	79.2	8.3	0.21**	0.19**
Parent Attends Meetings/Open Houses[h]											7.4	8.3	-0.9	-0.12*	-0.10*
Family Well-Being and Mental Health															
Depression[i]	15.4	15.4	-0.0	0.00	0.00	7.4	7.7	-0.3	-0.04	-0.04					
Parenting Distress	24.8	25.9	-1.2	-0.12*	-0.11*	24.7	25.5	-0.7	-0.08	-0.07					
Family Conflict	1.7	1.7	-0.1	-0.10*	-0.09*	1.7	1.7	-0.0	-0.04	-0.04					
Someone in Household Had Alcohol/ Drug Problem, Past Year											7.9	10.5	-2.5	-0.08+	-0.07
Child Witnessed Violence											11.4	11.2	0.1	0.0	0.00
Parent Self-Sufficiency															
Employed[j]	74.3	71.7	0.3	0.06	0.05	86.8	83.4	3.4	0.09+	0.08+	3.6	3.5	0.1	0.04	0.03
In School or Job Training[k]	46.9	41.9	5.0	0.10*	0.09*	60.0	51.4	8.6	0.17**	0.16**					
Income (dollars)[l]	14498.2	14864.2	-366.0	-0.03	-0.02	16871.7	17813.1	-941.4	-0.07	-0.07	2337.8	2258.6	79.3	0.04	0.03
Sample Size															
Parent interview	1,118	1,048	2,166			1,105	999	2,104			978	1,084	2,062		

(Continued)

TABLE 3. (Continued)

| | Program-Control Differences, Full Sample | | | | | | | | | | | | | | |
| | Age 2 | | | | | Age 3 | | | | | Age 5 | | | | |
Outcome	Program Group Participants[a]	Control Group[b]	Impact Estimate[c]	Effect Size (TOT)[d]	Effect Size (ITT)[d]	Program Group Participants[a]	Control Group[b]	Impact Estimate[c]	Effect Size (TOT)[d]	Effect Size (ITT)[d]	Program Group Participants[a]	Control Group[b]	Impact Estimate[c]	Effect Size (TOT)[d]	Effect Size (ITT)[d]
Parent–child interactions	941	855	1,796			874	784	1,658			827	890	1,717		
Bayley	931	850	1,781			879	779	1,658			NA	NA	NA		
Child assessments	994	918	1,912			928	832	1,760			836	919	1,755		

Source. Parent interviews, interviewer observations, and assessments of semistructured parent–child interactions conducted when children were in their prekindergarten year. HOME, Home Observation for Measurement of the Environment; CBCL, Child Behavior Check List; FACES, Family and Child Experiences Survey; PPVT, Peabody Picture Vocabulary Test; TVIP, Test de Vocabulario de Imagines Peabody.

Note. All impact estimates were calculated using regression models in which each site was weighted equally. All values in the tables are based on two-stage least squares analyses (treatment on treated); except for the columns that depict effect sizes based on ordinary least squares comparisons (intent to treat). Psychometric information on specific outcome measures, including descriptive statistics, is available in Chapter 2.

[a] A participant is defined as a program group member who received more than one Early Head Start home visit, met with an Early Head Start case manager more than once, received at least 2 weeks of Early Head Start center-based care, and/or participated in Early Head Start group parent–child activities.

[b] The control group mean is the mean for the control group members who would have participated in Early Head Start if they had been assigned to the program group instead. This unobserved mean was estimated as the difference between the program group mean for participants and the impact per participant.

[c] The estimated impact per participant is measured as the estimated impact per eligible applicant divided by the proportion of program group members who participated in Early Head Start services (which varied by site). The estimated impact per eligible applicant is measured as the difference between the regression-adjusted means for all program and control group members.

[d] The effect size was calculated by dividing the estimated impact per participant by the standard deviation of the outcome measure for the control group. For ease of reading, all statistically significant effect sizes appear in bold.

[e] Emotion regulation measured at ages 2 and 3 with the Bayley Behavior Rating Scales and at age 5 with the Leiter-R observer ratings.

[f] Reported as percentage of children who had received any immunizations by the time of each interview.

[g] At age 2 the time frame for this question is 15 months after random assignment. At age 3 the time frame is 26 months after random assignment. At ages 2 and 3 this item is measured as eligible for early intervention services.

[h] Includes only parents whose children were in a formal program. Sample sizes for this outcome were *N* = 440 and *N* = 467 for program and control groups, respectively.

[i] Depression measured with the Composite International Diagnostic Interview (CIDI) at age 2.

[j] At age 2 the time frame for this question is 15 months after random assignment, and at age 3 the time frame is 26 months after random assignment. At each earlier age the item is whether employed or not, but at age 5 we asked "How much time in the past 6 months have you held a job or jobs in which you worked at least 20 hr per week?" Answers were on a 5-point scale from 1 = *never* to 5 = *all of the time.*

[k] At age 2 the time frame for this question is 15 months after random assignment, and at age 3 the time frame is 26 months after random assignment.

[l] At age 2 the time frame for this question is 15 months after random assignment, and at age 3 the time frame is 26 months after random assignment. Amounts are annual income at ages 2 and 3 and monthly income at age 5.

+ *p* < .10; * *p* < .05; ** *p* < .01.

Child Social–Emotional Outcomes and Approaches to Learning Outcomes

We found positive impacts on several outcomes. By age 3, program group children exhibited less negativity toward their mother and were also more engaged with them (ES = .14, $p < .05$, and .20, $p < .01$, respectively).

The program group showed lower child aggression than the control group as reported by mothers at both ages 2 and 3. The effect sizes were .09, $p < .05$, and .11, $p < .05$. Group means were not significantly different at age 5 (ES = .05). However, at age 5, social behavior problems, as measured by the FACES scale, were significantly higher in the control group (ES = .12, $p < .05$).

Sustained attention with objects was higher in the program group at age 3 (ES = .16, $p < .01$) but not at age 2. Also, at age 5, the program group showed more positive approaches to learning (this FACES measure also taps social skills; ES = .14, $p < .01$) and better observed attention on the Leiter rating scales (ES = .09, $p < .10$). Emotion regulation as observed during the Bayley and Leiter Test assessments did not differentiate the groups.

Child Language, Cognitive, and Academic Skills

EHS enhanced children's cognitive skills at both ages 2 and 3, as evidenced by higher Bayley Mental Development Index (MDI) scores (ES = .16, $p < .01$, and .12, $p < .05$, respectively). Vocabulary was positively affected at both ages as well (ES = .12 for age 2 CDI vocabulary, $p < .05$, and .13 for the PPVT-III at age 3, $p < .05$). At age 5, PPVT-III scores were also positively affected (ES = .09, $p < .10$). For those children taking the Spanish version of the PPVT, we found no significant differences at age 3 (ES = .25), although these became significant at age 5 (ES = .29, $p < .10$). The group of children taking the TVIP was small, particularly at age 5.

In contrast, we found no group differences on the early achievement test scores at age 5 (Woodcock Johnson Letter-Word, Applied Problems, and Leiter Attention Sustained).

Child Health Outcomes

When children were ages 2 and 3, those in the program group were more likely to have had an immunization (ES = .10, $p < .05$, and .09, $p < .10$), although the overall rate of immunizations was very high (more than 95% in the control group at both ages). At age 5, somewhat fewer children in the program group had speech problems (ES = .09, $p < .10$). There were no differences in ER visits due to accidents or injuries.

Parenting and the Home Environment

When the children were ages 2 and 3, mothers in the program group reported engaging in more stimulating activities with their children than the

44

control group. EHS mothers had higher HOME language scores (ES = .12, $p < .01$ and ES = .10, $p < .05$), were more likely to read daily to their children (ES = .12, $p < .05$ and ES = .10, $p < .05$), initiated more teaching activities (ES = .11, $p < .05$ and ES = .09, $p < .10$), exhibited greater supportiveness during play (ES = .09, $p < .10$ and ES = .15, $p < .01$), and were more likely to set a regular bedtime at age 2 (ES = 12, $p < .05$). At age 5, effects were sustained for reading daily and for teaching activities (ES = .10, $p < .05$ at age 2, and ES = .11, $p < .05$ at age 3). Former EHS children were also somewhat more likely to have at least 26 books in their homes (ES = .08, $p < .10$), although there were no longer any significant differences for HOME language scores or supportiveness during play (ES = .03 and .06). In addition, mothers of the 5-year-olds who participated in EHS (and were enrolled in a formal program at that time) were more likely to attend meetings at the child's school (ES = .21, $p < .01$).

With respect to negative parenting, mothers in the program group were somewhat less likely to exhibit lower levels of detachment during play (ES = .10, $p < .05$, and ES = .09 at ages 2 and 3, respectively) and were less likely to report spanking their children (ES = .11, $p < .05$ at age 2 and ES = .14, $p < .01$ at age 3). These differences were not evident at age 5.

Family Well-Being and Mental Health

EHS lowered parenting distress and family conflict at age 2 (ES = .12, $p < .01$, and ES = .10, $p < .05$, respectively), but not at age 3 (ES = .08 and .04). Maternal depression scores were the same in the two groups when the children were 2 and 3 years of age; however, the mothers in the control group had higher depression scores at age 5 than those in the program group (ES = .12, $p < .05$).

In addition, at age 5, mothers in the program group were somewhat less likely to report that a household member had had an alcohol or drug problem in the past year (ES = .08, $p < .10$). There were no group differences in violence toward the mother or violence witnessed by the child at age 5.

Parental Self-Sufficiency

Mothers in the program group were somewhat more likely to be employed at age 3 (ES = .09, $p < .10$) but not at ages 2 or 5. The percentage of employed mothers was high—72% in the control group at age 2 and 83% at age 3. Additionally, at both ages 2 and 3, EHS mothers were more likely to be in school or in job training (ES = .10, $p < .05$, and .17, $p < .01$). Between 44% and 51% of the control group mothers and 48–60% of the EHS group were in school or in job training during the EHS program, which is relatively high, especially given their relatively high rate of employment (over 70%).

Apparently, many mothers were juggling work and training simultaneously. We found no group differences in income at any age point. Given that so many mothers in both the EHS and control groups were employed, this finding is not surprising.

GROWTH CURVE ANALYSES

Research Questions

In this section we report on using growth curves to examine when differences between the program and control groups emerged and whether those differences widened or narrowed over time. In most cases, the first time point examined corresponds to child age 2, and the additional points are ages 3 and 5. If differences between the program and control groups were to widen over time, it would suggest a "snowball effect" wherein early gains from EHS participation produced steeper growth over time. If differences were to narrow, it would be useful to pinpoint when they began to do so. It would also be useful to identify whether the narrowed treatment impact reflected a decline in status of the program group, a rise in status of the control group, or both. The answers could suggest when supportive services should be optimally offered to either or both groups.

The present analysis focuses on five of the outcomes: child cognitive ability, child aggressive behavior, maternal supportiveness, the home environment, and maternal depression. These outcomes were selected because they were assessed at all three time points, and were measured with continuous rather than categorical variables (both are requirements for growth curve analysis).

Our predictions were informed by findings from the cross-sectional impact analyses. First, given the consistent impacts over time for aggressive behavior and social problems, we expected that impacts would be seen at age 2 and continue, although the size of the effect would not increase over time. Second, because the cognitive measures exhibited more consistent program effects at ages 2 and 3 than at age 5, we expected that initial effects at age 2 would either continue at the same magnitude or become greater by age 3, followed by a diminution of effects at age 5. Third, we expected treatment effects for maternal supportiveness to appear at age 2, be sustained at age 3, and diminish somewhat at age 5. We expected impacts on the home language and learning environment to show a similar trend.

Fourth, we were unsure as to what the developmental pattern might be for treatment effects on maternal depressive symptoms. Some previous ECE evaluations have reported reductions in such symptoms though others have not. EHS did not influence maternal depressive symptoms at age 3; therefore, if effects were to be found, they would need to emerge at age 5.

Analytic Approach

Hierarchical linear models (HLMs) were computed with the HLM 6.0 software package (Raudenbush, Byrk, Cheong, & Congdon, 2004). All cases with valid data at one or more time points were included. HLM assumes that data are missing at random, which implies that the observed data can predict missingness adequately at any given time point. That assumption is reasonable in this study because of random assignment and the capture of control variables at baseline, before random assignment.

Child cognitive ability, child aggression, maternal supportiveness, and the home learning environment were assessed initially when children were 2 years of age. Maternal depression was first assessed when children were 14 months of age. Follow-up measures of all five constructs were administered when children were 3 years old, and then again at age 5.

We used two-level models to generate growth curves for each outcome. Individuals constituted the units of analysis at level 2, and outcome scores at each time point constituted the units of analysis at level 1. Specifically, we modeled within-individual growth over time at level 1, as shown in Equation (1a). For four of the five outcomes (child cognitive ability, child

$$Y_{ti} = \beta_{0i} + \beta_{1i}(\text{Age in months}_{ti} - 11.1)$$
$$+ \beta_{2i}(\text{Age in months}_{ti} - 11.1)^2 + e_{ti} \qquad (1a)$$

aggression, maternal supportiveness, and maternal depression), a quadratic term squaring age was found to be significant, indicating that growth was nonlinear over time. Thus, for those four outcomes, each individual i's score on outcome variable Y at time t was modeled as a function of an intercept (β_{0i}), a linear age term (β_{1i}), a nonlinear quadratic age term (β_{2i}), and an error term (e_{ti}). For the home learning environment score (see Eq. 1b), which exhibited purely

$$Y_{ti} = \beta_{0i} + \beta_{1i}(\text{Age in months}_{ti} - 11.1) + e_{ti} \qquad (1b)$$

linear growth over time, each individual i's score on outcome variable Y at time t was modeled as a function of an intercept (β_{0i}), a linear age term (β_{1i}), and an error term (e_{ti}). In all models, the age variable was centered around its minimum value (11.1 months). Thus the level-1 intercept (β_{0i}) is interpreted as individual i's score on outcome variable Y at the earliest age of assessment.

In level 2 models, time-invariant person-level characteristics were used to predict the intercept (β_{0i}) and linear slope (β_{1i}) terms from the level 1 models

(Equations 2a and 2b, respectively)

$$\beta_{0i} = \gamma_{00} + \gamma_{01}(\text{EHS program group}) + \gamma_{02}(\text{Number of moves})$$
$$+ \gamma_{03}(\text{Male child}) + \gamma_{04} \cdots \gamma_{06}(\text{Maternal education dummies})$$
$$+ \gamma_{07} \cdots \gamma_{09}(\text{Race/ethnicity dummies})$$
$$+ \gamma_{010} \cdots \gamma_{025}(\text{Site number dummies}) + u_{0i}$$

$$(2a)$$

$$\beta_{1i} = \gamma_{10} + \gamma_{11}(\text{EHS program group}) + \gamma_{12}(\text{Number of moves})$$
$$+ \gamma_{13}(\text{Male child}) + \gamma_{14} \cdots \gamma_{16}(\text{Maternal education dummies})$$
$$+ \gamma_{17} \cdots \gamma_{19}(\text{Race/ethnicity dummies})$$
$$+ \gamma_{110} \cdots \gamma_{125}(\text{Site number dummies}) + u_{1i}$$

$$(2b)$$

$$\beta_{2i} = \gamma_{20} \qquad (2c)$$

These characteristics included an indicator of EHS program status ($1 =$ program group) as well as characteristics of the children and families at baseline entered as controls. To achieve model stability it was necessary to limit the controls to a select group of those used in the models of program impacts. Those selected fit two criteria: they were not redundant with other characteristics, and they may be hypothesized to moderate the effects of EHS, and so should be held constant. These characteristics included maternal education (9th–11th grade only, high school diploma/GED, and education beyond high school/GED versus less than 9th grade), race/ethnicity (African American, Hispanic, and other versus White), the number of times families moved during the year prior to the baseline, child male, and EHS site (16 dummy variables comparing sites 2–17 to site 1). All controls were grand-mean-centered.

Person-level predictors of the linear slope, if significant, may be thought of as interactions with time. For example, if EHS program status significantly predicted the linear slope, it would indicate an interaction between program status and time, such that the program and control groups had different rates of linear change. Person-level characteristics were excluded as predictors of the linear slope in the final level 2 model if they were not statistically significant in order to clarify the interpretation of main effects (the effects of those characteristics on the intercept, or score at initial assessment).

48

Level 2 equations predicting level-1 intercepts (β_{0i}) and linear slopes (β_{1i}) also included error terms $(u_{0i}$ and u_{1i}; see Eqs. 2a and b). Because preliminary analyses failed to identify level-2 variability in nonlinear slopes (β_{2i}) for all five outcomes, equations predicting β_{2i} did not include level-2 predictors or error terms (see Eq. 2c).

The level-2 intercepts in Equations (2a–c) represent the parameters for an average growth curve when all level-2 predictors are set to zero (i.e., due to centering, its grand mean). In interpreting the level-2 program status indicators, γ_{01} represents the average effect of EHS on the level-1 intercept (i.e., the score at first assessment), and γ_{11} represents the average effect of EHS on linear growth in the level-1 outcome when the remaining level-2 predictors are set to zero.

We used an ITT approach to growth curve analysis due the capacities of the software program. As noted earlier in our previous tables, when the TOT estimates were compared with ITT-generated impacts in the original study, the results differ only in very minor ways.

Results

Growth in Children's Cognitive Skills

The Bayley MDI (Bayley, 1993) was used to measure cognitive ability at ages 2 and 3 but was no longer age-appropriate at age 5. We selected the Applied Problems subtest of the Woodcock-Johnson Test of Achievement (Woodcock & Johnson, 1990) to measure cognitive ability at age 5 because of all the age 5 measures, it is conceptually closest to the Bayley MDI. The level-1 model predicting cognitive ability therefore included a dummy variable to control for whether scores at each time t were based on the Bayley MDI or the Applied Problems subtest. Additional analyses substituting the PPVT-III as the measure of age 5 language skills produced comparable results.

As shown in Table 4, program status had a significant impact on children's cognitive ability at the initial age 2 assessment. The value of γ_{01} was 1.26 $(p < .01)$, indicating that children in the program group scored 1.26 points higher on cognitive ability than children in the control group (with all controls set to their grand mean; ES $= .08$). Program status did not, however, impact linear or nonlinear growth. That is, the rate of change between ages 2 and 5 was the same for the program and control groups. Both experienced nonlinear change in cognitive ability (linear slope x2014;γ_{10}[SE] $= 0.55[0.07]$, $t = 7.41$, $p < .001$; quadratic slope— γ_{20}[SE] $= -0.01[0.00]$, $t = -6.78$, $p < .001$; Table 4 and Figure 2). In both groups, children's scores on cognitive ability increased between ages 2 and 3 (inflection point[7] $= 35.96$ months), but declined thereafter.

TABLE 4

Gamma Coefficients, Standard Errors, and t-Ratios for Hierarchical Linear Models Predicting Selected Child Outcomes Over Time

	Child's Cognitive Ability			Child's Aggression		
	γ	SE	t-Ratio	γ	SE	t-Ratio
Intercept (initial assessment)	82.76	0.90	92.02***	14.88	0.40	36.79***
Program group	1.26	.47	2.71**	−0.41	0.23	−1.78+
Mother completed 9th–11th grade	0.30	1.35	0.22	−0.57	0.44	−1.31
Mother completed HS/GED	2.77	1.43	1.94+	−0.56	0.46	−1.21
Mother went beyond HS/GED	4.43	1.46	3.04**	−1.43	0.47	−3.00**
African American	−4.48	0.78	−5.77***	1.84	0.60	3.06**
Hispanic	−3.71	0.94	−3.94***	0.47	0.71	0.67
Other race/ethnicity	−1.93	1.25	−1.55	−0.87	0.96	−0.91
Number of moves, past year	−0.61	0.23	−2.68**	0.44	0.11	3.92***
Male child	−2.33	0.47	−4.99***	1.17	0.23	5.10***
Site No. 2	3.08	2.58	1.19	0.89	1.28	0.69
Site No. 3	7.96	2.18	3.64**	0.05	1.12	0.04
Site No. 4	12.06	2.18	5.52***	−2.12	1.16	−1.83+
Site No. 5	6.08	2.19	2.78**	−1.43	1.13	−1.26
Site No. 6	12.73	1.92	6.65***	1.31	0.99	1.33
Site No. 7	−2.34	2.19	−1.07	2.85	1.15	2.48*
Site No. 8	−0.59	1.95	−0.30	0.15	1.00	0.15
Site No. 9	15.64	2.19	7.15***	−0.55	1.19	−0.46
Site No. 10	1.52	2.26	0.67	0.64	1.19	0.54
Site No. 11	11.41	2.01	5.69***	−1.24	1.07	−1.16
Site No. 12	−4.25	2.23	−1.91+	−1.22	1.17	−1.04
Site No. 13	8.44	1.89	4.46***	0.70	0.99	0.71
Site No. 14	2.04	2.12	0.97	−1.02	1.13	−0.90
Site No. 15	6.66	1.99	3.35**	0.33	1.05	0.32
Site No. 16	8.80	2.10	4.20***	2.11	1.14	1.86+
Site No. 17	−0.85	2.05	−0.42	−1.66	1.07	−1.55
Linear Slope	0.55	0.07	7.41***	−0.19	0.03	−7.09***
Program group	—	—	—	—	—	—
Mother completed 9th–11th grade	0.10	0.05	2.26*	—	—	—
Mother completed HS/GED	0.07	0.05	1.41	—	—	—
Mother went beyond HS/GED	0.16	0.05	3.20**	—	—	—
African American	—	—	—	−0.08	0.02	−5.12***
Hispanic	—	—	—	−0.05	0.02	−3.01**
Other race/ethnicity	—	—	—	−0.01	0.03	−0.55
Number of moves, past year	—	—	—	—	—	—
Male child	—	—	—	—	—	—
Site No. 2	0.22	0.09	2.51*	−0.00	0.03	−0.14
Site No. 3	−0.11	0.07	−1.64	−0.03	0.03	−1.18
Site No. 4	−0.16	0.07	−2.41*	0.02	0.03	0.69
Site No. 5	−0.19	0.07	−2.64**	−0.00	0.03	−0.05
Site No. 6	−0.17	0.06	−2.81**	−0.04	0.02	−1.75+
Site No. 7	0.08	0.07	1.14	−0.08	0.03	−2.66**

(Continued)

TABLE 4. (*Continued*)

	Child's Cognitive Ability			Child's Aggression		
	γ	SE	t-Ratio	γ	SE	t-Ratio
Site No. 8	−0.09	0.06	−1.49	0.00	0.03	0.19
Site No. 9	−0.23	0.07	−3.31**	−0.05	0.03	−1.55
Site No. 10	−0.01	0.07	−0.14	−0.04	0.03	−1.15
Site No. 11	−0.34	0.06	−5.52***	0.03	0.03	1.23
Site No. 12	0.06	0.07	0.90	0.02	0.03	0.55
Site No. 13	−0.03	0.06	−0.46	−0.04	0.02	−1.83+
Site No. 14	0.11	0.07	1.55	−0.02	0.03	−0.75
Site No. 15	−0.06	0.06	−0.96	−0.03	0.03	−1.33
Site No. 16	−0.39	0.07	−5.89***	−0.07	0.03	−2.51*
Site No. 17	−0.07	0.06	−2.15	0.02	0.03	0.73
Quadratic Slope	−0.01	0.00	−6.78***	0.00	0.00	5.74***

Note: $^+p < .10$; $^*p < .05$; $^{**}p < .01$; $^{***}p < .001$.

Growth in Children's Aggressive Behavior

Children's aggressive behavior was reported by the mother at ages 2, 3, and 5 using the Aggressive Behavior scale from the CBCL (Achenbach & Rescorla, 2000). Program status had a marginally significant effect on children's aggressive behavior at the age 2 assessment ($\gamma_{01}[SE] = -0.41$ [0.23], $t = -1.78$, $p < .10$; Table 4), with children in the program group slightly less aggressive than children in the control group (ES = .06).

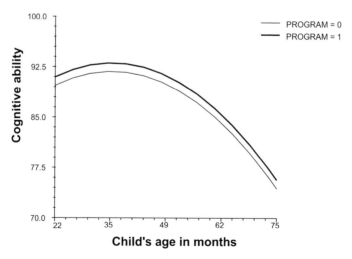

FIGURE 2.—Growth in child's cognitive ability.
Note: All level-2 covariates (number of moves, male child, race/ethnicity, maternal education, and site), and the level-1 dummy variable for the type of cognitive test administered, are set to grand means.

Program status did not have an effect on linear or nonlinear growth in aggression; thus, the difference between the program and control groups stayed constant over time. Both groups experienced nonlinear growth between ages 2 and 5 (linear slope—$\gamma_{10}[SE] = -0.19[0.03]$, $t = -7.09$, $p < .001$; quadratic slope $- \gamma_{20}[SE] = -0.00[0.00]$, $t = 5.74$, $p < .001$; Table 4 and Figure 3). In both groups, children's scores on aggression decreased from age 2 to age 4 and a half (inflection point $= 52.97$ months), but scores increased thereafter. However, aggression scores at age 5 did not exceed initial scores at age 2.

Growth in Maternal Supportiveness

Maternal supportiveness during play was assessed at child ages 2, 3, and 5 from the mother-child videotaped interaction. Program status had a significant impact on maternal supportiveness at age 2 ($\gamma_{01}[SE] = 0.07 [0.03]$, $t = 2.28$, $p < .05$; Table 5). Specifically, mothers in the program group scored 0.07 points higher on supportiveness than did mothers in the control group (ES $= .07$). Program status did not impact linear or nonlinear growth; thus, the differential between the program and control groups remained constant through age 5. Identical patterns of nonlinear growth in supportiveness were found for mothers in both groups (linear slope— $\gamma_{10}[SE] = -0.02[0.00]$, $t = -3.70$, $p < .001$; quadratic slope—$\gamma_{20}[SE] = 0.00[0.00]$, $t = 3.59$, $p < .01$; Table 5 and Figure 4). In both groups, mothers' scores on supportiveness declined slightly after child age 2, but at approximately age 4, they began to increase slightly (inflection point $= 45.98$ months).

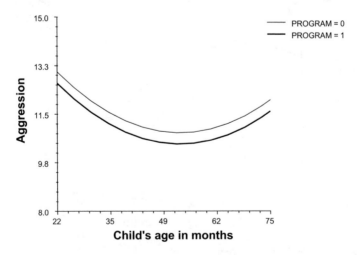

Figure 3.—Growth in child's aggression.
Note: All covariates (number of moves, male child, race/ethnicity, maternal education, and site) are set to grand means.

TABLE 5

Gamma Coefficients, Standard Errors and t-Ratios for Hierarchical Linear Models Predicting Selected Maternal Outcomes Over Time

	Maternal Supportiveness			Home Learning Environment			Maternal Depression		
	γ	SE	t-Ratio	γ	SE	t-Ratio	γ	SE	t-Ratio
Intercept (initial assessment)	4.15	0.06	63.94***	0.87	0.01	170.27***	9.13	0.20	46.07***
Program group	0.07	0.03	2.28*	0.02	0.00	3.36**	-0.23	0.22	-1.06
Mother completed 9th–11th grade	0.29	0.06	4.71***	0.06	0.01	7.20***	-0.19	0.42	-0.45
Mother completed high school/GED	0.50	0.06	7.6***	0.09	0.01	9.62***	-0.79	0.45	-1.76+
Mother went beyond high school/GED	0.77	0.07	11.58***	0.13	0.01	13.52***	-1.79	0.46	-3.91***
African-American	-0.33	0.09	-3.49**	-0.06	0.01	-8.16***	0.42	0.36	1.19
Hispanic	-0.28	0.11	-2.59*	-0.08	0.01	-8.07***	-1.35	0.43	-3.12**
Other race/ethnicity	-0.11	0.16	-0.71	-0.03	0.01	-2.79**	0.17	0.59	0.29
Number of moves, past year	0.01	0.02	0.88	-0.01	0.00	-2.68**	0.60	0.11	5.63***
Male child	-0.14	0.06	-2.52*	-0.01	0.00	-2.51*	0.12	0.22	0.54
Site No. 2	0.42	0.20	2.15*	-0.04	0.03	-1.53	-1.24	0.90	-1.38
Site No. 3	-0.05	0.17	-0.32	-0.00	0.02	-0.20	0.46	0.86	0.54
Site No. 4	0.41	0.18	2.34*	0.00	0.02	0.02	-0.90	0.88	-1.02
Site No. 5	0.09	0.17	0.53	-0.09	0.03	-2.98**	-0.88	0.85	-1.03
Site No. 6	0.16	0.16	0.99	0.02	0.02	0.77	-0.39	0.79	-0.50
Site No. 7	-0.23	0.18	-1.30	-0.04	0.03	-1.55	0.65	0.85	0.76
Site No. 8	-0.17	0.15	-1.13	-0.10	0.02	-4.37***	1.65	0.79	2.10*
Site No. 9	-0.18	0.19	-0.97	-0.04	0.03	-1.32	-2.24	0.88	-2.54*
Site No. 10	-0.05	0.18	-0.25	-0.03	0.03	-1.13	-0.96	0.90	-1.06
Site No. 11	-0.19	0.17	-1.15	0.00	0.03	0.12	1.11	0.82	1.35
Site No. 12	-0.14	-0.18	-0.75	-0.03	0.03	-0.98	-1.45	0.88	-1.65
Site No. 13	0.61	0.15	4.05***	0.01	0.02	0.28	0.19	0.78	0.24
Site No. 14	0.47	0.17	2.76**	0.08	0.03	3.24**	-0.62	0.84	-0.74
Site No. 15	0.23	0.16	1.41	0.02	0.03	0.92	0.41	0.82	0.50
Site No. 16	0.01	0.17	0.04	-0.14	0.02	-6.22***	-1.54	0.87	-1.77+

(Continued)

53

TABLE 5. (Continued)

	Maternal Supportiveness			Home Learning Environment			Maternal Depression		
	γ	SE	t-Ratio	γ	SE	t-Ratio	γ	SE	t-Ratio
Site No. 17	-0.41	0.17	-2.45*	-0.08	0.03	-2.81**	-2.56	0.83	-3.09**
Linear Slope	-0.02	0.00	-3.70***	-0.00	0.00	-13.23***	-0.06	0.01	-4.46***
Program group	—	—	—	—	—	—	—	—	—
Mother completed 9th–11th grade	—	—	—	—	—	—	—	—	—
Mother completed high school/GED	—	—	—	—	—	—	—	—	—
Mother went beyond high school/GED	—	—	—	—	—	—	—	—	—
African-American	0.00	0.00	1.52	—	—	—	—	—	—
Hispanic	0.01	0.00	2.63**	—	—	—	—	—	—
Other race/ethnicity	0.01	0.00	1.32	—	—	—	—	—	—
Number of moves, past year	—	—	—	—	—	—	—	—	—
Male child	0.00	0.00	2.18*	—	—	—	-0.07	0.02	-2.85**
Site No. 2	-0.01	0.01	-1.24	0.01	0.00	7.14***	-0.03	0.02	-1.29
Site No. 3	0.00	0.00	0.11	0.00	0.00	3.25**	0.01	0.02	0.50
Site No. 4	-0.01	0.00	-1.19	0.00	0.00	4.38***	-0.03	0.02	-1.11
Site No. 5	-0.00	0.00	-0.75	0.01	0.00	5.24***	-0.01	0.02	-0.53
Site No. 6	-0.00	0.00	-0.41	0.00	0.00	1.61	-0.02	0.02	-1.03
Site No. 7	0.00	0.01	0.28	0.00	0.00	1.01	0.01	0.02	0.34
Site No. 8	0.00	0.00	0.78	0.01	0.00	7.95***	0.03	0.02	1.52
Site No. 9	-0.00	0.00	-0.43	0.01	0.00	4.70***	-0.03	0.02	-1.11
Site No. 10	0.00	0.01	0.94	0.01	0.00	5.34***	-0.02	0.02	-0.75
Site No. 11	-0.00	0.00	-0.14	0.00	0.00	2.80**	-0.01	0.02	-0.36
Site No. 12	-0.00	0.00	-0.97	0.00	0.00	1.64	0.01	0.02	0.66
Site No. 13	-0.01	0.00	-2.13*	0.00	0.00	5.03***	-0.01	0.02	-0.56
Site No. 14	-0.00	0.00	-0.97	-0.00	0.00	-2.61**	-0.02	0.02	-1.15
Site No. 15	0.00	0.00	0.31	0.00	0.00	2.24*	0.00	0.02	0.18
Site No. 16	0.00	0.00	0.04	0.01	0.00	6.40***	0.05	0.02	2.33*
Site No. 17	0.01	0.00	1.94+	0.00	0.00	4.16***	0.00	0.02	
Quadratic Slope	0.00	0.00	3.59**	—	—	—	0.00	0.00	3.30**

Note: + p < .10; * p < .05; ** p < .01; *** p < .001.

54

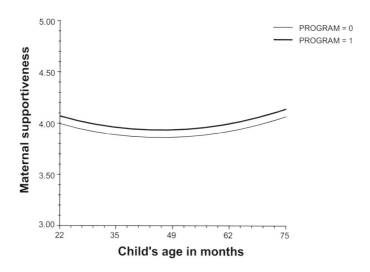

FIGURE 4.—Growth in maternal supportiveness.
Note: All covariates (number of moves, male child, race/ethnicity, maternal education, and site) are set to grand means.

Growth in the Home Language and Learning Environment

The quality of the home environment was measured at ages 2, 3, and 5 with a subscale of the HOME Inventory (Caldwell & Bradley, 1984; Fuligni et al., 2004). Because the number of items in the scale varied slightly across the three ages, scores at each time point were converted into proportions of the total possible score. Therefore, scores ranged from 0 to 1 ($M = .82$, $SD = .17$).

Program status had a significant impact on the home learning environment at the time of the age 2 assessment ($\gamma_{01}[SE] = 0.02[0.00]$, $t = 3.36$, $p < .01$; see Table 5). Mothers in the program group scored 2 percentage points higher on the home learning environment than mothers in the control group (ES = .11). However, their rate of change between ages 2 and 5 was identical to that of mothers in the control group. Both groups experienced only linear growth over time. Scores decreased from age 2 to age 5 (linear slope—$\gamma_{10}[SE] = -0.00[0.00]$, $t = -13.23$, $p < .001$; Table 5 and Figure 5).

Growth in Maternal Depression

At age 14 months, 3 years, and 5 years, mothers completed the CES-D scale (Radloff, 1977); at age 2, a different depression scale was administered, so we used the child age 14 months CES-D scores for this analysis. The long form was used at age 14 months (20 items) and the short form (12 items) at ages 3 and 5. To achieve consistency, we selected only the items from the age

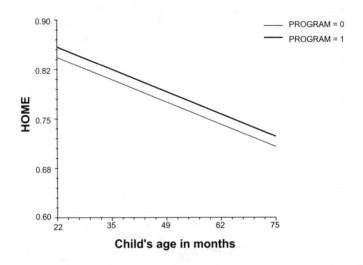

FIGURE 5.—Growth in home learning environment.
Note: All covariates (number of moves, male child, race/ethnicity, maternal education, and site) are set to grand means.

14 months form that appear in the short form for the present analyses (i.e., 12 items at each of the three ages).

Program status did not have a significant impact on maternal depression at the initial assessment at child age 14 months. Nor did program status have an effect on linear or nonlinear growth in maternal depression (Table 5 and Figure 6). Accordingly, growth curves, including intercept values, were identical, regardless of program status (linear slope—$\gamma_{10}[SE] = -0.06[0.01]$, $t = -4.46, p < .001$; quadratic slope—$\gamma_{20}[SE] = 0.00[0.00]$, $t = 3.30, p < .01$; Table 5 and Figure 6). Scores on maternal depression declined slightly after child age 14 months until child age 3 (inflection point = 38.30 months), when they started to increase slightly. Scores at age 5 resembled those at age 14 months.

MEDIATORS OF EHS PROGRAM IMPACTS AT AGE 5

Research Questions

If impacts are found at age 5, 2 years after the EHS program ended, it is likely that earlier effects account for sustained effects. Therefore, we conducted mediator analyses to investigate the extent to which impacts found earlier mediated or accounted for, at least in part, any impacts discovered later. A few previous evaluations of early childhood programs have reported such analysis. In one, based on the Abecedarian Project and Project

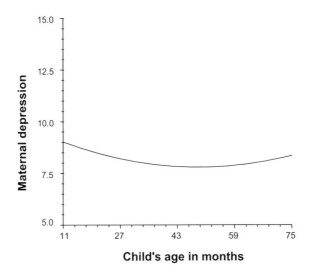

Figure 6.—Growth in maternal depression.
Note: All covariates (number of moves, male child, race/ethnicity, maternal education, and site) are set to grand means. Intercepts and slopes are identical for the program and control groups.

CARE, Burchinal, Campbell, Bryant, Wasik, and Ramey (1997) reported that sustained cognitive effects in childhood were in part due to program changes in infants' cognitive responsiveness. At the same time, the parenting behaviors measured (which were parental attitudes, not actually parenting behavior) were not influenced by the program and therefore could not have been operating as mediators. In the IHDP study, impacts on maternal depression when the children were 1 year of age influenced the later impact on behavior problems at age 3 (Klebanov, Brooks-Gunn, McCarton, & McCormick, 1998). In the same intervention program, effects on parenting behavior mediated program effects on cognitive development (Linver, Brooks-Gunn, & Kohen, 1999).

Based on the small research base, we did not have differential expectations for how intermediate and end-of-program impacts would mediate later outcomes, so we focused on end-of-program impacts. We expected impacts at the end of the program to mediate longer term impacts in the following ways (keeping in mind that at age 5, program impacts were found for behavior and attention, but not for achievement test scores). First, early program effects on child's language and cognition would be likely to mediate later program impacts on attention. Second, parenting behaviors, measured here as HOME language and literacy support, were expected to mediate later program impacts as well (both behavior and attention). Third, reductions in aggressive behavior at age 3 were expected to mediate impacts on behavior and attention at age 5.

Analytic Approach

Analyses were conducted using Mplus4 software. To test for mediation, we followed a procedure outlined by Kenny, Kashy, & Bolger, 1998. They defined the amount of mediation as the reduction in the direct effect of the initial variable (in this case, EHS Program) impact on the outcome variable (in this case, the age 5 impact variable) when the mediator is added. They demonstrate that this amount of reduction is equal to the products of the coefficients of the paths comprising the indirect effect. Mplus4 provides two tests relevant to examining mediation in this way. The first is the total indirect effect, which is the cumulative mediated effect through all mediators included in the model. This test answers the question of whether all the included (impact) mediator variables, taken together, mediate the effect of Program on the age 5 (impact) dependent variable. The second type of test is called the specific indirect effect. This is a test of the significance of the mediation through each of the mediators individually, controlling for the other mediators in the model. These tests answer the question of whether individual variables emerge as significant mediators of the effect of program on the age 5 dependent variable. All reported parameter estimates are standardized. In the models, random assignment to the EHS condition (Program) predicts the mediators, and the mediators, in turn, predict the age 5 outcome. Each model also includes a direct path from Program to the age 5 dependent variable. These models also include a group of covariates. The resulting models have no available degrees of freedom and are only identified, so fit statistics were not calculated.

We selected the outcomes and mediators as follows. All child outcomes were from the social, emotional, attention, and approaches to learning domains, given that no overall impacts were found for the cognitive, language, and academic skill domains at age 5. The outcomes include FACES social behavior problems, observed attention from the Leiter Scale, and FACES approaches to learning. The mediators to be examined include earlier aggressive behavior and engagement with the mother during play as well as the Bayley MDI and PPVT-III, all assessed at age 3. The language and literacy environment of the home also was included.

Results

Observed Attention at Age 5

Four of the five age 3 mediators significantly predicted observed attention at age 5 (Figure 7). Engagement during play and Bayley MDI were positively associated with observed attention, and aggressive behavior was negatively associated with it. The total indirect effect was significant ($b = .10$, $t = -3.40$, $p < .001$), indicating that the four age 3 mediators, as a group, significantly

58

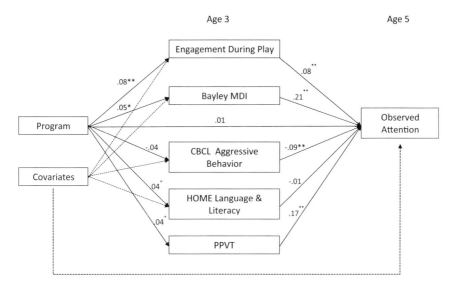

Figure 7.—Age 3 mediators of EHS impact on observed attention at age 5.
Note. All parameter estimates are standardized. Covariates include site, race/ethnicity, primary language at home, maternal education, whether child was first born, maternal employment status, living arrangement, number of children aged 0–5 in the household, number of children aged 6–17 in the household, child sex, whether the child was evaluated for concerns about health and development, whether the child was low birth weight, and whether the family received AFDC, food stamps, or WIC.

mediated the association between program and observed attention. There were two significant specific indirect effects (engagement during play: $b = .03$, $t = 2.44$, $p < .05$; and Bayley MDI: $b = .06$, $t = 2.42$, $p < .05$).

Approaches to Learning

Two of the four age 3 mediators significantly predicted FACES positive approaches to learning at age 5 (Figure 8). CBCL aggressive behavior was negatively associated with positive approaches to learning, whereas language and literacy in the home was positively associated with it. The total indirect effect was significant ($b = .04$, $t = 2.45$, $p < .05$), indicating that the group of four mediators significantly mediated the effect of EHS program on approaches to learning (Figure 8). There were no significant specific indirect effects. As with the model with age 2 mediators, the direct path from EHS program to approaches to learning was significant, indicated that the EHS Program had an impact on this outcome that was not mediated completely through the age 3 mediators.

Social Behavior Problems

Only one of the age 3 mediators, CBCL aggressive behavior, significantly predicted FACES social behavior problems (Figure 9). The total indirect

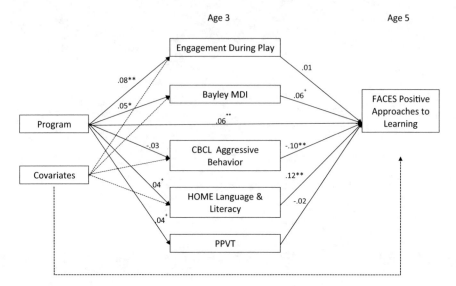

FIGURE 8.—Age 3 mediators of EHS impact on positive approaches to learning at age 5 (see Figure 7 note).

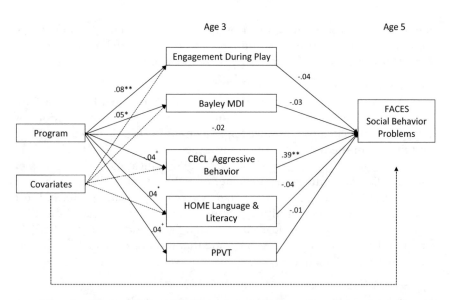

FIGURE 9.—Age 3 mediators of EHS impact on behavior problems at age 5 (see Figure 7 note).

effect of the mediators was significant and negative ($b = -.15$, $t = 2.37$, $p < .05$). None of the specific indirect effects was significant, but there was a trend for CBCL ($b = -.11$, $t = 1.75$, $p < .10$) to be a mediator.

DISCUSSION

The overall impacts suggest that the EHS program was effective in enhancing child, parent, and family outcomes at ages 2 and 3. The effects, although modest in size (with effect sizes of .15–.20), were found across a wide array of outcomes. In addition, the effects often appeared as early as age 2 and were for the most part maintained through age 3. At age 5, significant impacts continued to be seen for child social, emotional, attention, and approaches to learning outcomes. However, differences in vocabulary and achievement were not seen at age 5 (although Spanish-speaking 5-year-olds who participated in EHS had higher vocabulary scores than their control group counterparts). Parenting behaviors also were enhanced by the EHS program at age 2, with these effects, for the most part, being sustained at age 3 and some continued through age 5. Family well-being was enhanced at age 2, although these gains were not significant at age 3. By age 5, mothers in the EHS group had lower depression scores and were less likely to have someone in the household with an alcohol or drug problem. Furthermore, EHS was somewhat effective in getting children into formal program settings, including Head Start, following EHS, although more than half of the children were not in formal program continuously in the 2 years between EHS and kindergarten. As context for the impacts observed at age 5, we noted that EHS program participation had small (5–6 percentage points) but significant impacts on the percentage of children enrolled in formal early care and education programs, including Head Start, between ages 3 and 5.

The growth curve analyses indicate that the EHS program had a positive impact on four of the five potential outcomes considered here: child cognitive skills, child aggressive behavior, maternal supportiveness, and the home language and learning environment. By contrast, EHS had little impact on maternal depression in the growth curve analyses.

Notably, the results of growth curve analysis reveal a similar pattern for the four outcomes affected by EHS. First, the positive impacts of EHS appeared early; second, the magnitude of the impacts remained constant or diminished over the 3-year observation period. With respect to the first point, the current analyses show that EHS had a positive impact on children's cognitive ability and aggressive behavior, along with maternal supportiveness and the home learning environment, by the time children were 2 years old. By that age, families had participated in EHS for approximately 18 months, on

61

average. The current analysis shows that the differences in treatment and control families were similar over time (i.e., the growth curves for each did not converge, as would be expected if the treatment group become more like the control group, nor did they diverge, as would be expected if the treatment group became less like the control group). However, behavioral differences were seen at age 5, whereas cognitive ones were not in the cross-sectional analyses.

Although it is noteworthy that the program impacts did not diminish over time, neither did they increase. This was true when looking at the size of impacts during the program (ages 2 and 3) and after the program (age 5). These results are consistent with other effective early education programs, all of which have demonstrated steady or declining, but never increasing, impacts during or after the program ended (Barnett, 1995; Brooks-Gunn, 2004; Campbell, Pungello, Miller-Johnson, Burchinal, & Ramey, 2001; Currie, 2001; Gray & Klaus, 1970; Karoly et al., 2005; Lee, Brooks-Gunn, Schnur, & Liaw, 1990; McCarton et al., 1997; Schweinhart, Barnes, & Weikart, 1993).

Other program evaluations also have not reported increases in impact effect sizes over the life of the intervention (in the few evaluations for which data at ages 2 and 3 exist). However, such an increase could theoretically appear because with several child outcomes, early differences between children widen over time. Higher performing children have a stronger base of knowledge and awareness into which new lessons are incorporated, and their early successes might increase their motivation (Knudsen, Heckman, Cameron, & Shonkoff, 2006).

It is especially noteworthy that the curves for the treatment and control groups did not converge. Other evaluations suggest that impacts decline by more than one-half of a standard deviation a few years after the program has ended (Anderson, 2008; Karoly et al., 2005); however, the earlier results are based on cross-sectional analyses, not growth curve analyses. It has been suggested that the effects of Head Start fade over time because its graduates go on to attend poor-quality schools that undermine gains from the program (Lee & Loeb, 1995). A similar process might also apply to EHS graduates. The formal early care and education arrangements children entered after EHS may not have been of sufficiently high quality to augment, rather than merely sustain, the gains made during the program. And, in the EHS sample, many families did not receive any services in the 4th and 5th year of the study, after the end of the program, also mitigating against sustained effects. In Chapter VI we report that the children who displayed the most optimal outcomes at age 5 were those who went on to attend a formal early care and education program after EHS.

Finally, it is worth noting that the growth curve analysis was limited by the available measures. Ideally, such analysis would be based on identical measures administered at all time points. In the current study, legitimate concerns about age-appropriateness led to the use of a different assessment of children's cognitive ability at age 5 than at ages 2 and 3. Consequently, our analysis of children's growth in this area used two different tests, but we were able to compare them because they were scored on the same metric when standardized by national age norms. However, raw scores generally are preferred to standardized scores for the purposes of growth curve analysis. Unlike raw scores, which can be compared intuitively over time, standardized scores express children's achievement relative to those of their peers, thus limiting their interpretability over time.

The mediator analyses of the three child outcomes at age 5 were, for the most part, significant. For observed attention, the mediators accounted for all of the program impact, with children's earlier vocabulary, mental developmental index, and aggressive behavior accounting for the sustained effect. HOME language and literacy impacts at age 3 were not associated with a reduction in the EHS impact on observed attention at age 5. Reductions in children's aggression at age 3 accounted for the age 5 impacts on social behavior problems (while vocabulary, mental developmental index, and HOME language and literacy did not). Impacts on positive approaches to learning were accounted for, in part, by HOME language and literacy, as well as by earlier impacts on children's aggressive behavior.

NOTE

7. The inflection point is the value on the x-axis at which the curve bends.

IV. FAMILY SUBGROUPS AND IMPACTS AT AGES 2, 3, AND 5: VARIABILITY BY RACE/ETHNICITY AND DEMOGRAPHIC RISK

Helen H. Raikes, Cheri Vogel, and John M. Love

In 1989–1990, the Head Start "Blueprint" Commission convened experts from universities and the Head Start community to make recommendations for a new generation of Head Start research studies. Among the specific recommendations of that commission was to study what works for whom under what circumstances (US DHHS, 1990). This recommendation was made because, among other reasons, Head Start, as a national program, served diverse population groups. When Early Head Start (EHS) was created in 1995, it continued this Head Start tradition.

RACIAL/ETHNIC DIVERSITY AMONG EARLY HEAD START FAMILIES

Programs serve families diverse in race/ethnicity. The EHS sample included 37% Whites, 35% African Americans, 24% Hispanics, and 5% other ethnicities. To illustrate the diversity, EHS in Yakima, Washington, serves largely settled and former migrant Hispanic families, largely originating from Mexico. However, in McKenzie, Tennessee, EHS serves primarily African Americans, whereas the families in the Marshalltown, Iowa, site are primarily White in origin but with increasing numbers of Hispanics. EHS in New York City, located on East Broadway in Manhattan, serves families who are White, African American, and Hispanic (the Hispanics being primarily from Puerto Rico). Race/ethnicity provides important context for program participation but may also affect the pathways and mechanisms by which the program may have an impact. Differential patterns of participation in early childhood program types by race/ethnicity have been documented. For example, Hispanic families tend to be less frequent users of center-based early

Corresponding author: Helen Raikes, Child, Youth and Family Studies, 257 Mabel Lee Hall, University of Nebraska-Lincoln, Lincoln, Nebraska 68588-0236, email: hraikes2@unl.edu

childhood services than other racial/ethnic groups (Capizzano et al., 2007; Magnusson & Waldfogel, 2005). According to the previous infant-toddler intervention literature, African Americans consistently benefit from intervention programs (Garber & Heber, 1981; Ramey & Campbell, 1984) but few studies have followed Hispanics receiving 0–3 services longitudinally. This context introduces substantial variation in program use and effects in ways that have been little researched; race/ethnicity can also influence the choices and opportunities families have for subsequent experiences, for example, following EHS, which is the focus of later chapters of this monograph. In this chapter, we present findings from impact analyses for three racial/ethnic groups when children were 2, 3, and 5 years of age. These are essentially moderator analyses (i.e., treatment by race/ethnicity).

DEMOGRAPHIC RISKS AMONG EHS FAMILIES

Not only are there racial/ethnic differences, families in EHS are also diverse in terms of risk status. Nearly all EHS families are at risk by virtue of the fact that their annual incomes are at or below the federal poverty line. All these families encounter challenges due to poverty (Brooks-Gunn & Duncan, 1997; Duncan, Brooks-Gunn, & Klebanov, 1994), but many have additional challenges. Programs have a mandate to serve families with greatest needs within their communities but what this means may differ from one community to the next. For example, Sumter, South Carolina, serves single, teenage parents, so teenage parenthood is an additional risk factor for these parents. Other EHS programs add different risk factors to poverty in determining eligibility for the program. There are many ways to characterize risk factors. In the EHSREP, we identified five demographic risk factors measured at program entry—teenage parent status; single parent status; parent neither employed nor in school; parent receiving cash assistance; and parent not completed high school. Families were characterized according to whether they had 0–2 (low), 3 (moderate), or 4–5 (high) risk factors and EHS families tended to fall in roughly comparably sized groups across these three categories (45%, 30%, and 25% of the sample, respectively). In this chapter we examine impacts of the program at three ages for families at different risk levels, again conducting moderator analyses. Several studies have examined differential impacts according to risk; the Abecedarian study (Ramey & Campbell, 1984) found strongest impacts on children in highest risk families but the IHDP found stronger impacts among the heavier low-birthweight children than for the children who had very low birth weights (IHDP, 1990; McCormick et al., 2006). Using a cumulative risk framework for IHDP, moderate-risk poor children benefited the most (Liaw & Brooks-Gunn, 1994), with demographic risks mattering more than psychological risks (Klebanov &

Brooks-Gunn, 2006). These two studies used different ways of characterizing risk and illustrate that different definitions of risk together with varying sample characteristics with different cut points for highest risk make it difficult to compare findings about risk across studies.

METHODS FOR ANALYZING SUBGROUPS

Targeted analyses to examine whether there were program-control differences within subgroups were conducted at ages 2 and 3 and for the age 5 follow up. These analyses were conducted in the same way at each age and in a manner consistent with the analysis of overall impacts. Impacts were weighted equally by site, and sites were included in the analyses if they included 10 or more families in both the program and control groups that met the characteristic of the subgroup (in the case of the child and family subgroups). We also conducted chi-square tests to gauge whether the impacts differed across subgroups (e.g., whether impacts for African Americans, Hispanics, and Whites differed from each other). In these chi-square analyses, there were significant differences between groups for nearly half of the outcomes at age 2, two-thirds of outcomes at age 3, and one-quarter of outcomes at age 5— tables available from authors upon request. In this chapter, we report impacts for subgroups that pertain to race/ethnicity and risk and in Chapter V by program approach. We followed the same analytic procedures as those used for the sample overall, as described in Chapter III (i.e., both ITT and TOT estimates are reported in the tables).

Hypotheses

On the basis of the literature and early EHSREP findings, we developed six hypotheses to guide analysis of the race/ethnicity and risk subgroups.

First, given substantial EHS age 2 and age 3 positive impacts on African Americans (with many impacts showing effect sizes of about one half a standard deviation), we expected positive impacts at age 5 on many child and parenting outcomes to be maintained by virtue of the primacy of early experiences hypothesis and due to expected contemporaneous effects from sustained positive impacts on parents continuing to contribute to children's positive development during the years 3–5 (NICHD, 2005b).

Second, the impacts for Whites in the EHSREP tended to be concentrated on parents at age 2, with some child social–emotional impacts. For White families, it would be surprising for other effects to emerge at age 5 when they had not been seen at age 3. It is important to point out that White children in the control group were not faring as poorly as control group children of other racial/ethnic groups.

Third, for Hispanic children, a nonsignificant program effect size of around .38 on age 3 English receptive vocabulary might be expected to be significant by age 5. It is also possible that children's age 5 contemporaneous experiences in the home could be improved if early impacts on language and literacy stimulation and daily reading in the home continued, and parents continued with parenting practices seen when children were age 3.

Fourth, in the low-risk group, we might expect some relatively weak but significant impacts in the social–emotional area to be maintained. An interesting characteristic of this group is that it included a number of children who may have been in EHS due to having disabilities or suspected disabilities when they enrolled (and perhaps not as many other family risk factors). We expected that a higher proportion of children with fewer demographic risk factors in the program group would continue to present more disabilities.

Fifth, in the moderate-risk group, social, emotional and cognitive impacts, as well as parenting impacts at age 3 might be maintained due to the primacy hypothesis; we expected these to be augmented at age 5 due to a number of fairly strong effects on parenting at age 3 (thus providing new contemporaneous experiences for children during the prekindergarten years leading up to the age 5 assessment).

Sixth, in the highest risk group, at ages 2 and 3 there were few positive impacts and one negative trend (reduced child vocabulary in program children). According to Thoits's (2006) hypothesis that sometimes outcomes get worse in interventions before they get better, we might expect to see improvements by age 5 (assuming that age 3 was the "getting worse" part of the intervention). That is, if the intervention were really making families more open but temporarily more vulnerable, consistent with few positive impacts at age 3, then, possibly by age 5, the intervention might show positive effects. Clearly, this hypothesis is speculative.

RESULTS

We report impacts for subgroups of children and parents in this sequence: African American, White, Hispanic, low risk, moderate risk, and highest risk.

Subgroup Impacts by Race/Ethnicity

African American Families

Among African Americans at age 5 in regards to child and parent outcomes, the pattern of impacts was similar to what had been seen at ages 2 and 3 (Table 6). There remained significant impacts on children's social–emotional functioning at age 5 as were seen at ages 2 and 3. At age 5, EHS

67

TABLE 6

IMPACTS ON SELECTED CHILD AND FAMILY OUTCOMES AT AGES 2, 3, AND 5, BY AFRICAN AMERICAN RACE/ETHNICITY

Program-Control Differences, African American

Outcome	Age 2					Age 3					Age 5				
	Program Group Participants[a]	Control Group[b]	Impact Estimate[c]	Effect Size (TOT)[d]	Effect Size (ITT)[d]	Program Group Participants[a]	Control Group[b]	Impact Estimate[c]	Effect Size (TOT)[d]	Effect Size (ITT)[d]	Program Group Participants[a]	Control Group[b]	Impact Estimate[c]	Effect Size (TOT)[d]	Effect Size (ITT)[d]
Child Social-Emotional and Approaches to Learning Outcomes															
CBCL Aggressive Behavior	12.0	13.8	−1.9	−0.28**	−0.25**	9.1	11.4	−2.2	−0.35**	−0.29**	9.3	10.7	−1.4	−0.20*	−0.18+
FACES Social Behavior Problems											4.6	5.3	−0.7	−0.19+	−0.17+
Negativity Toward Parent During Play	2.1	2.2	−0.1	−0.12	−0.11	1.2	1.4	−0.2	−0.37**	−0.32**	1.2	1.3	−0.1	−0.10	−0.08
Engagement During Play	4.1	3.9	0.2	0.15	0.14	4.8	4.3	0.5	0.48**	0.41**	4.6	4.7	−0.1	−0.06	−0.06
Sustained Attention with Objects During Play	4.9	4.8	0.2	0.18	0.16	5.1	4.6	0.5	0.48**	0.41**					
FACES Positive Approaches to Learning											12.5	11.9	0.6	0.29**	0.26**
Observed Bayley Emotion Regulation[e]	3.6	3.6	0.1	0.08	0.04	4.0	4.0	0.0	0.04	0.05					
Observed Leiter Emotion Regulation											92.9	91.1	1.8	0.18+	0.14
Observed Attention											8.9	8.3	0.6	0.30**	0.24*
Leiter Attention Sustained											10.8	10.5	0.3	0.09	0.07
Family Well-Being and Mental Health															
MacArthur CDI Vocabulary	57.3	51.5	5.8	0.26**	0.22**										
English Receptive Vocabulary (PPVT)						82.6	78.8	3.8	0.23*	0.19*	88.3	84.9	3.4	0.23*	0.20*
Average Bayley MDI	88.9	85.4	3.5	0.26*	0.23**	88.5	86.9	1.6	0.13	0.11					
Percentage Bayley MDI <85	34.5	48.2	−13.7	−0.28*	−0.25*	36.0	37.5	−1.4	−0.03	−0.01					
Woodcock Johnson Letter-Word Identification (English)											91.4	91.5	−0.1	−0.01	0.00
Woodcock Johnson Applied Problems											86.2	85.0	1.2	0.06	0.05
Parent Self-Sufficiency															
ER Visits Due to Accident or Injury	7.5	7.6	−0.1	−0.00	−0.01	5.5	6.1	−0.5	−0.02	−0.02					
Any Immunizations[f]	97.1	96.1	1.0	0.06	0.05	97.8	98.1	−0.3	−0.02	−0.03					
Child Has Individualized Education Plan[g]	1.7	3.4	−1.7	−0.09	−0.09	9.2	4.8	4.3	0.19*	0.16+	6.7	7.1	−0.4	−0.01	−0.01

(Continued)

TABLE 6. (Continued)

Program-Control Differences, African American

Outcome	Age 2					Age 3					Age 5				
	Program Group Participants[a]	Control Group[b]	Impact Estimate[c]	Effect Size (TOT)[d]	Effect Size (ITT)[d]	Program Group Participants[a]	Control Group[b]	Impact Estimate[c]	Effect Size (TOT)[d]	Effect Size (ITT)[d]	Program Group Participants[a]	Control Group[b]	Impact Estimate[c]	Effect Size (TOT)[d]	Effect Size (ITT)[d]
Speech Problems (low score = fewer)											17.5	26.2	-8.7	-0.21+	-0.19*
Parenting and the Home Environment															
HOME Language and Literacy	10.3	10.0	0.4	0.20*	0.19*	10.6	10.1	0.5	0.23*	0.20*	10.1	10.7	-0.6	-0.18	-0.16
Percent Reading Daily	56.7	47.7	9.0	0.18+	0.15+	54.5	49.7	4.7	0.09	0.08	33.1	28.3	4.9	0.11	0.10
Percent Spanked Last Week	58.7	59.1	-0.4	-0.01	-0.01	60.7	65.5	-4.8	-0.10	-0.08	35.9	45.8	-9.9	-0.21+	-0.18+
Parent Supportiveness During Play	3.7	3.6	0.1	0.11	0.11	4.0	3.6	0.4	0.47**	0.40**	3.9	3.6	0.3	0.28*	0.23*
Parent Detachment During Play	1.6	1.7	-0.1	-0.09	-0.11	1.3	1.4	-0.1	-0.18	-0.17					
Percent Regular Bedtime	57.4	48.4	9.0	0.18+	0.15	60.0	48.5	11.5	0.23*	0.20*					
Teaching Activities	4.5	4.5	0.1	0.05	0.05	4.4	4.3	0.1	0.09	0.09	11.2	11.4	-0.2	-0.06	-0.06
Children's Books (26 or more)											60.4	47.5	12.9	0.26*	0.24*
Parent Attends Meetings/Open Houses[h]											78.2	76.1	2.0	0.05	0.05
Family Well-Being and Mental Health															
Depression[i]	13.0	17.7	-4.6	-0.14	-0.10	7.5	8.1	-0.5	-0.07	-0.07	7.7	9.7	-2.0	-0.28**	-0.24**
Parenting Distress	24.5	26.8	-2.3	-0.24*	-0.21*	24.3	26.2	-1.9	-0.20+	-0.16+					
Family Conflict	1.7	1.8	-0.0	-0.07	-0.06	1.6	1.7	-0.0	-0.07	-0.08					
Someone in Household Had Alcohol/ Drug Problem, Past Year											2.2	12.7	-10.5	-0.35**	-0.30**
Child Witnessed Violence											11.2	14.2	-3.0	-0.09	-0.10
Parent Self Sufficiency															
Employed[j]	73.3	68.1	5.2	-0.11	0.08	88.6	78.2	10.4	0.28**	0.23**					
In School or Job training[k]	52.2	49.7	2.5	0.05	0.06	64.0	59.9	4.1	0.08	0.08	3.8	3.6	0.2	0.11	0.10
Income (dollars)[l]	12933.6	12879.8	53.8	0.00	0.01	14477.5	14980.8	-503.3	-0.04	-0.04	2341.8	2159.8	182.0	0.10	0.09
Sample Size															
Parent interview	331	308				323	303				292	346			

(Continued)

TABLE 6. (Continued)

	Age 2					Age 3					Age 5				
Outcome	Program Group Participants[a]	Control Group[b]	Impact Estimate[c]	Effect Size (TOT)[d]	Effect Size (ITT)[d]	Program Group Participants[a]	Control Group[b]	Impact Estimate[c]	Effect Size (TOT)[d]	Effect Size (ITT)[d]	Program Group Participants[a]	Control Group[b]	Impact Estimate[c]	Effect Size (TOT)[d]	Effect Size (ITT)[d]
Parent-child interactions	266	232				245	220				217	264			
Bayley	269	228				262	220				NA	NA			
Child assessments	287	250				272	238				264	312			

Note. All impact estimates were calculated using regression models in which each site was weighted equally. All values in the tables are based on two-stage least squares analyses (treatment on treated) except for the columns that depict effect sizes based on ordinary least squares comparisons (intent to treat). Psychometric information on specific outcome measures, including descriptive statistics is available in Chapter 2.

[a] A participant is defined as a program group member who received more than one Early Head Start home visit, met with an Early Head Start case manager more than once, received at least 2 weeks of Early Head Start center-based care, and/or participated in Early Head Start group parent–child activities.

[b] The control group mean is the mean for the control group members who would have participated in Early Head Start if they had been assigned to the program group instead. This unobserved mean was estimated as the difference between the program group mean for participants and the impact per participant.

[c] The estimated impact per participant is measured as the estimated impact per eligible applicant divided by the proportion of program group members who participated in Early Head Start services (which varied by site). The estimated impact per eligible applicant is measured as the difference between the regression-adjusted means for all program and control group members.

[d] The effect size was calculated by dividing the estimated impact per participant by the standard deviation of the outcome measure for the control group. For ease of reading, all statistically significant effect sizes appear in bold.

[e] Emotion regulation measured at ages 2 and 3 with the Bayley Behavior Rating Scales and at age 5 with the Leiter-R observer ratings.

[f] Reported as percentage of children who had received any immunizations by the time of each interview.

[g] At age 2 the time frame for this question is 15 months after random assignment. At age 3 the time frame is 26 months after random assignment. At ages 2 and 3 this item is measured as eligible for early intervention services.

[h] Includes only parents whose children were in a formal program. Sample sizes for this outcome in the African American subgroup were $N = 104$ and $N = 120$ for program and control groups, respectively.

[i] Depression measured with the Composite International Diagnostic Interview (CIDI) at age 2.

[j] At age 2 the time frame for this question is 15 months after random assignment, and at age 3 the time frame is 26 months after random assignment. At each earlier age the item is whether employed or not, but at age 5 we asked "How much time in the past 6 months have you held a job or jobs in which you worked at least 20 hr per week?" Answers were on a 5-point scale from $1 = never$ to $5 = all\ of\ the\ time$.

[k] At age 2 the time frame for this question is 15 months after random assignment, and at age 3 the time frame is 26 months after random assignment.

[l] At age 2 the time frame for this question is 15 months after random assignment, and at age 3 the time frame is 26 months after random assignment. Amounts are annual income at ages 2 and 3 and monthly income at age 5.

[+] $p < .10$; [*] $p < .05$; [**] $p < .01$.

Source. Parent interviews, interviewer observations, and assessments of semistructured parent–child interactions conducted when children were in their prekindergarten year. HOME, Home Observation for Measurement of the Environment; CBCL, Child Behavior Check List; FACES, Family and Child Experiences Survey; PVT, Peabody Picture Vocabulary Test; TVIP, Test de Vocabulario de Imagines Peabody.

70

reduced CBCL aggressive behavior (ES = .20, $p < .05$), and perhaps FACES Social Behavior Problems (ES = .19, $p < .10$). EHS African American children also had greater positive approaches to learning (ES = .29, $p < .01$) and Leiter observed attention (ES = .30, $p < .01$), and somewhat greater Leiter observed emotion regulation (ES = .18, $p < .10$), although effect sizes were somewhat reduced from what had been seen in social-emotional functioning at age 3. The significant impact on receptive language as measured by the PPVT-III was the same as had been seen at age 3 (ES = .23, $p < .05$), and similar to what had been seen on the MacArthur CDI at age 2 (ES = .26, $p < .05$). Although there had been an impact on having an IEP at age 3, that did not remain at age 5; at age 5 there was a trend for EHS children to have fewer speech problems (ES = .21, $p < .10$).

The impacts on parenting variables seen at ages 2 and 3 among African Americans persisted. The age 3 impact on parenting support for language and literacy as a construct did not remain, but parents who had been enrolled in EHS provided significantly more books for their children at age 5 (ES = .26, $p < .05$), and parents were observed to be more supportive during play, although the effect size (ES = .28, $p < .05$) was smaller than at age 3 (ES = .47, $p < .01$). At age 5, there was a trend for parents to spank less (ES = .21, $p < .10$), and they less often reported depressive symptoms (ES = .28, $p < .01$), neither of which had been significant at age 3. The effects on depressive symptoms are probably related to impacts of reduced parenting distress seen at age 2 (ES = .24, $p < .05$) and a trend for that impact at age 3 (ES = .20, $p < .10$). Additionally, at age 5, former EHS parents significantly less often reported that someone in their household had a drug or alcohol problem (ES = .35, $p < .01$), which had not been measured at ages 3 or 2.

After leaving EHS, African American children had relatively high rates of participation in formal programs as 3- and 4-year-olds (59% of the program and 52% of the control group) and in Head Start specifically (68% of the program and 61% of the control group). However, EHS had no impact on use of formal programs in the 3–5 age period (not tabled).

White Families

White children and parents appeared to benefit most while the child was in the program, at age 2. The pattern of impacts seen at age 2 disappeared by age 3, except for a single impact on parents being in school or training (Table 7). At age 5 there were few impacts on children's development. At age 5, EHS White parents reported their children had somewhat fewer CBCL aggressive behavior problems (ES = .18, $p < .10$) than was reported for White control group children. EHS White children were more likely to have an IEP at age 5 (ES at age 5 = .25, $p < .05$) and were significantly more likely than control group children to have reported speech problems at age 5

TABLE 7

IMPACTS ON SELECTED CHILD AND FAMILY OUTCOMES AT AGES 2, 3, AND 5, BY WHITE RACE/ETHNICITY

Program-Control Differences, White

Outcome	Age 2					Age 3					Age 5				
	Program Group Participants[a]	Control Group[b]	Impact Estimate[c]	Effect Size (TOT)[d]	Effect Size (ITT)[d]	Program Group Participants[a]	Control Group[b]	Impact Estimate[c]	Effect Size (TOT)[d]	Effect Size (ITT)[d]	Program Group Participants[a]	Control Group[b]	Impact Estimate[c]	Effect Size (TOT)[d]	Effect Size (ITT)[d]
Child Social-Emotional and Approaches to Learning Outcomes															
CBCL Aggressive Behavior	11.8	12.8	−0.9	−0.14	**−0.14**[+]	11.9	12.3	−0.4	−0.07	−0.06	11.6	12.8	−1.2	**(0.18**[+]**)**	−0.16
FACES Social Behavior Problems											5.5	6.0	−0.5	−0.14	−0.12
Negativity Toward Parent During Play	1.6	1.8	−0.2	**−0.20***	**−0.20***	1.3	1.3	0.0	0.03	0.02	1.2	1.3	−0.1	−0.12	−0.11
Engagement During Play	4.5	4.4	0.2	**0.16**[+]	**0.16**[+]	4.9	4.8	0.1	0.09	0.08	4.8	4.8	−0.0	−0.01	−0.01
Sustained Attention with Objects During play	5.2	5.1	0.1	0.07	0.07	5.1	5.0	0.2	0.16	0.15					
FACES Positive Approaches to Learning						3.9	4.0	−0.1	−0.13	−0.12	12.3	12.1	0.2	0.11	0.09
Observed Bayley Emotion Regulation[e]	3.6	3.7	−0.1	**−0.15**[+]	−0.14										
Observed Leiter Emotion Regulation											90.7	90.6	0.0	0.00	0.01
Observed Attention											8.5	8.6	−1.0	−0.04	−0.03
Child Language/Cognitive/Academic Skills															
MacArthur CDI Vocabulary	58.1	56.0	2.1	0.09	0.10										
English Receptive Vocabulary (PPVT)						87.7	86.9	0.8	0.05	0.04	96.5	97.5	−1.0	−0.06	−0.06
Average Bayley MDI	92.2	90.9	1.3	0.10	0.09	94.8	93.3	1.5	0.12	0.12					
Percentage Bayley MDI <85	31.7	31.1	0.5	0.01	0.01	21.1	23.2	−2.1	−0.04	−0.05					
Woodcock Johnson Letter-Word Identification (English)											89.6	90.3	−0.7	−0.05	−0.05
Woodcock Johnson Applied Problems											93.4	93.1	0.3	0.02	0.01
Leiter Attention Sustained											11.4	11.5	0.0	−0.01	−0.01
Child Health															
ER Visit Due to Accident or Injury	10.0	10.4	−0.4	−0.02	−0.01	15.8	15.4	−0.4	0.01	0.00					
Any Immunizations[f]	98.5	97.6	0.9	0.05	0.05	99.3	98.1	1.2	0.09	0.09					
Child Has Individualized Education Plan[g]	7.7	7.0	0.8	0.04	0.04	13.5	8.8	4.7	0.21	0.17	17.9	11.1	6.8	**0.25***	**0.22**[+]
Speech Problems (low score = fewer)											32.8	19.6	13.2	**0.31****	**0.27****

(*Continued*)

TABLE 7. (Continued)

| | Program-Control Differences, White | | | | | | | | | | | | | | |
| | Age 2 | | | | | Age 3 | | | | | Age 5 | | | | |
Outcome	Program Group Participants[a]	Control Group[b]	Impact Estimate[c]	Effect Size (TOT)[d]	Effect Size (ITT)[d]	Program Group Participants[a]	Control Group[b]	Impact Estimate[c]	Effect Size (TOT)[d]	Effect Size (ITT)[d]	Program Group Participants[a]	Control Group[b]	Impact Estimate[c]	Effect Size (TOT)[d]	Effect Size (ITT)[d]
Parenting and the Home Environment															
HOME Language and Literacy	11.0	10.9	0.1	0.04	0.04	11.1	11.2	-0.1	-0.04	-0.04	10.4	10.3	0.1	0.04	0.04
Percent Reading Daily	69.9	64.9	5.0	0.10	0.10	66.6	62.7	3.9	0.08	0.07	42.1	36.8	5.3	0.12	0.12
Percent Spanked Last Week	39.2	50.7	-11.5	-0.23*	-0.22*	43.6	49.8	-6.3	-0.13	-0.13	31.6	36.5	-4.9	-0.10	-0.08
Parent Supportiveness During Play	4.4	4.3	0.1	0.06	0.06	4.1	4.1	0.1	0.08	0.07	4.2	4.2	-0.0	-0.03	-0.02
Parent Detachment During Play	1.3	1.4	-0.1	-0.10	-0.09	1.2	1.2	0.0	0.05	0.05					
Percent Regular Bedtime	65.9	62.3	3.7	0.07	0.07	62.8	68.1	-5.3	-0.11	-0.09					
Teaching Activities	4.7	4.6	0.1	0.13	0.13	4.5	4.5	-0.0	-0.02	0.00	11.6	11.1	0.4	0.14	0.13
Children's Books (26 or more)											87.7	85.6	2.1	0.04	0.04
Parent Attends Meetings/Open Houses[h]											85.2	80.3	4.9	0.12	0.12
Family Well-Being and Mental Health															
Depression[i]	20.2	19.3	0.9	0.03	0.01	8.6	8.9	-0.3	-0.05	-0.05	8.8	7.9	0.9	0.12	0.10
Parenting Distress	23.9	24.8	-0.9	-0.10	-0.11	25.3	24.6	0.7	0.07	0.04					
Family Conflict	1.6	1.8	-0.1	-0.19+	-0.18*	1.7	1.7	-0.0	-0.03	-0.04					
Someone in Household Had Alcohol/Drug Problem, Past Year											10.1	8.9	1.2	0.04	0.03
Child Witnessed Violence											17.4	9.7	7.8	**0.24***	**0.21***
Parent Self-Sufficiency															
Employed[j]	77.5	75.5	2.0	0.04	0.04	87.8	87.5	0.2	0.01	0.01	3.4	3.3	0.1	0.04	0.04
In School or Job Training[k]	40.7	39.3	1.4	0.03	0.03	58.4	48.5	9.8	**0.20***	**0.19***					
Income (dollars)[l]	16911.6	17078.6	-167.0	-0.01	0.00	18253.3	18731.9	-478.6	-0.04	-0.03	2351.9	2431.5	-79.6	-0.04	-0.02

(Continued)

TABLE 7. (*Continued*)

	Age 2					Age 3					Age 5				
Outcome	Program Group Participants[a]	Control Group[b]	Impact Estimate[c] (TOT)[d]	Effect Size (TOT)[d]	Effect Size (ITT)[d]	Program Group Participants[a]	Control Group[b]	Impact Estimate[c] (TOT)[d]	Effect Size (TOT)[d]	Effect Size (ITT)[d]	Program Group Participants[a]	Control Group[b]	Impact Estimate[c] (TOT)[d]	Effect Size (TOT)[d]	Effect Size (ITT)[d]
Sample Size															
Parent interview	379	363				366	346				346	361			
Parent-child interactions	298	289				279	263				257	270			
Bayley	286	291				272	267				NA	NA			
Child assessments	312	312				291	282				294	311			

Note. All impact estimates were calculated using regression models in which each site was weighted equally. All values in the tables are based on two-stage least squares analyses (treatment on treated) except for the columns that depict effect sizes based on ordinary least squares comparisons (intent to treat). Psychometric information on specific outcome measures, including descriptive statistics is available in Chapter 2.

Note that all footnotes are identical to those of Table 6.

Source. Parent interviews, interviewer observations, and assessments of semistructured parent–child interactions conducted when children were in their prekindergarten year. HOME, Home Observation for Measurement of the Environment; CBCL, Child Behavior Check List; FACES, Family and Child Experiences Survey; PPVT, Peabody Picture Vocabulary Test; TVIP, Test de Vocabulario de Imagines Peabody.

(ES = .31, p < .01). White former EHS children were significantly more likely to have witnessed violence (ES = .24, p < .05) than was true for control group children and there were no impacts for White parents.

After leaving EHS, among the high-risk group, 40% of former EHS White children and 41% of control group White children participated in formal programs ages 3 and 4, and 46% of the former EHS White children participated in Head Start specifically at some time between ages 3 and 5 compared to only 35% of the control group White children. The latter was a significant difference (p < .05; not tabled).

Hispanic Families

For Hispanic children and families, more positive impacts were seen at age 5 than at age 3 and age 2 (Table 8). At age 5, former EHS Hispanic children's parents reported significantly more positive approaches to learning (ES = .39, p < .05), and Spanish-speaking Hispanic children scored significantly higher on Spanish receptive vocabulary (ES = .29, p < .05), had significantly fewer reported speech problems (ES = .35, p < .05), and scored somewhat higher for engagement during play (ES = .23, p < .10). Impacts for Hispanic parents tended to cluster in two areas, support for children's learning and parent self-sufficiency activities. At ages 2 and 3, impacts were seen for daily reading and at age 3, support for language and literacy. Daily reading at age 5 was somewhat more likely in EHS than control group parents (27% vs. 15%; ES = .26, p < .10). EHS parents were also more likely to attend meetings and open houses at their child's school (ES = .29, p < .05). An EHS impact on being in school or job training was seen at both ages 2 and 3; but there were no differences in employment at age 5 (ES = .24).

After leaving EHS, 42% of former EHS children and 38% of control group children who are Hispanics attended formal programs when they were 3 and 4 years of age, whereas 53% of the program and 47% of the control group attended Head Start at some time during this period (nonsignificant differences; not tabled).

Subgroup Impacts for Groups Defined by Family Risk

Although nearly all EHS families may be considered high risk by virtue of income, some have additional characteristics that compound their level of risk and potentially create barriers to parenting and children's access to resources. Here we describe the impacts for the three subgroups (as defined earlier in this chapter) when children were 2, 3, and 5 years old.[8]

Low-Risk Families

For low-risk families, the pattern of impacts at age 5 was consistent with, but weaker than, impacts found at ages 3 and 2 (see Table 9). At age 5,

TABLE 8

IMPACTS ON SELECTED CHILD AND FAMILY OUTCOMES AT AGES 2, 3, AND 5, BY HISPANIC RACE/ETHNICITY

| | Program-Control Differences, Hispanic | | | | | | | | | | | | | | |
| | Age 2 | | | | | Age 3 | | | | | Age 5 | | | | |
Outcome	Program Group Participants[a]	Control Group[b]	Impact Estimate[c]	Effect Size (TOT)[d]	Effect Size (ITT)[d]	Program Group Participants[a]	Control Group[b]	Impact Estimate[c]	Effect Size (TOT)[d]	Effect Size (ITT)[d]	Program Group Participants[a]	Control Group[b]	Impact Estimate[c]	Effect Size (TOT)[d]	Effect Size (ITT)[d]
Child Social-Emotional and Approaches to Learning Outcomes															
CBCL Aggressive Behavior	12.9	12.2	0.6	0.09	0.09	11.7	10.4	1.2	0.19	0.19	10.0	9.9	0.2	0.02	0.06
FACES Social Behavior Problems											5.6	6.1	-0.5	-0.15	-0.10
Negativity Toward Parent During Play	1.5	1.5	-0.0	-0.01	-0.02	1.2	1.3	-0.1	-0.08	-0.09	1.2	1.2	0.0	-0.02	-0.02
Engagement During Play	4.4	4.4	0.0	0.03	0.03	4.7	4.7	-0.0	-0.01	-0.01	4.8	4.6	0.2	0.23[+]	0.21[+]
Sustained Attention with Objects During Play	4.9	4.9	-0.1	-0.05	-0.05	4.8	4.8	-0.0	-0.04	-0.04					
FACES Positive Approaches to Learning											12.0	11.2	0.8	0.39*	0.34**
Observed Bayley Emotion Regulation[e]	3.7	3.8	0.2	-0.18	-0.16	3.9	3.8	0.1	0.12	0.11					
Observed Leiter Emotion Regulation											89.9	92.0	-2.1	-0.22	-0.18[+]
Observed Attention											8.7	8.8	-0.1	-0.04	-0.01
Leiter Attention Sustained											11.0	10.6	0.4	0.12	0.08
Child Language/Cognitive/Academic Skills															
MacArthur CDI Vocabulary	53.4	52.8	0.6	0.03	0.02										
English Receptive Vocabulary (PPVT)						77.4	71.2	6.2	0.38	0.33	94.2	89.6	4.6	0.30	0.20
Spanish Receptive Vocabulary (TVIP)						97.2	94.9	2.3	0.27	0.25	90.0	83.0	7.0	0.29*	0.26*
Average Bayley MDI	87.7	86.2	1.5	0.11	0.11	92.0	91.3	0.7	0.05	0.04					
Percentage Bayley MDI <85	39.4	43.6	-4.3	-0.09	-0.08	20.3	28.1	-7.8	-0.17	-0.16					
Woodcock Johnson Letter-Word Identification (English)											86.9	88.8	-1.8	-0.13	-0.10
Woodcock Johnson Applied Problems											92.1	84.1	8.0	0.38	0.25

(*Continued*)

TABLE 8. (Continued)

Program-Control Differences, Hispanic

Outcome	Age 2					Age 3					Age 5				
	Program Group Participants[a]	Control Group[b]	Impact Estimate[c]	Effect Size (TOT)[d]	Effect Size (ITT)[d]	Program Group Participants[a]	Control Group[b]	Impact Estimate[c]	Effect Size (TOT)[d]	Effect Size (ITT)[d]	Program Group Participants[a]	Control Group[b]	Impact Estimate[c]	Effect Size (TOT)[d]	Effect Size (ITT)[d]
Child Health															
ER Visits Due to Accident or Injury	1.4	6.8	-5.4	-0.19*	-0.14+	4.0	4.1	-0.2	-0.01	-0.01					
Any Immunizations[f]	99.3	97.4	1.9	0.11	0.10	99.5	99.2	0.3	0.02	0.02					
Child Has Individualized Education Plan[g]	1.5	1.2	0.2	0.01	0.01	4.3	1.5	2.8	0.13	0.11	5.8	5.8	-0.1	0.00	0.04
Speech Problems (low score = fewer)											9.7	24.5	-14.8	-0.35*	-0.25*
Parenting and the Home Environment															
HOME Language and Literacy	9.6	9.3	0.3	0.17	0.16	10.3	9.8	0.5	0.21+	0.20+	10.5	9.9	0.6	0.18	0.15
Percent Reading Daily	48.9	36.3	12.7	0.25*	0.23*	45.1	30.9	14.3	0.29*	0.27*	27.1	15.3	11.8	0.26+	0.23*
Percent Spanked Last Week	36.9	44.2	-7.3	-0.15	-0.13	42.5	43.9	-1.4	-0.03	-0.02	30.3	27.7	2.6	0.05	0.07
Parent Supportiveness During Play	4.0	3.9	0.1	0.09	0.09	3.8	3.8	0.0	0.04	0.04	4.0	3.9	0.0	0.05	0.04
Parent Detachment During Play	1.2	1.3	-0.1	-0.11	-0.10	1.2	1.3	-0.0	-0.05	-0.04					
Percent Regular Bedtime	59.5	50.5	9.1	0.18	0.16	49.3	61.0	-11.7	-0.24+	-0.23+					
Teaching Activities	4.4	4.4	0.1	0.08	0.07	4.2	4.1	0.1	0.13	0.13	10.9	10.2	0.7	0.24	0.22+
Children's Books (26 or more)											52.1	44.4	7.7	0.16	0.10
Parent Attends Meetings/Open Houses[h]											97.8	86.1	11.6	0.29*	0.27
Family Well-Being and Mental Health															
Depression[i]	14.3	8.6	5.8	0.18	0.16	6.1	5.4	0.7	0.10	0.10	5.0	6.4	-1.4	-0.19	-0.14
Parenting Distress	25.9	26.4	-0.5	-0.05	-0.06	25.4	24.7	0.7	0.07	0.07					
Family Conflict	1.6	1.7	-0.1	-0.17	-0.15	1.7	1.7	-0.0	-0.00	-0.01					
Someone in Household Had Alcohol/Drug Problem, Past Year											9.6	8.3	1.2	0.04	0.04
Child Witnessed Violence											10.9	9.7	1.2	0.04	0.03

(Continued)

TABLE 8. (Continued)

| | Program-Control Differences, Hispanic | | | | | | | | | | | | | | |
| | Age 2 | | | | | Age 3 | | | | | Age 5 | | | | |
Outcome	Program Group Participants[a]	Control Group[b]	Impact Estimate[c]	Effect Size (TOT)[d]	Effect Size (ITT)[d]	Program Group Participants[a]	Control Group[b]	Impact Estimate[c]	Effect Size (TOT)[d]	Effect Size (ITT)[d]	Program Group Participants[a]	Control Group[b]	Impact Estimate[c]	Effect Size (TOT)[d]	Effect Size (ITT)[d]
Parent Self-Sufficiency															
Employed[j]	75.9	68.5	7.4	0.16	0.16	86.0	80.3	5.7	0.15	0.15	3.8	3.4	0.4	0.24	0.19[+]
In School or Job Training[k]	39.9	28.3	11.6	0.24*	0.22*	49.0	34.0	15.0	0.30*	0.28*					
Income (dollars)[l]	15358.4	16781.6	−1423.2	−0.12	−0.12	17131.1	18756.4	−1625.2	−0.12	−0.12	2317.2	2351.4	−34.1	−0.02	−0.07
Sample Size															
Parent interview	238	215				203	165				201	206			
Parent-child interactions	208	156				169	133				189	168			
Bayley	203	167				161	129				NA	NA			
Child assessments	219	184				169	140				115	124			

Note. All impact estimates were calculated using regression models in which each site was weighted equally. All values in the tables are based on two-stage least squares analyses (treatment on treated) except for the columns that depict effect sizes based on ordinary least squares comparisons (intent to treat). Psychometric information on specific outcome measures, including descriptive statistics is available in Chapter 2.

Note that all footnotes are identical to those of Table 6.

Source. Parent interviews, interviewer observations, and assessments of semistructured parent–child interactions conducted when children were in their prekindergarten year. HOME, Home Observation for Measurement of the Environment; CBCL, Child Behavior Check List; FACES, Family and Child Experiences Survey; PPVT, Peabody Picture Vocabulary Test; TVIP, Test de Vocabulario de Imagines Peabody.

TABLE 9

Impacts on Selected Child and Family Outcomes at Ages 2, 3, and 5, by Low-Risk Subgroup

| | Program-Control Differences, Low Risk | | | | | | | | | | | | | | |
| | Age 2 | | | | | Age 3 | | | | | Age 5 | | | | |
Outcome	Program Group Participants[a]	Control Group[b]	Impact Estimate[c]	Effect Size (TOT)[d]	Effect Size (ITT)[d]	Program Group Participants[a]	Control Group[b]	Impact Estimate[c]	Effect Size (TOT)[d]	Effect Size (ITT)[d]	Program Group Participants[a]	Control Group[b]	Impact Estimate[c]	Effect Size (TOT)[d]	Effect Size (ITT)[d]
Child Social-Emotional and Approaches to Learning Outcomes															
CBCL Aggressive Behavior	12.2	12.3	-0.1	-0.01	-0.01	11.0	11.5	-0.5	-0.07	-0.06	10.7	10.5	0.2	0.02	0.03
FACES Social Behavior Problems											5.4	5.7	-0.3	-0.07	-0.06
Negativity Toward Parent During Play	1.5	1.7	-0.2	-0.25**	-0.24**	1.2	1.3	-0.1	-0.17*	-0.17*	1.2	1.3	-0.1	-0.11	-0.10
Engagement During Play	4.5	4.4	0.1	0.10	0.09	4.9	4.7	0.2	0.20*	0.19*	4.8	4.7	0.0	0.05	0.04
Sustained Attention with Objects During play	5.1	5.0	0.1	0.15+	0.14+	5.0	4.9	0.1	0.14+	0.13					
FACES Positive Approaches to Learning											12.1	11.8	0.2	0.12+	0.11*
Observed Bayley Emotion Regulation[e]	3.7	3.7	-0.1	-0.06	-0.06	4.0	4.0	-0.0	-0.02	-0.02					
Observed Leiter Emotion Regulation											91.0	91.2	-0.2	-0.02	-0.02
Observed Attention											8.6	8.7	-0.1	-0.05	-0.05
Leiter Attention Sustained											11.2	11.6	-0.4	-0.12	-0.11
Child Language/Cognitive/Academic Skills															
MacArthur CDI Vocabulary	56.1	55.9	0.2	0.01	0.00										
English Receptive Vocabulary (PPVT)						86.0	84.3	1.7	0.11	0.09	95.7	95.3	0.4	0.02	0.02
Average Bayley MDI	91.4	90.5	0.9	0.07	0.06	92.0	92.1	-0.1	-0.01	-0.01					
Percentage Bayley MDI <85	32.7	32.2	0.5	0.01	0.01	24.5	28.4	-3.9	-0.08	-0.08					
Woodcock Johnson Letter-Word Identification (English)											90.7	90.3	0.3	0.02	0.02
Woodcock Johnson Applied Problems											91.2	90.0	1.2	0.06	0.05
Child Health															
ER Visits Due to Accident or Injury	4.9	6.4	-1.5	-0.05	-0.05	9.5	12.2	-2.7	-0.09	-0.09					
Any Immunizations[f]	99.5	97.4	2.1	0.12*	0.11*	100.0	98.8	1.3	0.09+	0.08+					
Child Has Individualized Education Plan[g]											12.2	8.1	4.1	0.15+	0.15+
Speech Problems (low score = fewer)	5.9	4.7	1.2	0.07	0.06	10.1	5.9	4.2	0.19*	0.17*	20.7	2.4	0.06	0.5	

(*Continued*)

TABLE 9. (*Continued*)

	Age 2					Age 3					Age 5				
					Program-Control Differences, Low Risk										
Outcome	Program Group Participants[a]	Control Group[b]	Impact Estimate[c]	Effect Size (TOT)[d]	Effect Size (ITT)[d]	Program Group Participants[a]	Control Group[b]	Impact Estimate[c]	Effect Size (TOT)[d]	Effect Size (ITT)[d]	Program Group Participants[a]	Control Group[b]	Impact Estimate[c]	Effect Size (TOT)[d]	Effect Size (ITT)[d]
Parenting and the Home Environment															
HOME Language and Literacy	10.5	10.3	0.2	0.10+	0.09+	10.8	10.9	−0.2	−0.08	−0.07	11.2	11.1	0.2	0.06	0.05
Percent Reading Daily	58.5	55.6	2.9	0.06	0.06	54.2	51.4	2.8	0.06	0.05	33.7	29.1	4.6	0.10	0.10
Percent Spanked Last Week	46.2	52.0	−5.7	−0.11	−0.11	40.4	51.8	−11.5	−0.23**	−0.22**	31.7	35.5	−3.8	−0.08	−0.07
Parent Supportiveness During Play	4.3	4.2	0.1	0.12	0.12	4.1	4.1	0.1	0.08	0.08	4.3	4.2	0.1	0.08	0.07
Parent Detachment During Play	1.3	1.4	−0.1	−0.16*	−0.16*	1.2	1.1	0.0	0.06	0.06					
Percent Regular Bedtime	65.7	58.6	7.1	0.14+	0.14+	62.5	61.5	1.0	0.02	0.02					
Teaching Activities	4.5	4.5	0.0	0.04	0.04	4.3	4.4	−0.0	−0.05	−0.04	11.2	10.9	0.2	0.08	0.08
Children's Books (26 or more)											71.5	67.9	3.6	0.07	0.07
Parent Attends Meetings/Open Houses[h]											91.7	84.5	7.2	0.18	0.15
Family Well-Being and Mental Health															
Depression[i]	15.0	12.0	3.0	0.09	0.08	7.1	7.4	−0.3	−0.04	−0.04	7.1	7.1	0.0	0.00	0.00
Parenting Distress	24.7	24.4	0.3	0.03	0.02	24.8	24.0	0.9	0.09	0.09					
Family Conflict	1.7	1.7	0.0	0.00	−0.01	1.6	1.7	−0.0	−0.08	−0.08					
Someone in Household Had Alcohol/Drug Problem, Past Year											7.4	9.8	−2.5	−0.08	−0.08
Child Witnessed Violence											10.2	6.9	3.3	0.10	0.10
Parent Self-Sufficiency															
Employed[j]	81.5	77.0	4.5	0.10	0.10	89.0	86.4	2.6	0.07	0.06	3.7	3.5	0.2	0.11	0.10
In school or Job Training[k]	34.1	33.1	1.1	0.02	0.02	47.9	42.6	5.3	0.11	0.09					
Income (dollars)[l]	17231.0	17383.3	−152.3	−0.01	−0.01	19633.4	20947.8	−1314.4	−0.10	−0.10	2530.3	2456.1	74.2	0.04	0.04

(*Continued*)

TABLE 9. (Continued)

| | Program-Control Differences, Low Risk | | | | | | | | | | | | | | |
| | Age 2 | | | | | Age 3 | | | | | Age 5 | | | | |
Outcome	Program Group Participants[a]	Control Group[b]	Impact Estimate[c]	Effect Size (TOT)[d]	Effect Size (ITT)[d]	Program Group Participants[a]	Control Group[b]	Impact Estimate[c]	Effect Size (TOT)[d]	Effect Size (ITT)[d]	Program Group Participants[a]	Control Group[b]	Impact Estimate[c]	Effect Size (TOT)[d]	Effect Size (ITT)[d]
Sample Size															
Parent interview	466	445				437	400				388	402			
Parent-child interactions	380	345				349	318				316	323			
Bayley	350	331				340	303				NA	NA			
Child assessments	404	378				363	318				296	320			

Note. All impact estimates were calculated using regression models in which each site was weighted equally. All values in the tables are based on two-stage least squares analyses (treatment on treated) except for the columns that depict effect sizes based on ordinary least squares comparisons (intent to treat). Psychometric information on specific outcome measures, including descriptive statistics is available in Chapter 2.

Note that all footnotes are identical to those of Table 6.

Source. Parent interviews, interviewer observations, and assessments of semistructured parent–child interactions conducted when children were in their prekindergarten year. HOME, Home Observation for Measurement of the Environment; CBCL, Child Behavior Check List; FACES, Family and Child Experiences Survey; PPVT, Peabody Picture Vocabulary Test; TVIP, Test de Vocabulario de Imagines Peabody.

EHS children had somewhat higher scores on positive approaches to learning (ES = .12, $p < .10$), consistent with significant positive impacts on sustained attention with objects, and reduced negativity toward parent during play at ages 2 and 3 and with engagement during play at age 3. EHS children were somewhat more likely to have an IEP than children in the control group at age 5 (ES = .15, $p < .10$), whereas these children had been significantly more likely to have an IEP at age 3 (some low-risk families may have been enrolled in EHS because their children had disabilities). At age 3, EHS parents spanked significantly less than control group parents but the difference was not significant at age 5. No other impacts on parenting were seen at age 5.

After leaving EHS, 48% of former EHS children and 36% of control group children who come from low-risk families attended formal programs when they were 3 and 4 years of age, a significant difference between EHS and control groups ($p < .01$). However, the difference between former EHS and control groups in ever attending Head Start during this period (47% and 44%, respectively) was not significant (not tabled).

Moderate-Risk Families

For children in moderate-risk families, impacts at age 5 were generally comparable in frequency and size to what had been seen at ages 3 and 2, but there were differences across domains (Table 10). The impacts on cognitive development seen at ages 2 and 3 and on language development at age 2 did not appear at age 5. At age 5, EHS children expressed significantly less negativity toward parent during play (ES = .21, $p < .05$), and somewhat greater positive approaches to learning (ES = .16, $p < .10$) and observed attention (ES = .18, $p < .10$), which had not been seen at the earlier ages. Impacts for parents at age 5 were consistent with those found at ages 3 and 2. At age 5, impacts were found on HOME Language and Literacy (ES = .42, $p < .01$), teaching activities (ES = .21, $p < .05$) and on the number of children's books in the home (trend, ES = .17, $p < .10$). These are consistent with a favorable impact on daily reading and teaching activities at ages 2 and 3, with parent detachment during play at age 3, and with a trend effect on parent supportiveness during play at age 3. At ages 2 and 3, EHS parents reported less parenting stress, whereas at age 5 they reported significantly fewer depressive symptoms (ES = .28, $p < .01$).

After leaving EHS, 46% of former EHS children and 41% of control group children in the moderate-risk group attended formal programs when they were both 3 and 4 years of age, whereas 60% of the EHS program and 51% of the control group ever attended Head Start specifically during this period (ES = .19, $p < .05$; not tabled).

TABLE 10
IMPACTS ON SELECTED CHILD AND FAMILY OUTCOMES AT AGES 2, 3, AND 5, BY MODERATE-RISK SUBGROUP

Program-Control Differences, Moderate Risk

Outcome	Age 2					Age 3					Age 5				
	Program Group Participants[a]	Control Group[b]	Impact Estimate[c]	Effect Size (TOT)[d]	Effect Size (ITT)[d]	Program Group Participants[a]	Control Group[b]	Impact Estimate[c]	Effect Size (TOT)[d]	Effect Size (ITT)[d]	Program Group Participants[a]	Control Group[b]	Impact Estimate[c]	Effect Size (TOT)[d]	Effect Size (ITT)[d]
Child Social–Emotional and Approaches to Learning Outcomes															
CBCL Aggressive Behavior	12.1	12.4	−0.3	−0.04	−0.06	10.9	11.3	−0.4	−0.06	−0.06	10.9	11.0	−0.0	−0.00	−0.01
FACES Social Behavior Problems											5.4	5.6	−0.2	−0.05	−0.05
Negativity Toward Parent During Play	1.7	1.8	−0.0	−0.01	−0.02	1.3	1.4	−0.1	−0.12	−0.11	1.2	1.3	−0.1	−0.21*	−0.20*
Engagement During Play	4.3	4.2	0.1	0.12	0.12	4.8	4.6	0.2	0.18	0.17	4.8	4.7	0.1	0.13	0.13
Sustained Attention with Objects During Play	5.0	5.1	−0.1	−0.10	−0.08	5.0	4.9	0.2	0.16	0.14					
FACES Positive Approaches to Learning											12.2	11.9	0.3	0.16+	0.14+
Observed Bayley Emotion Regulation[e]	3.7	3.7	0.0	0.02	0.02	3.9	3.8	0.1	0.10	0.09					
Observed Leiter Emotion Regulation											91.8	90.7	1.0	0.11	0.09
Observed Attention											8.8	8.4	0.4	0.18+	0.17+
Leiter Attention Sustained											10.9	11.0	−0.1	−0.04	−0.04
Child Language/Cognitive/Academic Skills															
MacArthur CDI Vocabulary	58.5	52.4	6.2	0.27**	0.26**										
English Receptive Vocabulary (PPVT)						85.1	84.1	1.0	0.06	0.06	92.8	91.3	1.4	0.10	0.07
Average Bayley MDI	91.4	86.2	5.2	0.39**	0.35**	93.7	90.0	3.6	0.28**	0.25*					
Percentage Bayley MDI <85	27.8	46.6	−18.8	−0.39**	−0.33**	24.8	25.6	−0.8	−0.02	−0.02					
Woodcock Johnson Letter-Word Identification (English)											88.8	90.6	−1.8	−0.13	−0.13
Woodcock Johnson Applied Problems											89.8	88.3	1.5	0.07	0.05
Child Health															
ER Visit Due to Accident or Injury	11.2	11.6	−0.4	−0.01	−0.01	14.2	10.3	3.9	0.13	0.10					
Any Immunizations[f]	98.0	95.8	2.2	0.12	0.10	98.6	97.4	1.2	0.09	0.07					

(Continued)

TABLE 10. (Continued)

| | Program-Control Differences, Moderate Risk | | | | | | | | | | | | | | |
| Outcome | Age 2 | | | | | Age 3 | | | | | Age 5 | | | | |
	Program Group Participants[a]	Control Group[b]	Impact Estimate[c]	Effect Size (TOT)[d]	Effect Size (ITT)[d]	Program Group Participants[a]	Control Group[b]	Impact Estimate[c]	Effect Size (TOT)[d]	Effect Size (ITT)[d]	Program Group Participants[a]	Control Group[b]	Impact Estimate[c]	Effect Size (TOT)[d]	Effect Size (ITT)[d]
Child Has Individualized Education Plan[g]	2.4	3.2	-0.8	-0.04	-0.05	6.1	6.0	0.2	0.01	-0.01	5.1	5.7	-0.6	-0.02	-0.03
Speech Problems (low score = fewer)											17.4	22.3	-4.9	-0.12	-0.10
Parenting and the Home Environment															
HOME Language and Literacy	10.4	10.0	0.3	0.18*	0.18*	10.7	10.4	0.3	0.13	0.12	11.4	10.1	1.3	0.42**	0.36**
Percent Reading Daily	58.6	44.8	13.9	0.28**	0.26**	64.4	46.5	17.9	0.36**	0.34**	32.9	29.2	3.7	0.08	0.06
Percent Spanked Last Week	46.6	54.2	-7.7	-0.15	-0.14	47.5	50.5	-3.0	-0.06	-0.06	36.3	34.4	1.9	0.04	0.04
Parent Supportiveness During Play	4.1	4.0	0.1	0.08	0.09	4.0	3.8	0.2	0.22+	0.20+	3.9	3.9	0.1	0.01	0.01
Parent Detachment During Play	1.4	1.5	-0.1	-0.10	-0.11	1.2	1.4	-0.2	-0.30*	-0.28*					
Percent Regular Bedtime	60.9	50.7	10.2	0.21*	0.19*	64.2	57.4	6.9	0.14	0.13					
Teaching Activities	4.6	4.4	0.2	0.28**	0.25**	4.5	4.2	0.3	0.39**	0.35**	11.5	10.8	0.6	0.21*	0.18+
Children's Books (26 or more)											66.2	57.9	8.3	0.17+	0.14+
Parent Attends Meetings/Open Houses[h]											34.8	126.6	-91.8	-2.3	-2.10
Family Well-Being and Mental Health															
Depression[i]	15.7	19.2	-3.5	-0.11	-0.10	7.7	8.1	-0.4	-0.06	-0.06	7.1	9.1	-2.0	-0.28**	-0.26**
Parenting Distress	25.0	26.8	-1.9	-0.20*	-0.20*	24.3	27.1	-2.8	-0.29**	-0.27**					
Family Conflict	1.7	1.8	-0.0	-0.05	-0.05	1.7	1.7	0.0	0.07	0.06					
Someone in Household Had Alcohol/Drug Problem, Past Year											8.1	10.8	-2.7	-0.09	-0.07
Child Witnessed Violence											10.7	11.2	-0.5	-0.02	-0.02
Parent Self-Sufficiency															
Employed[j]	72.7	67.7	5.0	0.11	0.12	87.6	81.9	5.7	0.15+	0.14+	3.6	3.5	0.1	0.08	0.05
In School or Job Training[k]	53.1	46.7	6.5	0.13	0.13	65.4	54.4	11.0	0.22*	0.21*					
Income (dollars)[l]	12378.5	11602.5	776.0	0.06	0.06	14856.8	14689.9	166.9	0.01	0.01	2125.20	2135.90	-10.7	-0.01	-0.01

(Continued)

TABLE 10. (Continued)

| | Program-Control Differences, Moderate Risk | | | | | | | | | | | | | | |
| | Age 2 | | | | | Age 3 | | | | | Age 5 | | | | |
Outcome	Program Group Participants[a]	Control Group	Impact Estimate[b]	Effect Size (TOT)[c,d]	Effect Size (ITT)[d]	Program Group Participants[a]	Control Group	Impact Estimate[b]	Effect Size (TOT)[c,d]	Effect Size (ITT)[d]	Program Group Participants[a]	Control Group	Impact Estimate[b]	Effect Size (TOT)[c,d]	Effect Size (ITT)[d]
Sample Size															
Parent interview	305	290				271	253				259	311			
Parent-child interactions	215	194				183	151				205	213			
Bayley	238	211				169	145				NA	NA			
Child assessments	271	228				193	169				215	230			

Note. All impact estimates were calculated using regression models in which each site was weighted equally. All values in the tables are based on two-stage least squares analyses (treatment on treated) except for the columns that depict effect sizes based on ordinary least squares comparisons (intent to treat). Psychometric information on specific outcome measures, including descriptive statistics is available in Chapter 2.

Note that all footnotes are identical to those of Table 6.

Source. Parent interviews, interviewer observations, and assessments of semistructured parent–child interactions conducted when children were in their prekindergarten year. HOME, Home Observation for Measurement of the Environment; CBCL, Child Behavior Check List; FACES, Family and Child Experiences Survey; PPVT, Peabody Picture Vocabulary Test; TVIP, Test de Vocabulario de Imagines Peabody.

For children in highest-risk families, the impacts story is most complex (Table 11). Analyses showed a negative impact of EHS on Woodcock-Johnson Letter-Word Identification at age 5 (ES = .28, $p < .05$) that was consistent with a negative trend effect on English receptive vocabulary found at age 3 and a negative trend on observed Bayley emotion regulation at age 2. Positive impacts were found at age 5 that had not been seen at age 3, although there had been one favorable social-emotional impact at age 2. At age 5 EHS children in the highest-risk group had more positive approaches to learning (ES = .29, $p < .05$) and showed a trend toward fewer speech problems (ES = .24, $p < .10$). Also, EHS parents in the highest-risk group were observed to be significantly more supportive during play (ES = .35, $p < .05$) and were considerably less likely to report someone in their household having a drug or alcohol problem (5% of EHS families vs. 15% of control group families; ES = .33, $p < .05$). There had not been positive impacts on parenting at age 3, but at age 2 EHS parents had reported less parenting distress but also less-regular bedtimes for children.

After leaving EHS, among the high-risk group, 42% of former EHS children and 45% of control group children in the moderate-risk group attended formal programs when they were both 3 and 4 years of age, whereas 60% of the EHS program and 56% of the control group ever attended Head Start during this period. Neither of these differences was statistically significant (not tabled).

DISCUSSION

We have argued that because EHS families are heterogeneous—the program serves different types of families in different localities—it is important to explore the impact of the program for subgroups defined by different family characteristics. Thus, we conducted targeted impact analyses where EHS participants in a subgroup were compared to the control group for that subgroup. We discuss the implications of findings for each subgroup.

Methodological issues are important in regards to family subgroups. The subgroup findings were conducted as impact analyses, using all controls that had been included in the overall impacts analyses, with all sites weighted equally. A site was included in the analyses only if it had a minimum of 10 program and control group families in a subgroup, thus not every site entered every subgroup analysis. Some suggest that subgroup findings within an overall impact study should be considered exploratory. In this study, it is certainly true that the subgroup analyses are underpowered relative to the overall sample, and reporting may be conservative or less reliable than the overall sample reporting. For example, effect sizes considerably larger than

TABLE 11

IMPACTS ON SELECTED CHILD AND FAMILY OUTCOMES AT AGES 2, 3, AND 5, BY HIGH-RISK SUBGROUP

Program-Control Differences, High Risk

Outcome	Age 2					Age 3					Age 5				
	Program Group Participants[a]	Control Group[b]	Impact Estimate[c]	Effect Size (TOT)[d]	Effect Size (ITT)[d]	Program Group Participants[a]	Control Group[b]	Impact Estimate[c]	Effect Size (TOT)[d]	Effect Size (ITT)[d]	Program Group Participants[a]	Control Group[b]	Impact Estimate[c]	Effect Size (TOT)[d]	Effect Size (ITT)[d]
Child Social-Emotional and Approaches to Learning Outcomes															
CBCL Aggressive Behavior	13.0	14.7	-1.7	-0.25[+]	-0.19	10.9	11.5	-0.6	-0.10	-0.07	10.1	11.5	-1.4	-0.20	-0.14
FACES Social Behavior Problems											5.6	6.2	-0.6	-0.16	-0.13
Negativity Toward Parent During Play	2.1	1.8	0.3	0.27	0.25	1.3	1.3	-0.0	-0.01	-0.01	1.2	1.2	-0.0	-0.04	-0.05
Engagement During Play	4.0	4.0	-0.1	-0.05	-0.07	4.5	4.6	-0.0	-0.03	-0.03	4.6	4.7	-0.2	-0.17	-0.16
Sustained Attention with Objects During Play	5.0	4.9	0.1	0.12	0.08	4.9	4.7	0.3	0.27	0.22					
FACES Positive Approaches to Learning											12.3	11.7	0.6	0.29*	0.24*
Observed Bayley Emotion Regulation[e]	3.5	3.7	-0.2	-0.21[+]	-0.23*	3.8	3.9	-0.1	-0.15	-0.15					
Observed Leiter Emotion Regulation											89.8	92.4	-2.6	-0.26	-0.21
Observed Attention											8.4	8.4	0.0	0.01	0.00
Leiter Attention Sustained											9.9	10.2	-0.3	-0.08	-0.08
Child Language/Cognitive/Academic Skills															
MacArthur CDI Vocabulary	52.6	48.5	4.1	0.18	0.17										
English Receptive Vocabulary (PPVT)						80.2	84.9	-4.7	-0.29[+]	-0.26[+]	83.0	84.7	-1.7	-0.11	-0.08
Average Bayley MDI	84.0	86.6	-2.6	-0.19	-0.18	88.5	90.1	-1.6	-0.13	-0.12					
Percentage Bayley MDI <85	48.6	44.0	4.6	0.09	0.08	39.2	28.2	11.1	0.24	0.21					
Woodcock Johnson Letter-Word Identification (English)											83.3	87.3	-4.0	-0.28*	-0.24*
Woodcock Johnson Applied Problems											80.4	82.5	-2.0	-0.10	-0.08
Child Health															
ER Visits Due to Accident or Injury	5.9	9.6	-3.7	-0.13	-0.10	7.9	7.4	0.5	0.02	0.01					
Any Immunizations[f]	94.9	96.7	-1.9	-0.11	-0.07	96.4	98.4	-2.0	-0.14	-0.10					

(Continued)

87

TABLE 11. (Continued)

Program-Control Differences, High Risk

Outcome	Age 2					Age 3					Age 5				
	Program Group Participants[a]	Control Group[b]	Impact Estimate[c]	Effect Size (TOT)[d]	Effect Size (ITT)[d]	Program Group Participants[a]	Control Group[b]	Impact Estimate[c]	Effect Size (TOT)[d]	Effect Size (ITT)[d]	Program Group Participants[a]	Control Group[b]	Impact Estimate[c]	Effect Size (TOT)[d]	Effect Size (ITT)[d]
Child Has Individualized Education Plan[g]	2.0	3.3	-1.3	-0.07	-0.08	5.9	4.7	1.2	0.06	0.04	3.9	5.9	-2.0	-0.07	-0.05
Speech Problems (low score = fewer)											16.9	26.7	-9.9	-0.24[+]	-0.19[+]
Parenting and the Home Environment															
HOME Language and Literacy	9.8	9.8	0.0	0.02	0.03	10.2	10.3	-0.1	-0.04	-0.04	9.5	9.9	-0.4	-0.13	-0.18
Percent Reading Daily	49.7	54.4	-4.7	-0.09	-0.06	42.8	44.4	-1.6	-0.03	-0.03	25.6	26.4	-0.8	-0.02	-0.03
Percent Spanked Last Week	57.7	66.2	-8.4	-0.17	-0.15	56.0	66.6	-10.7	-0.21	-0.15	43.1	36.9	6.2	0.13	0.11
Parent Supportiveness During Play	3.7	3.6	0.2	0.15	0.11	3.8	3.7	0.1	0.08	0.08	3.9	3.5	0.4	0.35*	0.32*
Parent Detachment During Play	1.6	1.8	-0.2	-0.20	-0.19	1.3	1.3	-0.1	-0.11	-0.08					
Percent Regular Bedtime	45.5	55.5	-10.0	-0.20	-0.19[+]	51.0	49.9	1.1	0.02	0.00					
Teaching Activities	4.4	4.6	-0.1	-0.15	-0.11	4.2	4.4	-0.1	-0.17	-0.16	11.0	10.9	0.1	0.04	0.03
Children's Books (26 or more)											46.7	47.7	-1.0	-0.02	-0.01
Parent Attends Meetings/Open Houses[h]											82.1	51.5	30.6	0.76	0.71
Family Well-Being and Mental Health															
Depression[i]	21.2	17.2	4.0	0.12	0.12	9.3	8.8	0.5	0.07	0.07	8.4	10.0	-1.6	-0.23	-0.16
Parenting Distress	25.8	28.3	-2.5	-0.26[+]	-0.22[+]	28.0	26.8	1.2	0.13	0.09					
Family Conflict	1.7	1.8	-0.1	-0.16	-0.16	1.8	1.8	0.1	0.10	0.08					
Someone in Household Had Alcohol/Drug Problem, Past Year											5.1	14.9	-9.8	-0.33*	-0.25*
Child Witnessed Violence											11.8	18.5	-6.7	-0.21	-0.16
Parent Self-Sufficiency															
Employed[j]	63.5	62.8	0.6	0.01	0.00	83.0	77.4	5.6	0.15	0.12	3.3	3.5	-0.2	-0.10	-0.11
In School or Job Training[k]	54.9	49.5	5.4	0.11	0.10	67.5	63.3	4.2	0.08	0.09					
Income (dollars)[l]	9993.8	10707.4	-713.6	-0.06	-0.07	10726.9	11005.0	-278.1	-0.02	-0.04	2209.0	1851.0	358.0	0.20	0.16

(Continued)

TABLE 11. (Continued)

| | Program-Control Differences, High Risk | | | | | | | | | | | | | | |
| | Age 2 | | | | | Age 3 | | | | | Age 5 | | | | |
Outcome	Program Group Participants[a]	Control Group[b]	Impact Estimate[c] (ITT)[d]	Effect Size (TOT)[d]	Effect Size (ITT)[d]	Program Group Participants[a]	Control Group[b]	Impact Estimate[c] (ITT)[d]	Effect Size (TOT)[d]	Effect Size (ITT)[d]	Program Group Participants[a]	Control Group[b]	Impact Estimate[c] (ITT)[d]	Effect Size (TOT)[d]	Effect Size (ITT)[d]
Sample Size															
Parent interview	191	182				178	172				185	218			
Parent-child interactions	138	128				93	78				127	130			
Bayley	122	118				100	95				NA	NA			
Child assessments	156	157				109	100				149	161			

Note. All impact estimates were calculated using regression models in which each site was weighted equally. All values in the tables are based on two-stage least squares analyses (treatment on treated) except for the columns that depict effect sizes based on ordinary least squares comparisons (intent to treat). Psychometric information on specific outcome measures, including descriptive statistics is available in Chapter 2.

Note that all footnotes are identical to those of Table 6.

Source. Parent interviews, interviewer observations, and assessments of semistructured parent–child interactions conducted when children were in their prekindergarten year. HOME, Home Observation for Measurement of the Environment; CBCL, Child Behavior Check List; FACES, Family and Child Experiences Survey; PPVT, Peabody Picture Vocabulary Test; TVIP, Test de Vocabulario de Imagines Peabody.

those for the overall sample are sometimes not significant because of high standard errors. Despite these drawbacks, we believe that family subgroup analyses are critical for distilling implications for program improvement and thus are central questions for evaluation studies. Our interpretation of subgroup findings has consistently focused on the presence of patterns of effects; consistency of findings over multiple time points in most family subgroups lends credibility to the results.

Ethnic/Racial Groups

Findings were most positive for African American children and families and the general pattern of significant impacts seen at ages 2 and 3 was maintained at age 5, as hypothesized. Children in EHS had better outcomes than control group children in terms of behavior problems, approaches to learning, attention, language development, and speech problems. When children were 5, EHS parents provided more children's books, were observed to be more supportive during play, spanked less, and had fewer depressive symptoms and less often reported someone in the household had a drug or alcohol problem.

These findings show that the program impacts were largely sustained for 2 years after the program was completed. Impacts may have been sustained for several reasons. First, a number of the age 3 impacts were rather robust, about half a standard deviation, and even though they were smaller at age 5, they were still meaningful and significant. Second, the substantial impacts on parents at age 5 could have facilitated outcomes. Third, African American children had the highest rates of sustained formal program participation at 59%, although the program group was not significantly ahead of the control group's 52%.

For Whites, the impacts seen at age 2 nearly disappeared by age 3, and by age 5 few impacts were found on children's development. However, the age 5 impacts were notable. In addition, former EHS Whites were significantly more likely to attend HS during the 3–5 age period. White children had the highest level of aggressive behavior of the racial/ethnic groups, and, at age 5, there was a trend toward EHS reducing these negative behaviors. It is possible that the higher rate of participation in HS may have contributed to this reduction of behavior problems at age 5 given that White EHS children did not have lower rates of behavior problems than the control group at age 3.

In addition, there had been indications that more White children than other groups had disabilities and White EHS children were more likely to have IEPs at age 5, in contrast with their control group. It is possible that some of these children were recruited into EHS because of their disabilities as throughout the study Whites had higher rates of IEPs than other racial/ethnic groups (e.g., disability rates at age 3 were 14%, 9%, and 4% for Whites, African

90

Americans, and Hispanics, respectively). Some of the children with IEPs may have had speech problems; at age 5, EHS White children were more likely to have an identified speech problem than their control group counterparts. The interpretation of the increase in IEPs and identified speech problems can be interpreted as a negative impact of the program on child outcomes, or that the program helped families to recognize developmental issues and obtain a diagnosis that leads to needed services. Given the emphasis that EHS and HS place on identifying disabilities, the latter interpretation is plausible.

That there were age 5 language impacts for Hispanics is encouraging given much smaller literatures to inform program development of services for low-income Hispanics. It is notable that early impacts for this group were centered on family support for child literacy and learning as well as a parent self-sufficiency outcome. However, findings were in general minimal for this group of children and families, which indicates the need to further develop effective program strategies to better serve this segment of the EHS population.

Risk Groups

We predicted, and found, relatively weak impacts on children in low-risk families. These children were more likely to have disabilities then those in the other two risk groups.

Although a somewhat substantial pattern of impacts remained among the children in the moderate-risk Group 2 years after the end of the program, the domains of impact changed. An impact was no longer found on cognitive development although impacts on social and emotional outcomes were found. The changing *pattern* of impacts on children may have been related to the influence of HS given that moderate-risk former EHS children were significantly more likely to attend HS than the moderate-risk control group. Impacts on positive parenting were more consistent across ages 3 and 5, as was the finding of less parenting stress at age 3 and reduced depression at age 5, lending some support for the role of the early experiences and possibly some for concurrent experiences, given that child domains affected by the program changed.

The story for highest-risk families is the most complex. At age 3, it certainly appeared that this group did not benefit from EHS services, although some important impacts emerged 2 years later. For this group, positive impacts of EHS emerged for social, emotional, and parenting outcomes at age 5, together with some reduction of "risky" behaviors in home life settings.

However, the impact on Letter-Word Identification at age 5 was negative, consistent with a negative trend on PPVT-III scores seen at age 3. It is further notable that highest-risk families were relatively unlikely to be in formal

91

program settings from ages 3 to 5 than other groups. Getting these highest-risk children into formal programs from EHS until kindergarten entry might be a priority given the negative achievement outcome.

NOTE

8. Because family risk level could be confounded with site, at age 3 we conducted a second set of analyses that pooled families and removed the weights by site. That is, with these new analyses, all respondents had equal opportunity to influence the outcomes. The comparability of these two analytic approaches (weighted by site or pooled) has been presented in other venues (Kisker et al., 2006).

V. PROGRAM SUBGROUPS: PATTERNS OF IMPACTS FOR HOME-BASED, CENTER-BASED, AND MIXED-APPROACH PROGRAMS

Rachel Chazan-Cohen, Helen H. Raikes, and Cheri Vogel

The overall goal of the federal Early Head Start (EHS) program is to enhance child development and family functioning. However, the approach taken to service delivery varies widely among local programs. As stated previously, the Head Start Program Performance Standards define four service delivery options that programs can choose for providing services to individual families.

The 17 EHS programs participating in the study were not randomly assigned to program approach. Each program selected a service delivery mode to best meet the needs of families and the community. The research empirically defined three program approaches based on services provided: (1) a home-based approach, in which all families received the home-based option; (2) a center-based approach, in which all families received the center-based option; and (3) a mixed approach, in which families were offered a combination of home-based and center-based care or home-based services to some families and center-based to others. Some mixed programs also moved families between home-based and center-based care over time depending on changing family needs.

Over the time of the study (1996–2002), approaches to delivering services increased in complexity as programs recognized the importance of having flexibility to meet the needs of individual families, especially as those needs changed over time with the implementation of welfare reform, which also began in 1996. The 17 research programs were initially divided about equally among center-based, home-based, and mixed-approach strategies. Within 1 year, however, a higher proportion of programs were providing home-based services.[9] For the impact analysis, program approach was defined as that offered in 1997, 1 year after the programs began serving families, because the

---

Corresponding author: Rachel Chazan-Cohen, Department of Psychology, George Mason University, 4400 University Drive, MS 6D5, Fairfax, VA 22030, email: rachelcc@gmail.com

majority of the study participants experienced the program approach that was being implemented in 1997.

This trend toward a mixed approach seems to be nationwide. The Survey of Early Head Start Programs (ACF, 2006) found that almost 60% of all programs provided either the combination option to all of their families or multiple options, whereas 17% were exclusively home based and 23% exclusively center based.

When asked about their theories of change, center-based programs emphasized direct pathways to improving children's development. Caregivers in these programs interacted directly with children to establish relationships and conduct activities designed to enhance their health and development. These programs also supported families through social services, parent education, and parent involvement, but most services were child-focused. The home-based programs emphasized indirect pathways to improving children's development. Home visitors interacted with parents to strengthen parent–child relationships, enhance parenting skills, and support parents' efforts to provide an educationally stimulating and emotionally responsive home environment. These activities were then expected to lead to changes in children's health and development. Mixed-approach programs combined these strategies (ACF, 2002a).

Given the variety of possible modes of service delivery and their underlying theories of change, it is important to look beyond the overall impacts to see if the patterns of impacts differed by program service delivery modality. EHS significantly increased services to program families during the first 2 years after enrollment, but most control group families received some services from other providers in the community (ACF, 2002b). Home-based and mixed-approach programs had the largest impacts on receipt of key services (center-based child care, home visits, case management, and group parent–child activities), and home-based programs had the largest impacts on receipt of core child development services. These differences reflect both lower levels of service receipt by program families and greater receipt of services by control families in center-based sites. Home-based and mixed-approach programs also had the largest impacts on receipt of a range of family development services.

HYPOTHESES

The underlying theories of change and the literature discussed in Chapter I lead to three hypotheses for EHS program subgroups.

First, programs that provide services through the home-based approach were expected to have greater impacts than center-based programs on parenting outcomes, parent–child relationships, family self-sufficiency, health, and child social–emotional outcomes. Furthermore, earlier impacts on parents are likely to lead to impacts on children after the program ends.

Second, programs that provide mainly center-based services with the required family support were expected to have more of an impact on child outcomes than on parenting, parent–child relationships, and family outcomes.

Third, those programs that have the capacity to offer both types of service options, referred to as mixed-approach programs, were expected to have the broadest pattern of impacts on parents and children across the developmental domains.

METHODS

The subgroup analyses reported in this chapter examine the same set of outcomes considered in the overall impact analyses. Since the mid-1990s, it has become more widely recognized that if a program is declared "effective" based on several of a larger group of impacts being statistically significant, then the probability of falsely identifying program impacts, both positive and negative (i.e., the probability of a Type I error) is much higher than the 5% reflected in an individual statistical test. Although we recognize the increased possibility of Type I error by not adjusting for multiple comparisons in the following analyses, the intent of the subgroup analyses is to inform program practice and guide future research. Thus, the consequences of having insufficient sample size to make multiple comparisons adjustments are less severe, and examining impact estimates in a more exploratory way without adjustments is appropriate.

To learn about impacts of different service delivery approaches, we focus primarily on the within-group impacts presented in Tables 12–14. These analyses were conducted in the same way at each age and in a manner consistent with the analysis of overall impacts (see Chapter III for details). We also conducted statistical tests to gauge whether the impacts differed across subgroups.

It is important to note that although the estimated impacts of EHS on outcomes within each subgroup based on program approach are based on the experimental study design (since families were randomly assigned to the treatment or control group within sites), programs were not randomly assigned to implement a particular program approach. Any differences in impacts by program approach may be due to other site-level factors that are associated with program approach. Thus, the results refer to the effectiveness of program approach *for programs that adopted that approach,* given their community contexts and eligible populations.

95

TABLE 12

IMPACTS ON SELECTED CHILD AND FAMILY OUTCOMES AT AGES 2, 3, AND 5, BY HOME-BASED PROGRAM APPROACH

Program-Control Differences, Home-Based

Outcome	Age 2 Program Group Participants[a]	Age 2 Control Group[b]	Age 2 Impact Estimate[c]	Age 2 Effect Size (TOT)[d]	Age 2 Effect Size (ITT)[d]	Age 3 Program Group Participants[a]	Age 3 Control Group[b]	Age 3 Impact Estimate[c]	Age 3 Effect Size (TOT)[d]	Age 3 Effect Size (ITT)[d]	Age 5 Program Group Participants[a]	Age 5 Control Group[b]	Age 5 Impact Estimate[c]	Age 5 Effect Size (TOT)[d]	Age 5 Effect Size (ITT)[d]
Child Social-Emotional and Approaches to Learning Outcomes															
CBCL Aggressive Behavior	12.9	13.2	-0.3	-0.04	-0.04	11.2	11.7	-0.5	-0.08	-0.07	10.6	11.3	-0.7	-0.10	-0.09
FACES Social Behavior Problems											5.5	6.1	-0.5	-0.15*	-0.13*
Negativity Toward Parent During Play	1.7	1.7	-0.0	-0.04	-0.04	1.3	1.3	-0.0	-0.07	-0.06	1.2	1.2	-0.0	-0.01	-0.01
Engagement During Play	4.3	4.3	0.0	0.03	0.03	4.8	4.6	0.2	0.19*	0.19*	4.7	4.6	0.0	0.05	0.04
Sustained Attention with Objects During Play	5.1	5.0	0.0	0.04	0.04	5.0	4.9	0.1	0.11	0.10					
FACES Positive Approaches to Learning											12.2	11.7	0.4	0.20**	0.18**
Observed Bayley Emotion Regulation[e]	3.6	3.6	-0.1	-0.06	-0.06	4.0	4.0	0.0	0.02	0.02	91.3	91.1	0.2	0.02	0.02
Observed Leiter Emotion Regulation											8.6	8.5	0.2	0.08	0.07
Observed Attention											10.9	10.6	0.3	0.10	0.09
Leiter Attention Sustained															
Child Language/Cognitive/Academic Skills															
MacArthur CDI Vocabulary	56.4	53.3	3.1	0.14+	0.13*	84.6	83.1	1.5	0.09	0.08	92.3	91.5	0.8	0.05	0.05
English Receptive Vocabulary (PPVT)	91.5	90.4	1.1	0.08	0.08	94.1	92.8	1.2	0.10	0.09					
Average Bayley MDI															
Percentage Bayley MDI < 85	31.7	32.8	-1.2	-0.02	-0.02	20.5	22.0	-1.4	-0.03	-0.03					
Woodcock Johnson Letter-Word Identification (English)											88.7	88.1	0.6	0.04	0.03
Woodcock Johnson Applied Problems											89.0	86.9	2.0	0.10	0.08
Child Health															
ER Visits Due to Accident or Injury	7.1	8.7	-1.6	-0.06	-0.05	11.3	11.8	-0.4	-0.01	-0.01					
Any Immunizations[f]	98.2	98.2	-0.0	-0.0	0.00	99.2	98.5	0.8	0.05	0.05					

(Continued)

TABLE 12. (*Continued*)

Program-Control Differences, Home-Based

	Age 2					Age 3					Age 5				
Outcome	Program Group Participants[a]	Control Group[b]	Impact Estimate[c]	Effect Size (TOT)[d]	Effect Size (ITT)[d]	Program Group Participants[a]	Control Group[b]	Impact Estimate[c]	Effect Size (TOT)[d]	Effect Size (ITT)[d]	Program Group Participants[a]	Control Group[b]	Impact Estimate[c]	Effect Size (TOT)[d]	Effect Size (ITT)[d]
Child Has Individualized Education Plan[g]	4.7	3.1	1.6	0.09	0.08	7.8	5.1	2.8	0.12+	0.12+	8.2	8.7	-0.5	-0.02	-0.02
Speech Problems (low score = fewer)											19.9	24.3	-4.4	-0.10	-0.10
Parenting and the Home Environment															
HOME Language and Literacy	10.3	10.1	0.2	0.11*	0.10*	10.9	10.7	0.2	0.07	0.06	11.2	10.6	0.6	0.18*	0.16*
Percent Reading Daily	55.8	54.7	1.1	0.02	0.02	54.5	55.7	-1.2	-0.02	-0.02	34.8	27.3	7.5	0.16*	0.15*
Percent Spanked Last Week	48.6	52.3	-3.7	-0.07	-0.07	44.1	49.6	-5.5	-0.11	-0.10	33.6	36.4	-2.8	-0.06	-0.06
Parent Supportiveness During Play	4.1	4.0	0.1	0.09	0.08	4.0	3.9	0.1	0.15*	0.15*	4.0	3.9	0.0	0.04	0.04
Parent Detachment During Play	1.4	1.5	-0.2	-0.16+	-0.15*	1.2	1.3	-0.1	-0.09	-0.09					
Percent Regular Bedtime	58.8	54.1	4.7	0.10	0.09	59.3	55.6	3.6	0.07	0.07					
Teaching Activities	4.6	4.5	0.0	0.04	0.04	4.4	4.4	-0.1	-0.06	-0.05	11.3	10.8	0.5	0.17*	0.15*
Children's Books (26 or more)											63.6	55.8	7.7	0.16*	0.14*
Parent Attends Meetings/Open Houses[h]											81.6	80.5	1.1	0.03	0.03
Family Well-Being and Mental Health															
Depression[i]	18.4	15.8	2.6	0.08	0.08	7.7	7.9	-0.1	-0.02	-0.01	7.6	8.3	-0.6	-0.09	-0.08
Parenting Distress	25.1	26.2	-1.2	-0.12+	-0.12+	24.9	26.3	-1.4	-0.14*	-0.13*					
Family Conflict	1.7	1.7	-0.1	-0.13+	-0.12+	1.7	1.7	-0.0	-0.01	-0.01					
Someone in Household Had Alcohol/Drug Problem, Past Year											8.6	9.7	-1.0	-0.03	-0.04
Child Witnessed Violence											12.3	12.9	-0.6	-0.02	-0.02
Parent Self-Sufficiency															
Employed[j]	69.0	70.1	-1.1	-0.02	-0.02	83.1	81.8	1.3	0.03	0.03	3.5	3.5	-0.0	-0.00	0.00
In School or Job Training[k]	43.6	37.9	5.7	0.12+	0.11+	53.1	45.5	7.6	0.15*	0.14*					
Income (dollars)[l]	13631.5	12312.3	1319.2	0.11+	0.10+	16268.5	15282.6	985.8	0.08	0.07	2408.3	2106.2	302.1	0.17*	0.16*
Sample Size															
Parent interview	500	466				502	446				448	479			

(*Continued*)

TABLE 12. (Continued)

Program-Control Differences, Home-Based

	Age 2					Age 3					Age 5				
Outcome	Program Group Participants[a]	Control Group[b]	Impact Estimate[c]	Effect Size (TOT)[d]	Effect Size (ITT)[d]	Program Group Participants[a]	Control Group[b]	Impact Estimate[c]	Effect Size (TOT)[d]	Effect Size (ITT)[d]	Program Group Participants[a]	Control Group[b]	Impact Estimate[c]	Effect Size (TOT)[d]	Effect Size (ITT)[d]
Parent–child interactions	429	374				392	348				405	424			
Bayley	432	387				396	350				NA	NA			
Child assessments	457	411				428	370				390	412			

Note. All impact estimates were calculated using regression models in which each site was weighted equally. All values in the tables are based on two-stage least squares analyses (treatment on treated) except for the columns that depict effect sizes based on ordinary least squares comparisons (intent to treat). Psychometric information on specific outcome measures, including descriptive statistics is available in Chapter 2.

[a] A participant is defined as a program group member who received more than one Early Head Start home visit, met with an Early Head Start case manager more than once, received at least 2 weeks of Early Head Start center-based care, and/or participated in Early Head Start group parent–child activities.

[b] The control group mean is the mean for the control group members who would have participated in Early Head Start if they had been assigned to the program group instead. This unobserved mean was estimated as the difference between the program group mean for participants and the impact per participant.

[c] The estimated impact per participant is measured as the difference between the program group mean for participants divided by the proportion of program group members who participated in Early Head Start services (which varied by site). The estimated impact per eligible applicant is measured as the difference between the regression-adjusted means for all program and control group members.

[d] The effect size was calculated by dividing the estimated impact per participant by the standard deviation of the outcome measure for the control group. For ease of reading, all statistically significant effect sizes appear in bold.

[e] Emotion regulation measured at ages 2 and 3 with the Bayley Behavior Rating Scales and at age 5 with the Leiter-R observer ratings.

[f] Reported as percentage of children who had received any immunizations by the time of each interview.

[g] At age 2 the time frame for this question is 15 months after random assignment. At age 3 the time frame is 26 months after random assignment. At ages 2 and 3 this item is measured as eligible for early intervention services.

[h] Includes only parents whose children were in a formal program. Sample sizes for this outcome in the home-based subgroup were $N = 175$ and $N = 184$ for program and control groups, respectively.

[i] Depression measured with the Composite International Diagnostic Interview (CIDI) at age 2.

[j] At age 2 the time frame for this question is 15 months after random assignment, and at age 3 the time frame is 26 months after random assignment. At each earlier age the item is whether employed or not, but at age 5 we asked "How much time in the past 6 months have you held a job or jobs in which you worked at least 20 hr per week?" Answers were on a 5-point scale from 1 = *never* to 5 = *all of the time.*

[k] At age 2 the time frame for this question is 15 months after random assignment, and at age 3 the time frame is 26 months after random assignment.

[l] At age 2 the time frame for this question is 15 months after random assignment, and at age 3 the time frame is 26 months after random assignment. Amounts are annual income at ages 2 and 3 and monthly income at age 5.

$+p < .10.$ $^{*}p < .05.$ $^{**}p < .01.$

Source. Parent interviews, interviewer observations, and assessments of semistructured parent–child interactions conducted when children were in their prekindergarten year. HOME, Home Observation for Measurement of the Environment; CBCL, Child Behavior Check List; FACES, Family and Child Experiences Survey; PPVT, Peabody Picture Vocabulary Test; TVIP, Test de Vocabulario de Imagines Peabody.

TABLE 13

IMPACTS ON SELECTED CHILD AND FAMILY OUTCOMES AT AGES 2, 3, AND 5, BY CENTER-BASED PROGRAM APPROACH

Program-Control Differences, Center-Based

Outcome	Age 2					Age 3					Age 5				
	Program Group Participants[a]	Control Group[b]	Impact Estimate[c]	Effect Size (TOT)[d]	Effect Size (ITT)[d]	Program Group Participants[a]	Control Group[b]	Impact Estimate[c]	Effect Size (TOT)[d]	Effect Size (ITT)[d]	Program Group Participants[a]	Control Group[b]	Impact Estimate[c]	Effect Size (TOT)[d]	Effect Size (ITT)[d]
Child Social-Emotional and Approaches to Learning Outcomes															
CBCL Aggressive Behavior	11.7	12.3	-0.54	-0.07	-0.08	9.6	10.8	-1.2	-0.18	-0.12	10.8	11.0	-0.2	-0.03	0.00
FACES Social Behavior Problems											5.5	5.4	0.1	0.03	0.05
Negativity Toward Parent During Play	1.8	1.7	0.1	-0.08	0.06	1.2	1.4	-0.2	-0.27*	-0.22*	1.3	1.3	0.0	0.01	-0.03
Engagement During Play	4.4	4.4	-0.1	-0.05	-0.03	4.9	4.7	0.2	0.17	0.09	4.6	4.7	-0.1	-0.12	-0.06
Sustained Attention with Objects During Play	5.0	5.1	-0.1	-0.09	-0.09	5.0	5.0	0.0	0.00	-0.01					
FACES Positive Approaches to Learning						4.0	4.0	0.0	0.01	0.01	12.2	12.0	0.2	0.10	0.08
Observed Bayley Emotion Regulation[e]	3.7	3.7	0.1	0.06	0.07										
Observed Leiter Emotion Regulation											92.0	91.3	0.7	0.07	0.04
Observed Attention											8.8	8.3	0.4	0.22	0.17
Leiter Attention Sustained											11.2	10.8	0.4	0.12	0.09
Child Language/Cognitive/Academic Skills															
MacArthur CDI Vocabulary	54.9	55.2	-0.3	-0.1	-0.02	83.2	81.8	1.5	0.09	0.06					
English Receptive Vocabulary (PPVT)						89.8	88.9	0.9	0.07	0.05	91.8	89.7	2.1	0.14	0.10
Average Bayley MDI	90.1	87.0	3.1	0.23*	0.09										
Percentage Bayley MDI < 85	31.8	43.9	-12.1	-0.25+	-0.19+	26.5	36.1	-9.7	-0.21	-0.15					
Woodcock Johnson Letter-Word Identification (English)											89.7	92.0	-2.4	-0.17	-0.14
Woodcock Johnson Applied Problems											90.3	88.6	1.8	0.08	0.07
Child Health															
ER Visit Due to Accident or Injury	7.8	9.8	-1.9	-0.07	-0.05	9.1	11.9	-2.7	-0.09	-0.06					
Any Immunizations[f]	98.1	96.4	1.7	0.09	0.09	98.5	98.3	0.3	0.02	0.02					
Child Has Individualized Education Plan[g]						8.3	3.7	4.6	0.21	0.15	4.4	5.8	-1.5	-0.05	-0.02
Speech Problems (low score = fewer)	3.5	2.4	1.0	0.06	0.03						17.9	23.5	-5.5	-0.13	-0.08
Parenting and the Home Environment															
HOME Language and Literacy	10.3	10.3	-0.0	-0.02	-0.01	10.7	10.5	0.3	0.13	0.10	10.6	10.6	0.1	0.02	-0.02
Percent Reading Daily	58.2	49.0	9.2	0.18	0.15	57.9	50.9	7.0	0.14	0.11	27.7	26.4	1.3	0.03	0.01

(Continued)

TABLE 13. (Continued)

| | Program-Control Differences, Center-Based | | | | | | | | | | | | | | |
| | Age 2 | | | | | Age 3 | | | | | Age 5 | | | | |
Outcome	Program Group Participants[a]	Control Group[b]	Impact Estimate[c]	Effect Size (TOT)[d]	Effect Size (ITT)[d]	Program Group Participants[a]	Control Group[b]	Impact Estimate[c]	Effect Size (TOT)[d]	Effect Size (ITT)[d]	Program Group Participants[a]	Control Group[b]	Impact Estimate[c]	Effect Size (TOT)[d]	Effect Size (ITT)[d]
Percent Spanked Last Week	52.4	55.7	-5.3	-0.11	-0.10	51.4	61.0	-9.6	-0.19	-0.15	40.1	38.0	2.2	0.05	0.05
Parent Supportiveness During Play	4.0	4.1	-0.1	-0.08	-0.05	4.1	4.0	0.1	0.09	0.03	4.1	4.1	-0.0	-0.02	-0.04
Parent Detachment During Play	1.5	1.4	0.1	0.10	0.08	1.2	1.1	0.1	0.16	0.15					
Percent Regular Bedtime	68.5	57.3	11.2	0.22+	0.16+	58.7	57.0	1.8	0.04	0.05					
Teaching Activities	4.5	4.5	0.0	0.08	0.05	4.6	4.3	0.2	0.26+	0.17+	11.3	10.9	0.3	0.11	0.08
Children's Books (26 or more)											63.6	58.7	4.9	0.10	0.07
Parent Attends Meetings/Open Houses[h]											89.0	82.7	6.2	0.16	0.12
Family Well-Being and Mental Health															
Depression[i]	12.8	11.6	1.2	0.04	0.04	7.3	7.1	0.2	0.03	0.01	7.5	8.0	-0.5	-0.06	-0.03
Parenting Distress	24.7	24.8	-0.1	-0.01	0.00	23.9	25.0	-1.1	-0.12	-0.08					
Family Conflict	1.7	1.7	0.0	-0.02	0.00	1.6	1.7	-0.1	-0.11	-0.08					
Someone in Household Had Alcohol/Drug Problem, Past Year											7.8	13.3	-5.5	-0.18	-0.14
Child Witnessed Violence											13.6	9.4	4.3	0.13	0.10
Parent Self-Sufficiency															
Employed[j]	84.9	79.4	5.5	0.12	0.10	91.3	87.3	4.1	0.11	0.08	3.8	3.7	0.2	0.09	0.05
In School or Job Training[k]	50.9	50.5	0.4	0.01	0.00	65.1	61.5	3.6	0.07	0.05					
Income (dollars)[l]	14882.6	17918.4	-3035.8	-0.25	-0.20	18647.4	22085.5	-3438.2	-0.26+	-0.23+	2322.4	2163.6	158.8	0.09	0.04
Sample Size															
Parent interview	240	203				253	210				210	240			
Parent–child interactions	236	195				227	181				165	183			
Bayley	217	181				217	172				NA	NA			
Child assessments	242	208				226	187				197	220			

Note. All impact estimates were calculated using regression models in which each site was weighted equally. All values in the tables are based on two-stage least squares analyses (treatment on treated) except for the columns that depict effect sizes based on ordinary least squares comparisons (intent to treat). Psychometric information on specific outcome measures, including descriptive statistics is available in Chapter 2.

Note that all footnotes are identical to those of Table 12.

Source. Parent interviews, interviewer observations, and assessments of semistructured parent–child interactions conducted when children were in their prekindergarten year. HOME, Home Observation for Measurement of the Environment; CBCL, Child Behavior Check List; FACES, Family and Child Experiences Survey; PPVT, Peabody Picture Vocabulary Test; TVIP, Test de Vocabulario de Imagines Peabody.

TABLE 14

IMPACTS ON SELECTED CHILD AND FAMILY OUTCOMES AT AGES 2, 3, AND 5, BY MIXED-BASED PROGRAM APPROACH

Program-Control Differences, Mixed Approach

Outcome	Age 2 Program Group Participants[a]	Control Group[b]	Impact Estimate[c]	Effect Size (TOT)[d]	Effect Size (ITT)[d]	Age 3 Program Group Participants[a]	Control Group[b]	Impact Estimate[c]	Effect Size (TOT)[d]	Effect Size (ITT)[d]	Age 5 Program Group Participants[a]	Control Group[b]	Impact Estimate[c]	Effect Size (TOT)[d]	Effect Size (ITT)[d]
Child Social-Emotional and Approaches to Learning Outcomes															
CBCL Aggressive Behavior	11.8	13.3	-1.5	-0.23+	-0.21*	10.7	11.3	-0.6	-0.09	-0.08	10.1	10.8	-0.7	-0.10	-0.09
FACES Social Behavior Problems											5.0	5.6	-0.6	-0.18*	-0.16*
Negativity Toward Parent During Play	1.8	2.0	-0.2	-0.18+	-0.17+	1.3	1.3	-0.1	-0.15	-0.14	1.2	1.3	-0.0	-0.03	-0.02
Engagement During Play	4.3	4.1	0.2	0.20*	0.19*	4.7	4.4	0.3	0.30**	0.28**	4.7	4.7	-0.0	-0.05	-0.05
Sustained Attention with Objects During Play	5.0	4.9	0.2	0.16+	0.16+	5.0	4.7	0.3	0.31**	0.29**					
FACES Positive Approaches to Learning											12.2	11.9	0.3	0.14+	0.12
Observed Bayley Emotion Regulation[e]	3.6	3.7	-0.0	-0.05	-0.05	4.0	4.1	-0.1	-0.08	-0.08					
Observed Leiter Emotion Regulation											90.0	90.7	-0.7	-0.08	-0.07
Observed Attention											8.4	8.5	-0.1	-0.03	-0.03
Leiter Attention Sustained											10.8	11.4	-0.5	-0.16+	-0.15+
Child Language/Cognitive/Academic Skills															
MacArthur CDI Vocabulary	57.5	53.2	4.3	0.19*	0.18*										
English Receptive Vocabulary (PPVT)						82.2	78.5	3.7	0.23*	0.21*	91.3	90.6	0.8	0.05	0.05
Average Bayley MDI	88.2	86.4	1.5	0.11	0.10	89.3	87.9	1.4	0.11	0.11					
Percentage Bayley MDI<85	38.0	45.2	-7.2	-0.15	-0.14	36.1	38.4	-2.2	-0.05	-0.05					
Woodcock Johnson Letter-Word Identification (English)											90.6	92.1	-1.5	-0.11	-0.10
Woodcock Johnson Applied Problems											90.5	90.1	0.4	0.02	0.01
Child Health															
ER Visits Due to Accident or Injury	6.5	8.2	-1.7	-0.06	-0.06	9.6	8.7	0.9	0.03	0.03					
Any Immunizations[f]	98.3	95.5	2.9	0.16+	0.15+	98.5	97.3	1.2	0.08	0.08					
Child Has Individualized Education Plan[g]						7.1	7.1	0.1	0.00	0.00	10.0	7.1	3.0	0.11	0.11
Speech Problems (low score = fewer)	2.7	5.3	-2.6	-0.14	-0.13						20.1	19.0	1.1	0.03	0.02
Parenting and the Home Environment															
HOME Language and Literacy	10.4	10.0	0.4	0.22**	0.20**	10.3	10.1	0.2	0.09	0.08	9.4	9.7	-0.3	-0.11	-0.09
Percent Reading Daily	60.4	48.6	11.9	0.24**	0.22**	59.0	45.0	14.0	0.28**	0.26**	38.8	32.5	6.3	0.14	0.13
Percent Spanked Last Week	43.9	52.3	-8.4	-0.17+	-0.16+	46.6	57.6	-10.9	-0.21*	-0.21*	34.9	35.9	-1.0	0.02	-0.02

(Continued)

TABLE 14. (Continued)

Program-Control Differences, Mixed Approach

Outcome	Age 2 Program Group Participants[a]	Age 2 Control Group[b]	Age 2 Impact Estimate[c]	Age 2 Effect Size (TOT)[d]	Age 2 Effect Size (ITT)[d]	Age 3 Program Group Participants[a]	Age 3 Control Group[b]	Age 3 Impact Estimate[c]	Age 3 Effect Size (TOT)[d]	Age 3 Effect Size (ITT)[d]	Age 5 Program Group Participants[a]	Age 5 Control Group[b]	Age 5 Impact Estimate[c]	Age 5 Effect Size (TOT)[d]	Age 5 Effect Size (ITT)[d]
Parent Supportiveness During Play	4.1	3.9	0.2	0.18*	0.17*	4.0	3.8	0.2	0.21*	0.20*	4.0	3.8	0.2	0.16	0.15
Parent Detachment During Play	1.4	1.5	-0.2	-0.16+	-0.16+	1.2	1.4	-0.2	-0.24*	-0.23*					
Percent Regular Bedtime	59.6	54.7	4.9	0.10	0.09	59.3	62.4	-3.1	-0.06	-0.06					
Teaching Activities	4.6	4.4	0.2	0.22**	0.21**	4.4	4.2	0.2	0.18+	0.17+	11.5	11.2	0.2	0.07	0.07
Children's Books (26 or more)											67.0	64.1	3.0	0.06	0.06
Parent Attends Meetings/Open Houses[h]											89.5	77.6	11.9	0.30*	0.28*
Family Well-Being and Mental Health															
Depression[i]	13.9	15.3	-1.4	-0.04	-0.04	7.2	7.8	-0.6	-0.08	-0.08	7.3	8.4	-1.1	-0.16+	-0.15+
Parenting Distress	24.7	27.0	-2.3	-0.24**	-0.23**	24.8	25.9	-1.1	-0.11	-0.11					
Family Conflict	1.7	1.7	0.0	-0.08	-0.09	1.7	1.7	-0.00	-0.05	-0.05					
Someone in Household Had Alcohol/Drug Problem, Past Year											7.2	9.7	-2.6	-0.08	-0.08
Child Witnessed Violence											8.3	10.8	-2.5	-0.08	-0.07
Parent Self-Sufficiency															
Employed[j]	74.0	67.1	6.9	0.15+	0.14+	88.6	82.0	6.5	0.17*	0.16*	3.6	3.6	0.0	0.0	0.01
In School or Job Training[k]	49.1	40.2	8.9	0.18*	0.16*	65.1	51.3	13.8	0.28**	0.25**					
Income (dollars)[l]	15009.7	16002.9	-993.2	-0.08	-0.07	16500.6	18178.0	-1677.3	-0.13	-0.12	2347.60	2432.80	-85.20	-0.05	-0.04
Sample Size															
Parent interview	352	352				350	343				320	365			
Parent-child interactions	276	286				251	255				255	280			
Bayley	282	282				266	257				NA	NA			
Child assessments	295	299				274	275				248	286			

Note. All impact estimates were calculated using regression models in which each site was weighted equally. All values in the tables are based on two-stage least squares analyses (treatment on treated) except for the columns that depict effect sizes based on ordinary least squares comparisons (intent to treat). Psychometric information on specific outcome measures, including descriptive statistics is available in Chapter 2.

Note that all footnotes are identical to those of Table 12.

Source. Parent interviews, interviewer observations, and assessments of semistructured parent–child interactions conducted when children were in their prekindergarten year. HOME, Home Observation for Measurement of the Environment; CBCL, Child Behavior Check List; FACES, Family and Child Experiences Survey; PPVT, Peabody Picture Vocabulary Test; TVIP, Test de Vocabulario de Imagines Peabody.

102

Not surprisingly, characteristics of communities and families differed according to program approach, as they would in a real world setting in which programs choose services intended to best meet the needs of their community. In this study, center-based programs were more likely to be urban and serve working parents, whereas home-based programs were less likely to serve African American parents and parents who were employed or in job training at the time of enrollment into the program. In addition, mixed-approach programs were more likely to serve pregnant women and women who were more likely to score above the clinical cutoff on a measure of depressive symptoms at the time of enrollment (ACF, 2002a, Volume II).

RESULTS

Impacts for Home-Based Programs

Child Outcomes

At age 2, home-based programs had no impacts on children's social–emotional outcomes (Table 12). By age 3 one positive impact emerged, on child engagement of parent coded from videotaped parent–child interactions during a play interaction (ES = .19, $p < .05$), and at age 5, there was a favorable impact on parent report of behavior problems (i.e., reducing reported behavior problems) (ES = .15, $p < .05$) and a positive impact on parent report of approaches to learning (ES = .20, $p < .01$). There were no impacts on child negativity or sustained attention to objects during play with parents at any age and no impacts on rater observations of child behavior during the structured direct assessment at any age.

Home-based programs had no significant impacts on children's vocabulary, cognitive, and academic outcomes at any age. At age 2, a somewhat positive impact on a parent report of child vocabulary was found (ES = .14, $p < .10$).

The analyses revealed little indication that home-based programs had impacts in the area of child health and disabilities. There was a statistical trend indicating an increase in children having an Individualized Education Program (IEP) at age 3 (ES = .12, $p < .10$).

Parent and Family Outcomes

Early analyses indicated that home-based programs were enhancing parenting, especially support for learning. At age 2, a positive impact on the HOME language and literacy subscale was found (ES = .11, $p < .05$) and at age 5 (ES = .18, $p < .05$), but not at age 3 (ES = .07). Although there was no significant impact at age 2 on parental supportiveness during play, it was significant at age 3 (ES = .15, $p < .05$), but then no longer significant at age 5.

At age 2 parent detachment during play was somewhat lower for the EHS group (ES = .16, p < .10).

At age 5, three new positive impacts emerged: daily reading (ES = .16, p < .05), the number of parent teaching activities with the child (ES = .17, p < .05), and the likelihood that parents reported a large number of children's books in the home, which was assessed only at age 5 (ES = .16, p < .05). We found no impacts on parent spanking, child having a regular bedtime, or parent attending meetings or open houses at the child's early care and education program (only assessed at age 5).

The analyses revealed few impacts of home-based programs on family well-being and mental health. There were no impacts on parental depressive symptoms at any age or risk factors assessed at age 5, including child living with someone with a drug or alcohol problem or child witnessing violence. The one significant impact in this domain was reduced parenting distress at age 3 (ES = .14, p < .05). There were two statistical trends suggesting positive impacts, or reductions, in both parenting distress (ES = .12, p < .10) and family conflict (ES = .13, p < .10) at age 2.

Home-based programs had early and sustained impacts on family self-sufficiency. Parents were somewhat more likely to be in school or job training at age 2 (ES = .12, p < .10) and signficantly so at age 3 (ES = .15, p < .05). Similarly, we found a statistical trend indicating an increase in income at age 2 (ES = .11, p < .10) that was not significant at age 3 but became significant at age 5 (ES = .17, p < .04). The analyses revealed no impacts on employment at any age.

Home-based programs were effective in transitioning children into formal early care and education programs. Former EHS children were more likely than control children to attend a formal program at both ages 3 and 4 than non-EHS children (p < .05) and were also somewhat more likely to have attended Head Start during this period (p < .10; not tabled).

Impacts for Center-Based Programs

Child Outcomes

One impact for center-based programs was found on children's social emotional functioning at age 3, a reduction in child negativity toward the parent as coded from videotaped parent–child interactions (ES = .27, p < .05) (Table 13). We found no other significant impacts on parent report of child behavior, behavior coded from videotapes of parent–child play, or rater observations of child behavior during the structured direct assessments at any age.

Center-based programs had early impacts on child cognitive functioning at age 2: a positive impact for higher average Bayley scores (ES = .23, p < .05) and a somewhat lower percentage of children scoring in the at-risk range of functioning with a Bayley MDI < 85 (ES = .25, $p < .10$). However, no other impacts on child language or cognitive and academic skills were found. No impacts in the area of child health were seen.

Parent and Family Outcomes

Center-based programs did not have significant impacts on parent outcomes. Two statistical trends emerged, however (Table 13); EHS children were somewhat more likely than control children to have a regular bedtime at age 2 (ES = .22, $p < .10$) and EHS families earned somewhat less money than control group families (ES = .26, $p < .10$) when children were 3 years old.

Center-based programs were effective in transitioning children into formal early care and education programs. Former EHS children were more likely than control children to attend a formal program at both ages 3 and 4 than non-EHS children ($p < .01$) and were also somewhat more likely to have attended Head Start during this period ($p < .10$; not tabled).

Impacts for Mixed-Approach Programs

Child Outcomes

When children were 2 and 3 years old, mixed-approach programs had a pattern of positive impacts on children's social and emotional outcomes, but at age 5, only one significant impact remained (Table 14). At age 2, parents reported somewhat lower aggressive behavior in the EHS group (ES = .23, $p < .10$), although no impact was found at age 3. At age 5, mixed-approach programs had a positive impact on parent report of behavior problems on the FACES measure (ES = .18, $p < .05$), but no impact on the CBCL. Children who had been in EHS were reported by their parents to have somewhat more-positive approaches to learning (ES = .14, $p < .10$) at age 5. Positive impacts were also seen in behaviors coded from videotaped parent–child interactions during a play interaction, specifically child engagement of the parent at ages 2 (ES = .20, $p < .05$) and 3 (ES = .30, $p < .01$) and sustained attention to objects during play (a trend) at age 2 (ES = .16, $p < .10$) and significant at age 3 (ES = .31, $p < .01$). There were no impacts on child negativity during play with parents at any age and no impacts on any child behaviors during play when children were 5. There were no impacts on rater observations of child behavior during the structured direct assessment at any age.

Mixed-approach programs had early impacts on children's vocabulary but no positive impacts on children's cognitive and academic outcomes. At age 2, mixed programs had an impact on parent report of child vocabulary (ES = .19, $p < .05$) and at age 3 on children's PPVT-III scores (ES = .23, $p < .05$). At age 5, there was a statistical trend for a negative impact on the Leiter Scale of Attention Sustained (ES = .16, $p < .10$).

105

Mixed-approach programs had no significant impacts on child health, although a statistical trend suggesting an increase in immunizations was found at age 2 (ES = .16, $p < .10$).

Parent and Family Outcomes

Similar to their effects on child outcomes, mixed-approach programs had a strong pattern of impacts on parents at ages 2 and 3, but the impacts were largely gone at age 5 (Table 14). Mixed-approach programs enhanced support for language and literacy in the home at ages 2 and 3. Specifically, positive impacts were seen for the HOME language and literacy subscale at age 2 (ES = .22, $p < .01$), daily reading at ages 2 (ES = .24, $p < .01$) and at age 3 (ES = .28, $p < .01$), as well as the number of teaching activities in the home when children were 2 (ES = .22, $p < .01$) and 3 (ES = .18, $p < .10$). Mixed-approach EHS programs also had impacts on discipline techniques; EHS parents were somewhat less likely than control group parents to report spanking their children in the last week at age 2 (ES = .17, $p < .10$) and signicantly more likely at age 3 (ES = .21, $p < .05$). Mixed approach programs had favorable impacts on parent behavior coded from videotaped play interaction, including supportiveness at age 2 (ES = .18, $p < .05$) and 3 (ES = .21, $p < .05$), and parent detachment at age 2 (a trend, ES = .16, $p < .10$) and age 3 (ES = .24, $p < .05$). The mixed-approach programs did not have a significant impact on children having a regular bedtime. At age 5, we found some indication that former EHS parents remained more engaged in their children's learning; there was a significant impact on parents attending a meeting or open house in their children's formal program and education setting (ES = .30, $p < .05$).

Mixed-approach programs had some impacts on family well-being and parent self-sufficiency outcomes. EHS mothers reported less parenting stress than control group mothers at age 2 (ES = .24, $p < .01$) and fewer depressive symptoms at age 5 (ES = .16, $p < .10$). There were no other well-being impacts at any age. Mixed-approach programs had impacts on mothers' self-sufficiency outcomes when children were 2 and 3, specifically, mother being employed (ES = .15, $p < .10$ at age 2, and ES = .17, $p < .05$ at age 3) and being in school or job training (ES = .18, $p < .05$ at age 2 and ES = .28, $p < .01$ at age 3), but not at age 5. No impacts were found on family income at any age. Finally, mixed programs had no effect on the percentages of children participating in formal care and education programs in the 3–5 age period (not tabled).

Across-Group Differences

For about one-quarter of the outcomes, there was a significant chi square, indicating a significant difference in impact across the three subgroups (tables available from authors upon request). There were no significant differences at age 5.

At all three ages, no statistically significant differences were seen among the three subgroups on children's social and emotional outcomes. In the area of cognitive and language outcomes, only the impacts on percentage scoring in the at-risk range on the Bayley MDI (less than a standard score of 85) differed among programs at ages 2 and 3. In both cases, it was center-based programs that had the larger impact. Mixed-approach programs were somewhat more likely to be in the negative direction and home- and center-based programs in the positive direction on sustained attention.

In the area of health, the impacts on three outcomes differed significantly at ages 2 and 3: emergency room visits due to accident or injury, with center based having a slightly larger impact at both ages; child immunizations, with mixed-approach programs having a larger impact at both ages; and child having an IEP, with home- and center-based programs having a larger impact at both ages.

In the area of parenting, the impacts on five outcomes differed significantly across program approaches: Daily reading at ages 2 and 3, with mixed-approach and center-based programs having the larger effects; spanking at ages 2 and 3, with mixed-approach programs having the larger impacts; parent detachment during play at age 3, with mixed-approach programs have the largest positive impact; child having a regular bedtime at ages 2 and 3, with center-based programs having the larger impact at age 2 and both center- and home-based programs having the larger impacts at age 3; and parent engagement in teaching activities with the child at age 3, with mixed-approach programs having the larger impact. There were no differences among impacts on parent mental health and well-being.

In the area of self-sufficiency outcomes, impacts on three outcomes differed significantly among the program-type subgroups at ages 2 and 3: parent employed, with mixed-approach programs having the larger impacts; parent being in school or job training, with mixed-approach and home-based programs having the larger impacts; and family income, with home-based programs having the larger impact.

DISCUSSION

The impact findings for program subgroups do not totally align with previous studies in that center-based programs had fewer impacts than expected. Although there was some indication of an impact on cognition at age 2, it was not sustained at ages 3 or 5. As expected, at ages 2 and 3, while the program was still in progress, mixed-approach programs providing both center- and home-based services had the greatest impacts across child and parent outcomes, but these impacts were not sustained at age 5, 2 years after the end of the program. Again, as hypothesized, home-based programs were more effective for parents than for children, and impacts were sustained 2 years after the end of the program.

Like other intervention studies of home-based programs (Howard & Brooks-Gunn, 2009; Sweet & Appelbaum, 2004), EHS home-based programs tended to have continued modest-sized impacts on parents. Unlike other intervention studies, however, EHS home-based programs had less of an impact on health and emotional well-being and more of an impact on parent support for language and literacy, perhaps reflecting EHS's focus on this topic. EHS home-based programs replicated important and sustained impacts on parent self-sufficiency outcomes found in other studies (e.g., Barnet, Liu, DeVoe, Alperovitz-Bichell, & Duggan, 2007; Olds, 2007; Olds, 1999), particularly for education and family income. Two years after the end of the program, those families who had been in EHS home-based programs earned, on average, $300 more per month than control group families.

EHS center-based programs had fewer than expected impacts for children and families, especially in the areas of children's cognitive and language outcomes (NICHD Early Child Care Research Network, 2005a). Although most impacts were not significantly different from those of the other program approaches, showing that center-based programs contributed to the overall impacts reported in Chapter III, we found no pattern of impacts specific to these programs. It may be that the small number of sites (four) and families did not provide the power necessary to show the pattern of impacts. Alternatively, it may be that intensity of services must be taken into account. For instance, Hill et al. (2003) report a dosage effect with large effect sizes on cognitive development at age 8 among children who experienced more than 300 days of center-based care in the IHDP study. Perhaps an analysis of dosage would provide insight to the lack of impacts for EHS center-based programs.

Similar to the literature on programs providing both center- and home-based services (Brooks-Gunn et al., 1993; Johnson & Blumenthal, 1985; Martin, Brooks-Gunn, Klebanov, Buka, & McCormick, 2008; McCormick et al., 2006; Seitz & Provence, 1990; Seitz et al., 1985; Zigler et al., 1992), EHS mixed-approach programs had a broad pattern of impacts on child and parent outcomes at ages 2 and 3. Child impacts included gains in child cognitive, language, social, emotional, and approaches to learning outcomes. Impacts for parents included positive parenting behaviors during parent–child play, support for language and literacy, and discipline as well as parent well-being and self-sufficiency. However, unlike the findings of earlier model programs, the EHS mixed-program impacts in cognition were not sustained 2 years after the end of the program. Sustained impacts were seen in approaches to learning (specifically in reduced behavior problems and improved approaches to learning).

108

These findings leave some unanswered questions and directions for programs and future research. For home-based programs, further work needs to explore ways to augment impacts so that they include child cognitive and language outcomes as well as the parent and child social–emotional impacts found here. Earlier analysis of the EHS home-based programs may point to some ways to achieve these additional impacts. When home-based programs fully implemented the HS Program Performance Standards, focusing on child development as well as supporting family functioning, they did have impacts on child language and cognitive functioning, at age 3 (ACF, 2002a).

Additional work also needs to explore the lack of impacts for center-based programs, and especially why early gains in cognition were not sustained. Is this an issue of insufficient or varying dosage, or might the lack of impacts relate to activities occurring or not occurring during program hours? Finally, for the mixed-approach programs, unanswered questions relate to why the larger and broader impacts were not sustained 2 years after the end of the program. Perhaps gains were not sustained because these programs were not effective in transitioning children info formal early care and education programs in the 3- to 5-year age period, a hypothesis we explore in Chapter VI.

NOTE

9. Nevertheless, 2 years later, only two home-based programs continued to rely exclusively on the home-based approach; the others began delivering center-based services to some families either directly or through formal partnerships with child care providers. After one year, four programs were exclusively center-based programs, and they remained center-based programs throughout the evaluation period.

VI. LINKS BETWEEN EARLY CARE AND EDUCATION EXPERIENCES BIRTH TO AGE 5 AND PREKINDERGARTEN OUTCOMES

Rachel Chazan-Cohen and Ellen E. Kisker

When children enter kindergarten, their development and skills reflect the cumulative effects of the in-home and out-of-home experiences they have had up to that time. In previous chapters we have documented the lasting contribution of EHS experiences between birth and age 3 to parenting and children's outcomes at kindergarten entry. This chapter investigates two questions: (1) What are the potential effects of formal early care and education experiences between ages 3 and 5 on parenting practices and children's development and skills at kindergarten entry? and (2) How do subsequent formal early care and education experiences build on or expand the effects of EHS? In other words, what are the cumulative influences of early care and education experiences birth to age 5?

The Advisory Committee responsible for designing EHS (USDHHS, 1994) knew that some programs would not be connected to HS programs and that many preschool HS programs do not serve 3-year-olds. Furthermore, it knew that some families would no longer be income eligible for HS services and that some families would not need or choose to participate in comprehensive services offered by HS. Given that a smooth transition to HS would not always be possible or even optimal, the Advisory Committee chose to stress the need for continued high-quality services rather then continued HS services. Following from their vision, we look first at the influences of formal programs in the 3–5 years. We then look at influences of EHS birth to age 3 in combination with formal programs ages 3–5. We also ask whether implications of continued formal program participation differ if it includes any HS experience, and we include a special look at families at highest demographic risk, who appear to show a pattern that is different from the overall sample.

Corresponding author: Rachel Chazan-Cohen, Department of Psychology, George Mason University, 4400 University Drive, MS 6D5, Fairfax, VA 22030, email: rachelcc@gmail.com

HYPOTHESES

We hypothesized that children who had both EHS birth to age 3 and formal programs ages 3–5 would fare the best at age 5, consistent with the original theory of change for EHS that emphasized assisting families in finding formal early childhood education programs for their children at the conclusion of the birth to age 3 intervention (USDHHS, 1994). This thinking is consistent with the Incremental and Augmented Experiences premise described in Chapter I. We envisioned EHS and services for children ages 3–5 playing a different role for different domains of functioning. Based on the Early Experiences premise described in Chapter I, we predict a greater role of EHS services for children's positive social and emotional outcomes and parenting behaviors. Although participation in EHS would be more important in determining these outcomes, later services might play a role as well, providing their own effects as well as supporting earlier gains. For cognitive and school achievement-related outcomes, we predicted, as has been found in other studies (e.g., Gormley et al., 2005), that contemporaneous effects from formal early care and education would be strongest. Thus, we expect to see formal program experiences 3–5 to be especially linked with achievement-related outcomes. However, we had seen cognitive impacts from EHS at age 3 and, therefore, it was reasonable to expect higher scores for children who had both EHS birth to age 3 and formal programs ages 3–5 than for those who had attended formal programs ages 3–5 only. The domain of negative emotional outcomes was more difficult to predict. Whereas the Early Experiences premise would predict that participation in EHS would be most important, we expected to find small negative effects of preschool education programs in this domain (Magnuson et al., 2007; NICHD ECCRN, 2005a). Thus, in this one instance, the Incremental and Augmented Experiences theories lead to the prediction that participation in EHS would offset or protect against the possible negative effects from later formal early care and education.

Attending HS, with comprehensive services for both children and parents, could affect outcomes differently than other types of formal early care and education for children. The combination of EHS and HS is of particular policy interest. Thus, we posed questions related to HS participation as well as with preschool education more generally. Those children with both EHS and HS experiences are expected to have the most optimal outcomes, with benefits in the academic outcomes primarily coming from HS and benefits in the domains of children's social and emotional outcomes and parenting coming primarily from EHS. We anticipated that for those families at highest risk, who did not appear to benefit from EHS at the end of the program, continued comprehensive services 0–5, that is EHS followed by HS, might be particularly beneficial (although previous literature is silent on this point).

111

ANALYTIC APPROACH

The randomized design of EHS ended at age 3. After age 3, families in both the program and control groups could have enrolled their children in any formal early care and education programs that existed in their communities. We defined formal programs as consisting of HS (state) prekindergarten programs, or center-based child care. In fact, experience with formal early care and education was nearly universal. As a large majority of children (89%) experienced some formal early care and education between the ages of 3 and 5, and just over half were enrolled in HS at some point during that period (see Chapter III, Table 2).

Given that children were not randomly assigned to enter formal preschool programs or not, controlling for any observed differences between the groups will help minimize selection bias, but the possibility of selection bias due to unobserved differences that cannot be controlled will remain. To minimize potential selection bias, in all analysis we controlled for child and family background characteristics that could influence outcomes as well as community factors captured in the site identifier.

Contributions of Formal Programs at Ages 3–5

Regression analyses were conducted to assess the contribution of formal programs during both preschool years (3–4 and 4–5)[10] to children's outcomes, controlling for other observed differences between children and their families. Analysis included observations only for the sample members with data for the prekindergarten outcome being analyzed and did not rely on any imputed outcomes (see discussion of nonresponse in Chapter II). Models were estimated with maximum likelihood estimation methods using Mplus4 software (Kenny, Kashy, & Bolger, 1998).[11] In order to assess the magnitude of the associations between formal programs and the outcome we converted the raw regression coefficients from natural or scaled units into effect size units. Because the age 3 measures were not always exactly the same as the prekindergarten outcome measures, we calculated effect sizes by dividing the coefficient by the standard deviation of the prekindergarten outcome for the control group. We present findings overall and then for those families at highest levels of demographic risk.

Contribution of Early Childhood Education Experiences 0–5

We defined four groups based on service use in the birth to age 3 and 3–5 age periods. Services in the birth to age 3 period were defined by membership in either the EHS or control group. Use of formal programs during both ages of the 3–5 age period was defined by whether children were in formal programs (center-based care, prekindergarten, or HS) at both the 3–4 age period *and* the 4–5 age period.[12] To explicate the combined influences of early education experiences birth to age 3 and ages 3–5, we examined the outcomes of four groups of children:

1. Neither EHS nor formal programs: control group children who could not participate in EHS and who did not experience formal programs at both ages 3 and 4.
2. EHS birth to age 3: children in the EHS program group who did not experience formal programs at both ages 3 and 4.
3. Formal programs ages 3–5: children who did not have the opportunity to enroll in EHS (i.e., the control group) but experienced formal programs at both ages 3 and 4.
4. Both EHS birth to age 3 and formal programs ages 3–5: children in the EHS program group who also experienced formal programs at both ages 3 and 4.

Twenty-nine percent of the sample had neither experience; 30% EHS only; 19% formal program 3–5 only; and 22% had both EHS and formal program 3–5.[13] We then conducted similar analysis of HS experience: 25% neither EHS nor HS; 25% EHS only; 22% HS only; 28% both EHS and HS.[14]

We then take a special look at the subsample of families at highest demographic risk.[15] Twenty-eight percent had neither EHS nor formal program 3–5; 32% had EHS only; 19% had formal program 3–5 only; and 21% had both EHS and formal program 3–5. In terms of HS experience in the 3–5 age range, 22% had neither EHS nor HS; 23% EHS only; 26% HS only; and 29% both EHS and HS.

We used analysis of covariance procedures to calculate mean outcomes adjusted for differences in background characteristics. Because not all potential differences among the groups of children could be controlled in the analyses, caution must be exercised in interpreting the results. Outcomes were classified into the following domains: child approaches to learning (4 measures); child vocabulary (2 measures); parenting and home environment (7 measures); family well-being (3 measures); child academic skills (3 measures); and child negative social–emotional outcomes (4 measures). To compare the patterns of means hypothesized above, we computed post hoc contrasts for the following patterns of adjusted means. Weights are in parentheses.

- Linear contrasts for outcomes where EHS provides most of the benefit (approaches to learning, vocabulary, parenting, and family well-being outcomes); contrast weights are in parentheses: Both

113

(2) > EHS birth to age 3 (1) > either HS (HS) or formal programs ages 3–5 (−1) > neither (−2).

- Linear contrasts for outcomes where formal programs or HS provides most of the benefit (academic outcomes), contrast weights are in parentheses: Both (2) > either HS or formal programs ages 3–5 (1) > EHS birth to age 3 (−1) > neither (−2).
- Contrast for the special case in which EHS *buffers* the negative effect of formal programs on negative social–emotional outcomes, contrast weights are in parentheses: Formal programs ages 3–5 (2) > Both EHS birth to age 3 and formal programs ages 3–5 (1) > neither (0) > EHS birth to age 3 (−3).

A significant contrast indicates that the obtained pattern of means is not significantly different from the expected pattern. We present overall results followed by those for families at highest demographic risk.

RESULTS

Associations Between Formal Program Participation 3–5 and Outcomes

Child Social and Emotional Outcomes

Controlling for other factors, formal early care and education program participation during both preschool years was associated with more-aggressive behavior and greater behavior problems as reported by parents when their children were entering kindergarten. This pattern of findings is consistent across several measures of negative social and emotional outcomes (Table 15): Children with formal program participation at both preschool ages received Family and Child Experiences Survey (FACES) behavior problems aggression scale scores that were higher by .17 (ES = .10, $p < .05$); scores on the CBCL measure of aggressive behavior problems were higher by .65 (ES = .09, $p < .05$); and FACES social behavior problems index scores that were .41 higher (ES = .11, $p < .01$). Children's observed negativity during a play task with their parent did not differ significantly among children who were in formal programs during both preschool years and children who were not.

Formal program participation in both age periods 3–5 was not significantly associated with children's positive social–emotional outcomes (Table 15).

Child Vocabulary and Academic Skills

Formal program participation in both age periods 3–5 was associated with higher scores on the Woodcock-Johnson Letter-Word Identification subtest (at the trend level; 1.03 points higher, ES = .07, $p < .10$), but was

114

TABLE 15

Associations of Continuous Formal Program Participation and Head Start Experience with Outcomes, Controlling for Fixed Effects, in Effect Size Units

	Formal Program Participation Ages 3 and 4	Any Preschool Head Start Experience
Child Negative Social–Emotional Outcomes		
CBCL Aggressive Behavior	0.09*	−0.01
FACES Aggression	0.10*	−0.03
FACES Social Behavior Problems	0.11**	−0.03
Negativity During Play	0.00	0.00
Child Approaches Toward Learning		
FACES Positive Approaches to Learning	−0.03	0.01
Emotion Regulation	0.01	−0.01
Attention Sustained	−0.03	−0.01
Engagement During Play	0.16	0.07
Sustained Attention to Objects	0.09	0.12+
Child Academic Outcomes		
Woodcock-Johnson-R Letter-Word Identification: English	0.07+	0.09*
English Receptive Vocabulary (PPVT)	0.03	0.06
Woodcock-Johnson-R Applied Problems	−0.04	0.08+
Child Health		
Child Has Speech Problems	0.01	0.04
Child Has an Individualized Education Program	0.09*	0.17***
Parenting and the Home Environment		
Parent Supportiveness	0.07	−0.02
Percent Reading Daily	0.12**	0.05
HOME Learning Environment Subscale	0.08	0.04
Percent Spanked Last Week	0.05	−0.02
Eight Teaching Activities	−0.03	0.06
Child Has at Least 26 Books	0.09*	0.08*
Parent Well-Being		
Depressive Symptoms	−0.02	−0.04
Someone in Household Has Drug/Alcohol Problem	−0.07	0.06
Child Witnessed Violence in Past Year	−0.05	0.06
Parent Abused in Past Year	0.03	0.08+
Sample Sizes	1,118–2,063	1,118–2,063

***$p < .001$. **$p < .01$. *$p < .05$. +$p < .10$.

not associated with better vocabulary or math skills (Table 15). These findings reflect the results for children to whom the test was administered in English.

It is notable that any experience in preschool HS was associated with more-positive prereading and math skills (Table 15): 1.3 points on the Woodcock-Johnson-R Letter-Word Identification subtest (ES = .09, $p < .05$)

115

and 1.7 points on the Woodcock-Johnson Applied Problems subtest
(ES = .08, $p < .05$).

Child Disability Services

The analyses reveal that formal program participation at both ages was
associated with a higher likelihood that the child had an Individualized
Educational Plan (IEP: 2.4 percentage points more likely than other children
to have an IEP, ES = .09, $p < .05$), and any participation in HS was strongly
associated with a higher likelihood that the child had an IEP (4.5 percentage
points more likely, ES = .17, $p < .001$). The higher proportion with an IEP
may indicate that children with formal program participation in both age
periods 3–5 and HS experience received better screening to identify a
disability, or it may reflect a higher incidence of disabilities, or both.

Parenting

Formal program participation in both the 3–4 and 4–5 age periods was
associated with more daily reading with children (by 5.5 percentage points,
ES = .12, $p < .01$) and having more books in the home (4.3 percentage
points more likely to have 26 books, ES = .09, $p < .05$).

Any HS participation also was associated with a significant increase in the
percentage of children who were reported to own at least 26 books (by 4.1
percentage points, ES = .08, $p < .05$). For five other parenting measures,
however, we found no significant associations with HS participation.

Parent Well-Being

The analyses showed no significant associations of formal program
participation in both preschool age periods with parent well-being (Table 15).

Families With Highest Number of Demographic Risks

In highest risk families (those with 4 or 5 of the risk factors used to define
our risk index),[16] many of whom had been teenage parents, formal program
participation at both ages was associated with more-negative child and parent
outcomes (Table 16). Highest-risk children who were enrolled in formal
programs during both years received lower scores on the Woodcock-Johnson
Applied Problems subtest (3.6 points lower, ES = .17, $p < .05$), and they were
more likely to have an IEP (6 percentage points higher, ES = .20, $p < .05$).
There was a trend suggesting that the parents of the highest risk children
provided less support of learning at home (they were 8 percentage points less
likely to report that their child had at least 26 books, ES = .15, $p < .10$, and
they received lower scores (by .8 points) on the HOME Learning
Environment subscale, ES = .23, $p < .10$).

Among the highest risk families, enrollment in HS was associated with
some more positive outcomes for children and parents, suggesting that the
type of program in which the highest risk children enrolled may have been
important. Higher risk parents whose children were ever enrolled in HS were

TABLE 16

	Formal Program Participation at Both Preschool Ages	Any Preschool Head Start Experience
Child Negative Social–Emotional Outcomes		
CBCL Aggressive Behavior	0.11	0.04
FACES Aggression	0.08	0.04
FACES Social Behavior Problems	0.17^+	0.03
Negativity During Play	0.06	−0.03
Child Approaches Toward Learning		
FACES Positive Approaches to Learning	−0.06	−0.01
Emotion Regulation	0.05	−0.01
Attention Sustained	−0.04	0.02
Sustained Attention to Objects	0.01	0.13
Engagement During Play	−0.02	0.15
Child Academic Outcomes		
Woodcock-Johnson-R Letter-Word Identification (English)	−0.12	0.37^{***}
English Receptive Vocabulary (PPVT)	−0.09	0.10
Woodcock-Johnson-R Applied Problems	$−0.17^*$	0.15^+
Child Health		
Child Has Speech Problems	0.06	0.01
Child Has an Individualized Education Program	0.20^*	0.16^*
Parenting and the Home Environment		
Parent Supportiveness	0.11	−0.01
Percent Reading Daily	0.00	0.24^{***}
Child Has at Least 26 Books	$−0.15^+$	0.29^{***}
HOME Learning Environment Subscale	$−0.23^+$	0.27^*
Percent Spanked Last Week	−0.04	0.04
Eight Teaching Activities	−0.09	0.08
Parent Well-Being		
Depressive Symptoms	−0.08	$−0.20^*$
Someone in Household Has Drug/Alcohol Problem	−0.06	−0.05
Child Witness Violence in Past Year	−0.02	$−0.15^+$
Parent Was Abused in Past Year	0.04	0.09
Sample Sizes	361–472	361–472

$^{***}p < .001.^{**}p < .01.^*p < .05.^+p < .10.$

more likely to report reading to their children daily (11 percentage points
more likely, ES = .24, $p < .001$), more likely to report that their child had at
least 26 books (15 percentage points, ES = .29, $p < .001$), and they received
higher scores on the HOME (0.9 points higher, ES = .27, $p < .05$). These

parents also reported significantly fewer depressive symptoms than higher-risk parents whose children were never enrolled in HS (1.4 points lower score on the CES-D Short Form, ES = .20, $p < .05$). Children in the highest-risk families who were ever enrolled in HS received significantly higher scores on the Woodcock-Johnson-R Letter-Word Identification subtest (5.5 points higher, ES = .37, $p < .001$), and there was a trend to higher scores on the Woodcock-Johnson-R Applied Problems subtest (3.3 points higher, ES = .15, $p < .10$).

Associations of Early Childhood Education Experiences 0–5 With Outcomes: EHS and Formal Programs

For four domains—child approaches to learning, child vocabulary, parenting and home environment, and family well-being—we hypothesized that those children with both EHS birth to age 3 and formal programs ages 3–5 would fare best, followed by those with EHS birth to age 3, followed by those with formal programs ages 3–5, and finally, those with neither experience.

The expected pattern of means was supported for the FACES positive approaches to learning ($F = 10.72$, $p < .01$), and there was a trend for receptive vocabulary for those children assessed in English on the PPVT-III ($F = 3.63$, $p < .10$) (Table 17). We did not detect linear patterns for receptive vocabulary for children assessed in Spanish, the Leiter-R Attention Sustained score, the Leiter-R observed emotion regulation, or observed child engagement during interaction with their parents.

The expected pattern of means was supported for the following parenting and home environment and family well-being outcomes: Observed home support for language and literacy ($F = 6.37$, $p < .05$), daily reading ($F = 7.75$, $p < .01$), number of books in the home ($F = 9.66$, $p < .01$), parent teaching behaviors ($F = 4.74$, $p < .05$), parent depressive symptoms ($F = 3.98$, $p < .05$), and child living with someone with a drug or alcohol problem ($F = 4.12$, $p < .05$). The contrasts were not significant for parent report of spanking, child witnessing community violence, or observed parent behavior during play.

For children's academic functioning, it was hypothesized that those children with both EHS birth to age 3 and formal programs ages 3–5 would fare best, followed by those with formal programs ages 3–5, followed by those with EHS birth to age 3, and finally, those with neither experience.

Overall, the expected pattern of means was supported for the Woodcock-Johnson-R Letter Word Identification administered in English ($F = 7.44$, $p < .01$), for child having an IEP ($F = 12.20$, $p < .001$). The expected pattern was not found for Woodcock-Johnson Applied Problems (Table 17).

We hypothesized that although formal program participation was associated with an increase in negative social and emotional behaviors, this

TABLE 17

ADJUSTED MEANS FOR EARLY HEAD START AND FORMAL PROGRAM EXPERIENCES

	EHS 0–3 & FP 3–5	EHS 0–3	FP 3–5	Neither	F-Test and Significance of Post Hoc Contrast
Early Head Start Confers Most of Benefit:					
Linear Contrast Both (2) > EHS 0–3 (1) > FP 3–5 (−1) > Neither (−2)					
Child Approaches Toward Learning					
FACES Positive Approaches to Learning	12.08	12.18	11.82	11.85	10.72**
Observed Emotion Regulation	91.23	91.21	90.73	91.21	ns
Leiter-R Attention Sustained	11.18	10.67	10.92	10.88	ns
Engagement During Play	4.72	4.66	4.75	4.64	ns
Child Vocabulary					
English Receptive (PPVT-III)	92.92	90.90	91.38	90.70	3.63+
Spanish Receptive (TVIP)	85.97	87.55	85.36	80.14	ns
Parenting and Home Environment					
Parent Supportiveness During Play	4.19	4.04	4.12	4.05	ns
Parent Negative Regard During Play	1.16	1.19	1.23	1.21	ns
Reading Daily	.37	.31	.33	.27	7.75**
HOME Language and Literacy	11.10	10.59	10.76	10.35	6.37*
Child Spanked Within Last Week	.36	.36	.39	.35	ns
Teaching Activities	11.23	11.28	11.03	10.92	4.74*
Children's Books (26 or more)	.69	.60	.62	.59	9.66**
Family Well-Being					
Depressive Symptoms (CES-D)	7.60	7.97	8.36	8.37	3.98*
Child Witnessed Violence	.16	.14	.13	.17	ns
Someone in Household With Drug/ Alcohol Problem	.07	.09	.09	.11	4.12*

	EHS 0–3 and FP 3–5	FP 3–5	EHS 0–3	Neither	F-Test and Significance of Post Hoc Contrast
Formal Program Confers Most of Benefit:					
Linear Contrast Both (2) > FP 3–5 (1) > EHS 0–3 (−1) > Neither (−2)					
Child Academic Skills					
Woodcock Johnson-R Letter-Word Identification (English)	90.53	90.11	87.79	89.05	7.44**
Woodcock Johnson Applied Problems	89.09	88.18	88.51	87.20	ns
Child Has Individualized Education Plan	.11	.10	.06	.06	12.20***

	FP 3–5	EHS 0–3& FP 3–5	Neither	EHS 0–3	F-Test and Significance of Post Hoc Contrast
Early Head Start Buffers Against Negative Effects of Formal Program:					
Contrast FP 3–5 (2) > Both (1) > Neither (0) > EHS 0–3 (−3)					
Child Negative Social–Emotional Outcomes					
CBCL Aggressive Behavior	11.53	11.23	10.84	10.46	6.48*
FACES Aggression	2.80	2.67	2.60	2.48	8.09**
FACES Social Behavior Problems	6.06	5.72	5.68	5.27	11.38***
Negativity During Play	1.28	1.21	1.22	1.25	ns

Note. EHS = Early Head Start; HS = Head Start; FP = Formal Programs; ns = not significant. Contrast weights are in parentheses.
$^+p < .10.$ $^*p < .05.$ $^{**}p < .01.$ $^{***}p < .001.$

119

would be less so for those children who had also experienced EHS. Highest scores in negative behavioral outcomes were expected for those with formal programs ages 3–5 alone, followed by those with EHS and formal programs 3–5, followed by children who had neither experience. Children with EHS only were expected to have the lowest scores.

The expected pattern of means was supported for parent report of CBCL aggressive behavior ($F = 6.48$, $p < .05$), FACES aggressive behavior ($F = 8.09$, $p < .01$), and FACES social behavior problems ($F = 11.38$, $p < .001$). We did not detect the expected pattern for observed child negativity while in play with the parent.

In summary, the expected pattern of adjusted means was seen, particularly in the domains of parenting and home environment, family well-being, child academic functioning, and child negative social and emotional outcomes. There is less support for the expected pattern for child approaches to learning and child vocabulary.

Associations of Early Childhood Education Experiences 0–5 With Outcomes: EHS and HS

Similar to the previous set of analyses examining formal program experiences, for approaches to learning, children's vocabulary, parenting and home environment, and family well-being, we hypothesized that those children with both EHS birth to age 3 and HS ages 3–5 would fare best, followed by those with EHS birth to age 3, followed by those with HS ages 3–5, and finally, those with neither experience. As explained above, we also expected the same pattern for children's negative social–emotional outcomes.

The expected pattern of means was supported for FACES positive approaches to learning ($F = 13.13$, $p < .001$) and receptive vocabulary for those children assessed in Spanish ($F = 4.99$, $p < .05$). The linear contrast was not significant for receptive vocabulary for children assessed in English, the Leiter-R Attention Sustained score and observed emotion regulation scales, observed child engagement and negativity during interaction with their parents, or parent report of aggressive behaviors and total social behavior problems (Table 18).

The expected pattern of means was supported for the following parenting and home environment and family well-being outcomes: Observed HOME support for language and literacy ($F = 3.59$, $p < .05$), daily reading ($F = 5.87$, $p < .05$), number of books in the home ($F = 6.28$, $p < .05$), and parent teaching behaviors ($F = 6.08$, $p < .05$). The expected pattern was not detected for parent report of spanking, child witnessing community violence, child living with someone with a drug or alcohol problem, parent depression, or observed parent behavior during play.

120

TABLE 18
Adjusted Means for Early Head Start and Head Start Experiences

	EHS 0–3 and Any HS	EHS 0–3	Any HS	Neither	F-Test and Significance of Post Hoc Contrast
Early Head Start Confers Most of Benefit: Linear Contrast Both (2) > EHS 0–3 (1) > Any HS (−1) > Neither (−2)					
Child Negative Social–Emotional Outcomes					
CBCL Aggressive Behavior	10.89	10.68	11.46	10.74	ns
FACES Aggression	2.59	2.53	2.71	2.64	ns
FACES Social Behavior Problems	5.54	5.36	5.88	5.75	ns
Negativity During Play	1.23	1.23	1.27	1.23	ns
Child Approaches Toward Learning					
FACES Positive Approaches to Learning	12.19	12.07	11.76	11.90	13.13***
Observed Emotion Regulation	91.38	91.12	90.80	91.25	ns
Leiter-R Attention Sustained	11.05	10.74	10.84	10.94	ns
Engagement During Play	4.65	4.73	4.75	4.63	ns
Child Vocabulary					
English Receptive (PPVT-III)	92.23	91.44	90.89	91.07	ns
Spanish Receptive (TVIP)	87.91	86.64	80.34	82.45	4.99*
Parenting and Home Environment					
Supportiveness During Play	4.09	4.15	4.07	4.09	ns
Negative Regard During Play	1.15	1.21	1.23	1.21	ns
Reading Daily	.36	.31	.30	.29	5.87*
HOME Language and Literacy	10.89	10.71	10.47	10.53	3.59*
Child Spanked Within Last Week	.34	.38	.39	.34	ns
Teaching Activities	11.34	11.18	10.98	10.96	6.08*
Children's Books (26 or more)	.67	.60	.60	.60	6.28*
Family Well-Being					
Depressive Symptoms (CES-D)	7.87	7.91	8.79	8.36	ns
Child Witnessed Violence	.15	.14	.17	.14	ns
Someone in Household With Drug/Alcohol Problem	.08	.08	.12	.09	ns

	EHS 0–3 and Any HS	Any HS	EHS 0–3	Neither	F-Test and Significance of Post Hoc Contrast
Head Start Confers Most of Benefit: Linear Contrast Both (2) > Any HS (1) > EHS 0–3 (−1) > Neither (−2)					
Child Academic Skills					
Woodcock Johnson-R Letter-Word Identification (English)	90.07	89.58	87.81	89.35	2.83+
Woodcock Johnson Applied Problems	89.68	88.06	87.69	86.98	4.15*
Child Has Individualized Education Plan	.11	.11	.05	.05	23.06***

Note. EHS = Early Head Start; HS = Head Start; FP = Formal Programs; ns = not significant.
Contrast weights are in parentheses.
$^{+}p < .10.$ $^{*}p < .05.$ $^{**}p < .01.$ $^{***}p < .001.$

For children's academic functioning, we hypothesized a somewhat different pattern. We expected that those children with both EHS birth to age 3 and HS ages 3–5 would fare best, followed by those with HS ages 3–5, followed by those with EHS birth to age 3, and finally, those with neither experience.

The expected pattern of means was supported for the Woodcock-Johnson Applied Problems ($F = 4.15$, $p < .05$) as well as for the child having an IEP ($F = 23.06$, $p < .001$), and there was a trend for the Woodcock-Johnson-R Letter Word Identification administered in English ($F = 2.83$, $p < .10$) (Table 18).

In summary, for children whose participation in EHS is followed by participation in HS, there is some support for the expected patterns of adjusted means, especially in the domains of parenting and home environment and child academic functioning. There is less support for the expected patterns in the domains of child vocabulary and approaches to learning, and no support for child negative social–emotional outcomes and family well-being.

Highest Risk Families: EHS and Formal Programs

For child approaches to learning, child vocabulary, parenting and home environment, and family well-being, we hypothesized that those with both EHS birth to age 3 and formal programs ages 3–5 would fare best, followed by those with EHS birth to age 3, followed by those with formal programs ages 3–5, and finally, those with neither experience. However, due to the lack of associations of formal programs with positive outcomes for this subgroup of children and families, we did not expect to find a strong pattern of effect for the combined effects of EHS plus formal programs for families at highest risk.

The expected pattern of means was found for FACES positive approaches to learning ($F = 3.97$, $p < .05$), but no other child outcomes (Table 19). There was a trend for the expected pattern of means for observed parent negative regard during play ($F = 3.85$, $p < .10$). No other parenting and home environment or family well-being outcomes were significant.

For children's academic functioning, we hypothesized that those children with both EHS birth to age 3 and formal programs ages 3–5 would fare best, followed by those with formal programs ages 3–5, followed by those with EHS birth to age 3, and finally, those with neither experience. However, due to the lack of associations of formal programs with positive outcomes for this subgroup of children and families, we did not expect to find a strong pattern of effect for the combined effects of EHS plus formal programs for families at highest risk. Overall, the expected pattern of means was supported only for the child having an IEP ($F = 7.16$, $p < .01$) (Table 19).

We hypothesized that although participation in formal programs was associated with an increase in children's negative social and emotional behaviors, this would be less so for those children who had also experienced EHS. The expected pattern of means was supported for the parent report on the CBCL aggressive behavior scale ($F = 4.68$, $p < .05$), the FACES scale of aggressive behavior ($F = 5.34$, $p < .05$), and the FACES scale of social

122

TABLE 19

ADJUSTED MEANS FOR EARLY HEAD START AND FORMAL PROGRAM EXPERIENCES FOR
Highest RISK FAMILIES

	EHS 0–3 and FP 3–5	EHS 0–3	FP 3–5	Neither	F-Test and Significance of Post Hoc Contrast
Early Head Start Confers Most of Benefit: Linear Contrast Both (2) > EHS 0–3 (1) > FP 3–5 (−1) > Neither (−2)					
Child Approaches Toward Learning					
FACES Positive Approaches to Learning	12.19	12.22	11.66	11.92	3.97*
Observed Emotion Regulation	91.04	90.24	90.22	91.07	ns
Leiter-R Attention Sustained	10.70	10.00	9.67	10.56	ns
Engagement During Play	4.60	4.51	4.57	4.67	ns
Child Vocabulary					
English Receptive (PPVT)	86.41	84.98	85.34	87.92	ns
Parenting and Home Environment					
Supportiveness During Play	3.99	3.79	3.75	3.74	ns
Negative Regard During Play	1.17	1.22	1.29	1.35	3.85*
Reading Daily	.30	.29	.29	.27	ns
HOME Language and Literacy	9.51	10.06	9.07	9.80	ns
Child Spanked Within Last Week	.38	.41	.40	.37	ns
Teaching Activities	11.25	10.90	10.79	11.26	ns
Children's Books (26 or more)	.54	.48	.44	.54	ns
Family Well-Being					
Depressive Symptoms (CES-D)	8.92	8.72	8.84	10.22	ns
Child Witnessed Violence	.22	.13	.17	.30	ns
Someone in Household With Drug/Alcohol Problem	.07	.11	.14	.12	ns

	EHS 0–3 and FP 3–5	FP 3–5	EHS 0–3	Neither	F-Test and Significance of Post Hoc Contrast
Formal Program Confers Most of Benefit: Linear Contrast Both (2) > FP 3–5 (1) > EHS 0–3 (−1) > Neither (−2)					
Child Academic Skills					
Woodcock Johnson-R Letter-Word Identification (English)	85.40	87.73	85.49	88.08	ns
Woodcock Johnson Applied Problems	82.36	82.59	84.17	85.37	ns
Child has Individualized Education Plan	.11	.14	.04	.05	7.16**

	FP 3–5	EHS 0–3 and FP 3–5	Neither	EHS 0–3	F-Test and Significance of Post Hoc Contrast
Early Head Start Buffers Against Negative Effects of Formal Program: Contrast FP 3–5 (2) > Both (1) > Neither (−2) > EHS 0–3 (−3)					
Child Negative Social–Emotional Outcomes					
CBCL Aggressive behavior	12.54	11.64	12.17	10.38	4.68*
FACES Aggression	3.00	2.74	2.83	2.42	5.34*
FACES Social Behavior Problems	6.81	6.17	6.19	5.35	7.61**
Negativity During Play	1.25	1.29	1.17	1.27	ns

Note. EHS = Early Head Start; HS = Head Start; FP = Formal Programs; ns = not significant.
Contrast weights are in parentheses.
+p < .10. *p < .05. **p < .01. ***p < .001.

behavior problems ($F = 7.61$, $p < .01$). The expected pattern was not found for observed child negativity while in play with their parent (Table 19).

In summary, for those families at highest demographic risk, there is support for the expected patterns of adjusted means in the area of child negative social–emotional outcomes, where EHS appears to have buffered children from the negative behaviors associated with formal programs. There is little support for the expected patterns in other domains of child and family functioning. This is most likely due to the lack of associations between positive outcomes and formal program experiences ages 3–5 for this subgroup of families. Though the overall hypotheses remain the same for this group of families, the nonexperimental findings indicate a more complex relationship between parenting and home environment and family well-being, with some benefits coming from HS as well. Therefore, we tested some parenting and home environment and family well-being outcomes under both the mostly EHS and mostly HS patterns to see which achieved a better fit.

Highest Risk Families: EHS and HS

For the domains of child negative social and emotional outcomes, child approaches to learning, child vocabulary, parenting and home environment, and family well-being, we hypothesized that children with both EHS birth to age 3 and HS ages 3–5 would fare best, followed by those with EHS birth to age 3, followed by those with HS ages 3–5, and finally, those with neither experience (Table 20).

The expected pattern of means was found for FACES social behavior problems ($F = 4.06$, $p < .05$) and somewhat supported for parent report of aggressive behaviors on the CBCL ($F = 3.12$, $p < .10$) and FACES ($F = 3.28$, $p < .10$) as well as for FACES positive approaches to learning ($F = 3.57$, $p < .10$), but not for the other child outcomes (Table 19). Trends suggested support for the expected pattern of means for the following family well-being outcomes: Child witnessing community violence ($F = 3.72$, $p < .10$) and parental depression ($F = 2.75$, $p < .10$). There was no support for the expected pattern of means for parenting and home environment outcomes.

For children's academic functioning we hypothesized that those children with both EHS birth to age 3 and HS ages 3–5 would fare best, followed by those with HS ages 3–5, followed by those with EHS birth to age 3, and finally, those with neither experience. The nonexperimental findings suggest that HS confers benefits to some parenting and home environment and family well-being factors for the highest risk families, so we explored whether the mostly HS pattern was a good fit for the following outcomes: someone in the household reads to the child daily, number of books in the home, home support for language and literacy, and maternal depression. The expected pattern of means was supported for the Woodcock-Johnson-R Letter Word

124

TABLE 20
Adjusted Means for Early Head Start and Head Start Experiences for Highest Risk Families

	EHS 0–3 and Any HS	EHS 0–3	Any HS	Neither	F-Test and Significance of Post Hoc Contrast
Early Head Start Confers Most of Benefit: Linear Contrast Both (2) > EHS 0–3 (1) > Any HS (−1) > Neither (−2)					
Child Negative Social–Emotional Outcomes					
CBCL Aggressive Behavior	10.95	10.83	12.47	12.0	3.12$^+$
FACES Aggression	2.57	2.52	2.91	2.84	3.28$^+$
FACES Social Behavior Problems	5.88	5.44	6.30	6.57	4.06*
Negativity During Play	1.26	1.29	1.21	1.21	ns
Child Approaches Toward Learning					
FACES Positive Approaches to Learning	12.26	12.09	11.67	12.02	3.57$^+$
Observed Emotion Regulation	90.20	90.82	90.51	90.97	ns
Leiter-R Attention Sustained	10.31	10.19	10.26	10.05	ns
Engagement During Play	4.57	4.51	4.70	4.52	ns
Child Vocabulary					
English Receptive (PPVT-III)	86.80	83.58	86.22	87.93	ns
Parenting and Home Environment					
Supportiveness During Play	3.90	3.85	3.75	3.75	ns
Negative Regard During Play	1.16	1.26	1.35	1.27	ns
Reading Daily	.36	.21	.32	.24	ns
HOME Language and Literacy	10.15	9.47	9.95	9.16	ns
Child Spanked Within Last Week	.37	.44	.42	.32	ns
Teaching Activities	11.23	10.77	10.95	11.27	ns
Children's Books (26 or more)	.56	.43	.54	.45	ns
Family Well-Being					
Depressive Symptoms (CES-D)	7.94	9.95	9.30	10.03	2.75$^+$
Child Witnessed Violence	.14	.22	.21	.29	3.72$^+$
Someone in Household With Drug/Alcohol Problem	.07	.12	.14	.10	ns

	EHS 0–3 and Any HS	Any HS	EHS 0–3	Neither	F-Test and Significance of Post Hoc Contrast
Head Start Confers Most of Benefit: Linear Contrast Both (2) > Any HS (1) > EHS 0–3 (−1) > Neither (−2)					
Child Academic Skills					
Woodcock Johnson-R Letter-Word Identification (English)	87.76	89.39	82.02	85.62	7.78**
Woodcock Johnson Applied Problems	84.92	84.34	81.55	83.83	ns
Child has Individualized Education Plan	.10	.11	.02	.06	5.35*
Parenting and Home Environment					
Reading Daily	.36	.21	.32	.24	6.34*
HOME Language and Literacy	10.15	9.95	9.47	9.16	3.23$^+$
Children's Books (26 or more)	.56	.54	.43	.45	4.80*
Family Well-Being					
Depressive Symptoms (CES-D)	7.94	9.30	9.95	10.03	4.75*

Note. EHS = Early Head Start; HS = Head Start; FP = Formal Programs; ns = not significant.
Contrast weights are in parentheses.
$^+p < .10.$ $^*p < .05.$ $^{**}p < .01.$ $^{***}p < .001.$

125

Identification administered in English ($F = 7.78$, $p < .01$) as well as for the child having an IEP ($F = 5.35$, $p < .05$) (Table 20).

For the parenting and home environment and family well-being factors examined, the pattern with the primacy of HS was supported for daily reading ($F = 6.34$, $p < .05$), number of books in the home ($F = 4.80$, $p < .05$), and maternal depression ($F = 4.75$, $p < .05$); there was a trend for home support for language and literacy ($F = 3.23$, $p < .10$).

In summary, for those families at highest demographic risk, some support exists for the premise of EHS and HS working together to enhance parenting and family well-being as well as children's social and emotional and cognitive outcomes. The benefits for children's social and emotional outcomes come primarily from EHS, whereas benefits in the areas of child achievement and family well-being come from HS.

DISCUSSION

In general, this chapter presents evidence for the importance of services across the period from birth to age 5 and supports the guidance of the Secretary's Advisory Committee on Services for Families with Infants and Toddlers (USDHHS, 1994) that EHS programs focus on transitioning children into high-quality early childhood education programs as they leave the program.

Controlling for outcomes at age 3 and other background characteristics, enrollment in formal early care and education programs during both preschool years (ages 3 to 4 and 4 to prekindergarten) was associated primarily with more favorable prekindergarten outcomes related to reading, both child ability and family support for literacy in the home (more daily reading to children by parents, more children's books, and a trend to higher scores on a prereading achievement test). In contrast, the results also show that formal program participation at both ages 3–4 and 4–5 was associated with an increase in parent-reported aggressive behavior and behavior problems. These associations with aggressive behavior are consistent with the findings from other studies (NICHD ECCRN, 2003a, 2003b).

Levels of parent-reported aggressive behavior were similar at age 3 for children who subsequently enrolled in formal programs at both ages and children who did not. For children with formal program participation at both preschool ages, levels of aggressive behavior remained at the same level at kindergarten entry as they had been at age 3, on average, whereas for other children, levels of aggressive behavior diminished modestly, consistent with expected developmental patterns (Degnan, 2006).

Although the pattern of significant associations between formal program participation at ages 3–4 and 4–5 and more aggressive behavior and behavior problems at age 5 (prekindergarten) is troubling, the effect sizes are modest. Moreover, although the associations of formal program participation with these more-negative social–emotional outcomes are statistically significant, they are not substantial in terms of differences in behavior and do not raise children's behavior problems to levels indicating a need for clinical intervention.

For children from the highest risk families, there are indications that children who were in formal programs at both preschool ages also were not faring as well academically as other children from highest risk families. In this group, any participation in a HS program was associated with better child and parent outcomes, suggesting that the type of program in which children were enrolled may matter most for the highest risk children. Among the highest-risk families, associations of HS participation with literacy-related parenting and child academic outcomes were relatively strong and consistent. In this group, HS participation was also associated with several indicators of parent and child well-being.

When we look at the combined influence of services birth through age 5, we find support for our hypothesis that those children and families who experienced EHS followed by services in the 3- to 5-year-old age period fared the best overall, with benefits in social–emotional, vocabulary, parenting and home environment, and family well-being outcomes coming primarily from EHS, and the benefits in achievement-oriented outcomes coming from the preschool services.

For most outcomes in the domains of approaches to learning, vocabulary, parenting and home environment, and family well-being, there was support for the expected pattern of adjusted means, a linear pattern with most of the benefit from EHS. In the domain of academic skills, there was support for the expected linear trend with most of the benefit coming from formal preschool programs. Finally, in the domain of negative social–emotional outcomes, there was strong support for the expected pattern: EHS appears to have been a protective factor that buffered children from the negative associations with formal program participation.

Somewhat surprisingly, when we looked at experience of HS in combination with EHS, we found less support for the expected patterns. Support for the benefit of both experiences with the primary benefit from EHS was found for parenting, especially in the area of support for learning, and child academic outcomes as well as receptive vocabulary for Spanish speakers. However, there was less support for this pattern for children's social–emotional outcomes and family well-being. There are several possible reasons for these findings. We were not able to get an accurate report of total amount of time in HS, so some of the children in the HS groups may have been in HS only briefly. Also, it may be that higher earning and functioning families, whose children may have been doing better, were no longer eligible for HS services.

The roles of formal programs and HS in the 3–5 age period are somewhat different for those families at highest risk. Formal programs did not seem to confer benefits to highest risk families unless the formal program was HS. For these highest risk children who attended formal preschool programs, previous EHS experience protected them somewhat from the increases seen in aggressive behaviors and behavior problems. EHS buffers children at highest risk from the negative effects of formal programs on aggression and problem behavior. Furthermore, whereas EHS benefits the well-being of these families, if HS follows the program, it confers additional benefits to family well-being. HS also confers additional benefits for children's achievement outcomes, which are not found for other forms of formal programs. In summary, for these families at highest demographic risk, following EHS with HS supports these families in the critical domains of children's achievement and social–emotional outcomes as well as family well-being; children and families at highest risk appear to benefit from comprehensive services from birth to age 5.

The findings for children's academic achievement and social–emotional outcomes are especially consistent. Parent report on approaches to learning shows a primacy for the birth to age 3 EHS experience with added benefit of the ages 3–5 experience across both formal programs and HS and both the overall sample and those families at highest risk. For aggression and behavior problems, it appears that formal program participation does confer risk, but less so for those who had experienced EHS. Thus, EHS may have served as a protective factor. As expected for academic outcomes, the preschool experience, be it HS or some other type of formal program, confers most of the benefit. Children getting both EHS and formal preschool experiences were also more likely to have an IEP, with most of the identification coming from being in a formal preschool setting. This likely reflects the fact that children in EHS with special needs were more likely to be identified (ACF, 2002a), that identified children were more likely to be transitioned into formal settings, and that children in formal settings were more likely to be identified than children in less formal settings.

This work has important limitations. First, although we tried to identify and control for biases due to nonrandom formal program choices, some findings could be due to unobserved differences and caution needs to be used in interpreting the findings. Furthermore, in these analyses we did not take into account aspects of the preschool programs at ages 3–5 other than their type, and in the case of formal programs, the age periods of children's participation. Taking into account other aspects such as number of settings and length of time in HS would have been illuminating, but these data were not available.

The overall message from this chapter is that it is important for infant and toddler services to be followed by preschool services. Those children with both experiences appear to reap benefits from both. Our findings suggest that early intervention should be followed by continued supportive services, and that for those at highest risk, continued comprehensive services from birth to age 5 is the most beneficial sequence.

NOTES

10. The effects of formal early care and education programs between ages 3 and 5 on parenting and children's outcomes are expected to be greatest for children who were in formal programs for a substantial portion of that period. Approximately 43% of children in the research sample were enrolled in formal early care and education programs during both preschool years.

11. In a test of the sensitivity of results to approach for handling missing data, multiple imputation procedures in SAS yielded results that were comparable to those produced by Mplus4.

12. Many children assigned to the control group for the birth to age 3 phase of the study, who were not allowed to participate in EHS, did experience other forms of early childhood care settings. Although EHS children were significantly more likely than control children to be in child care in the birth to age 3 phase, most families in both program and control groups used child care, and the percentages in child care rose as children got older. At 14 months of age, 66% of EHS children were in child care compared to 57% of control group children; by 36 months of age, 84% of EHS children were in child care compared to 78% of control group children (ACF, 2004).

13. The analyses were conducted using the sample of 2,273 children for whom program settings at ages 3 and 4 were obtained.

14. The analyses were conducted using the sample of 2,316 children for whom prekindergarten data were collected. There were 43 cases in which setting at either age 3 or 4 was ambiguous. These cases were not used in the formal programs analyses, but they were included in the Head Start analyses.

15. The sample of highest risk children for whom formal program information at ages 3–5 was available was 522, and 533 for whom any HS participation was available. The difference in sample size is due to some ambiguity in formal program settings for either age 3 or age 4 in 11 cases.

16. To distinguish families with different levels of risk, we counted up to five demographic risk factors that families had when they enrolled: (1) being a single parent; (2) receiving public assistance; (3) being neither employed nor in school or job training; (4) being a teenage parent; and (5) lacking a high school diploma or GED. To form subgroups of reasonable size, families were divided into three subgroups based on the number of risk factors they had when they enrolled: (1) lower risk families who had zero, one, or two risk factors; (2) moderate-risk families who had three risk factors; and (3) highest risk families who had four or five risk factors.

VII. CONCLUSIONS AND IMPLICATIONS

Jeanne Brooks-Gunn, John M. Love, Helen H. Raikes, and Rachel Chazan-Cohen

In 1996 and 1997, several thousand low-income families across the country responded to outreach efforts by 17 newly created EHS programs. Thus began one of this country's largest, multi-site, multi-state, longitudinal experiments of a program that began before some (about 25%) of the participating children were born and all were under 1 year of age, and followed them until they were getting ready to enter kindergarten. This monograph provides a picture of the development of these low-income families and children, from early assessments and interviews when children were about 2 years old (capturing the impacts of the program over the first 2 years of their lives), through the age 3 impacts (at the end of the program), to the age 5 impacts two years after the end of the program. In this monograph we have presented the background of the study and its methods along with our analysis and findings. In this final chapter, we highlight the findings and lessons that pertain to two broad arenas: how to better plan and implement effective intervention strategies in the first 5 years of life and how understanding changing and diverse developmental trajectories can contribute to more effective early childhood programs and the public policies that shape them.

The monograph includes the information that followers of early childhood intervention evaluations expect: Impacts of the intervention are presented when children were 5 years old, 2 years after its conclusion (Chapter III) in the context of the impacts found while families were still enrolled in the program—at ages 2 and 3. These findings are also considered in terms of the experiences the children had in the years between leaving their EHS program (for the treatment group) and entering kindergarten (impacts on program participation in Chapters III, IV, and V, and nonexperimental analysis Chapter VI). Our analyses have gone beyond the standard program evaluation report and investigated children's early care and education

Corresponding author: Jeanne Brooks-Gunn, Teachers College, and the College of Physicians and Surgeons, Columbia University, 525 West 120th Street, New York, New York 10027, email: brooks-gunn@columbia.edu

experiences after the program ended, which puts the evaluation in a community and birth-to-age-5 context. We also examined impacts for subgroups of children and families (Chapter IV), and for different types of programs (Chapter V). Mechanisms by which the intervention may have exerted its effects on children's developmental outcomes are also considered (Chapters III, IV, V, and VI).

DEVELOPMENTAL CONTEXT AND THEORETICAL FRAMEWORK

Little is known about the cumulative effects of out-of-home, formal program experiences starting in the first years of life on low-income families. Much of what we do know comes from a small number of program evaluations and longitudinal studies. Of the three most well-known (and cited) early childhood interventions that have followed children into adulthood (Abecedarian, Perry Preschool, and Child Parent Centers in Chicago, the last of which is quasi-experimental), only the first provided services in the first three years of life (Barnett, 2011). These three critical evaluations focus on early childhood education for the most part, not the mix of services that young children typically receive (Leventhal, Brooks-Gunn, McCormick, & McCarton, 2000). Many longitudinal studies focus on the development of young children in the U.S., including two nationally representative birth cohorts (the Early Childhood Longitudinal Study-Birth Cohort and the Fragile Families and Child Well-Being Study; see Brooks-Gunn et al., 2000; 2003; Reynolds, Temple, Ou, Arteaga, & White, 2011). This entire body of research provides a rich understanding of children's experiences, with the birth cohort studies continuing to yield insights on early developmental trajectories as a function of home and services provisions, albeit in a nonexperimental context. This combined experimental and nonexperimental research supports the notion that early care experiences, both parental and nonparental care, are important predictors of later functioning. It is important to note that many of these early intervention studies have been conducted as single-site evaluations, unlike the EHSREP, an evaluation of a nationally implemented program.

This monograph addresses issues relevant to at least four audiences: practitioners who concern themselves with program operations, policy makers who design policies and programs for young children, developmental psychologists and other researchers who investigate developmental phenomena in the early years, and evaluators of interventions for low-income families and children in their early years. In particular, this research can be useful to (1) programs that desire to fine-tune the timing and intensity of their interventions, (2) policy makers who wish to optimize early childhood investments, (3) developmental scientists who search for better understanding of trajectories of development in the context of multiple environmental influences over a longer period before school entry than is typically studied, and (4) evaluators of early intervention programs interested in strategies for examining both experimental and nonexperimental questions in the context of a randomized program evaluation design.

It is particularly important to note how our work is grounded. We began with a program evaluation of EHS. The evaluation design provided a large sample of low-income families with young children who came to enroll in a new federal program, which in itself establishes certain boundaries on the applicability and generalizability of the findings. The families live in cities, small towns, and rural areas across the country, yet they are not a statistically representative sample of low-income families, or even of EHS families, although the original sample reflected the racial and geographic make-up of the national EHS program at the time the sample was selected (i.e., at the beginning of the program). The families are highly diverse so that within the low-income population, the sample includes the three most prevalent racial/ethnic groups found in the U.S. and families with substantial differentiation along a number of risk indicators. And, of course, all the families applied for EHS services (like all experimental evaluations of early childhood programs). Half the families in the sample, as determined by random assignment, attended the federal program designed to promote both child and family development; the other half had, as far as we know, experiences with various programs and services that low-income families may generally obtain when they do not have access to a formal program like EHS.[17] For 5 years, extensive and intensive data about both the program and control group families were collected; we learned about the experiences the families had, the programs they participated in, the services they received, and how they fared on a wide range of child, parenting, and family functioning measures.

As one might expect of a study initiated to address specific questions about a particular program's effectiveness, this research was not originally designed from a particular theoretical point of view. Nevertheless, we find that the research is relevant to three converging theoretical perspectives seen in the developmental literature. One is the notion that developmental processes are amplified by transactional processes between the child and others in various contexts (Sameroff & Fiese, 2000). A second is the concept that development of skills at one age influences further development (Heckman & Masterov, 2004). Third is the principle of developmental timing, suggesting that experiences (in this case, a program intervention and other program participation after the intervention) may have different effects at different times during a child's development (NICHD ECCRN, 2005a). For all four audiences we have identified (practitioners, policy makers, developmentalists, and program evaluators), issues with respect to the timing of developmental experiences are central.

As discussed in Chapter I, we identified four ways in which the timing of life experiences interacts with the nature of development as children age: (1) Experiences at specific points in development (effects of experiences relate to specific periods in development); (2) early experiences (early experiences outweigh later ones); (3) contemporaneous experiences (current experiences outweigh earlier ones); and (4) incremental and augmented experiences (effects of early experiences are maintained and perhaps augmented by later experiences). The EHSREP provides data obtained throughout the first 5 years of life—data on children's experiences (across multiple spheres) as well as their development across the broad range of developmental domains. This has provided the opportunity to examine the extent to which what is learned about the influences of children's programmatic experiences tends to support these different ways that experiences influence different aspects of development. Perhaps surprisingly, the timing of early childhood services has not been systematically examined previously. That is, do poor children benefit from services provided in infancy or toddlerhood more than from services offered in the preschool years? An ancillary question has to do with intensity or dosage, or the cumulative effect of multiple years of services.

SUMMARY OF THE MAIN RESEARCH FINDINGS

The central purpose of the research reported in this monograph was to examine the impacts of EHS on children and parents, the role of program features in modifying the overall impacts, and the extent to which families that differ in key demographic characteristics were differentially affected by their intervention experience. During the intervention (at ages 2 and 3), a variety of child impacts were seen for the full sample benefiting the EHS group. These included enhanced cognitive and language skills, reduced aggressive behaviors, higher engagement with the parent during play, and higher rates of immunizations. The effect sizes for these varied child impacts were around .20.

A number of these impacts (i.e., intervention-control group differences) on children, parents, and parenting that were seen at ages 2 and 3 were still present when children were assessed at age 5. As detailed in Chapter III, 2 years after the EHS program ended, the intervention significantly reduced behavior problems and enhanced positive social skills and approaches to learning. EHS increased vocabulary scores in Spanish-speaking children (but not in English speakers). On the other hand, no impacts were found on school-related achievement outcomes such as letter-word identification and applied problems or on observed parent–child play interactions. In growth curve analyses, no significant change in patterns between the treatment and control groups was seen across ages 2–5. When significant cross-sectional impacts were no longer found at age 5, this means that no interaction between treatment and age was found. The EHS longitudinal research base provided opportunities not only to examine program impacts (on child and family outcomes and program participation), as just described, but to undertake a series of mediational analyses that would move toward greater understanding of the mechanisms by which EHS might influence outcomes. One benefit of such analyses is providing information that can inform program development and improvement. Earlier impacts on children's vocabulary, cognition, and aggressive behavior were associated with the sustained effect on observed attention at age 5. Reductions in children's aggression at ages 2 and 3 related to the age 5 impacts on social behavior problems. Impacts on positive approaches to learning were associated with the earlier impacts on HOME language and literacy, vocabulary, and aggressive behavior.

The Advisory Committee on Services for Children with Infants and Toddlers (USDHHS), which was responsible for designing EHS, charged programs to ensure a smooth transition for children as they continued services after EHS, be it Head Start or other preschool programs of high quality. They believed that continued services would be necessary to sustain and further build on the benefits of EHS. Thus, to understand the contribution of post-EHS experiences, our research looked at children's participation in "formal" preschool programs, which could be any center-based program serving primarily 3- and 4-year-olds (i.e., children who were between 3 and 4 and between 4 and 5 years of age). It is important to note that despite the Advisory Committee's vision of a smooth transition to other preschool services, only about one-half of former EHS children were in formal programs at age 3–4. This rate rose to 82% at age 4–5, and about one-half of these children were in HS programs. African American children were somewhat more likely to enroll in HS and experience some formal programs between ages 3 and 5 than children from other racial/ethnic groups. Compared with control group children, the EHS group experienced higher rates of enrollment in any formal program between age 3 and 4 and in the combined 3–4 and 4–5 age period.

We reported differential program impacts according to two key subgroups based on child and family demographic characteristics: racial/ethnic groups and family demographic risk factors. African Americans experienced the greatest benefits from EHS at both age 3 and 5. By cumulating up to five family risk factors in addition to being low-income (as all sample families were), high-, moderate-, and low-risk groups were formed. We found very few significant impacts for the lowest risk group and none for the high-risk group at ages 2 and 3, but some positive impacts emerged for the highest-risk families and their children at age 5.

We also created three subgroups based on the programming approach programs took to delivering EHS services: programs were either home-based, center-based, or a mixed approach. It is important to note that although the estimated impacts of EHS within each program type are based on the experimental study design (since families were randomly assigned to the treatment or control group within sites), programs were not randomly assigned to implement a particular program approach. Any differences in impacts by program approach may be due to other site-level factors that are associated with program approach. Thus, the results refer to the effectiveness of program approach *for programs that adopted that approach*, given their community contexts and eligible populations. Looking at effect sizes for the three types of programs suggests that home-based programs were most effective in improving parenting and home environment outcomes, along with family self-sufficiency, and this pattern was seen at all three ages studied. In addition, however, a few positive impacts emerged at age 5 for children's social and emotional development and important family risk factors. We observed few impacts for the children and families who were enrolled in center-based programs. Although there was an early indication of center-based programs having an impact on cognitive development at age 2, this did not appear at age 3 and did not appear as any academic-skill impacts at age 5. Children and families in the EHS mixed-approach programs experienced the largest number of impacts and the largest impacts of any subgroup at ages 2 and 3. However, at age 5, few of the mixed-approach program impacts remained. Given that each program site was free to offer a mix of services (i.e., no standard curriculum was used across sites or within program types), caution should be taken when interpreting these results.[18]

We also conducted a series of nonexperimental analyses to examine the role of early care and education experiences beyond EHS (described in Chapter VI). Although participation in formal early care and education programs at both age 3–4 and 4–5 was associated with an increase in aggressive behaviors (unless the formal program was Head Start), program participation may have enhanced children's academic readiness for school. Enrollment in formal early care and education both during age 3–4 and in the 4–5 age period was associated with higher prekindergarten reading skills. Among the highest-risk families, enrollment in Head Start was associated with more-positive outcomes for children and parents, suggesting that the type of program in which the highest-risk children enrolled after EHS may have been particularly important.

Finally, it appears that those children and families who experienced EHS followed by services in the 3- to 5-year age period fared the best overall, but the various outcomes were associated with program experiences in different ways (Chapter VI). Benefits in social, emotional, and parenting outcomes came primarily from EHS, whereas the benefits in achievement-oriented outcomes

135

appeared to stem from formal program participation between ages 3 and 5. For aggression and behavior problems, formal programs confer risk, but less so for those who had experienced EHS. The roles of early childhood services in the 3–5 age period are somewhat different for those families who are at highest risk. For these families, following EHS with HS seems to be associated with children's achievement and social–emotional outcomes as well as with family well-being. We infer from the findings that early intervention may have its strongest effects when followed by preschool-age early childhood education, and that children at highest risk benefit from comprehensive services birth through age 5.

INTERPRETATIONS OF THE RESULTS

What are we to make of these findings? In terms of emotional and attentional processes, it seems as though EHS children continued to do better than their peers in the control group 2 years after program participation. However, the gains seen in cognitive and language scores were not (with the exception of Spanish-speaking children) sustained. Several explanations are outlined here, the first having to do with the size of the initial effects, the second with services received in the years following EHS by the control group, the third with the intensity of the EHS program, and the fourth with curriculum services.

First, the effect sizes were smaller than those for earlier evaluations of smaller scale programs for children under 3, at least for those programs that offered center-based care or center-based care with home visiting. At the end of these earlier programs, effects sizes ranged from .40 to 1.25 of a standard deviation for cognitive and language outcomes (Campbell & Ramey, 1994; IHDP, 1990; Karoly et al., 2005). In previous evaluations following children after a program ends, the impacts, although sustained, drop by perhaps one-third to one-half (Brooks-Gunn et al., 1994; Campbell & Ramey, 1995; McCarton et al., 1997; Zigler, Gilliam, & Barnett, 2011). If a program's impact is about one-fifth to one-quarter of a standard deviation at the end of a program, two years later it would be about .12 of a standard deviation or less (Brooks-Gunn, 2011). The EHSREP, like others before it, does not have the power to detect such differences. A meta-analysis of 123 preschool education programs (Camilli et al., 2010) estimates that the reduction in standard deviation differences is about .23; therefore, a program would theoretically have to have an initial effect size of .43 to show a .20 effect several years after the invention ended. And the effect sizes in EHS, for the entire sample, did not reach .40. It is noteworthy, however, that the initial effect sizes for African American children were in that range, and that significant effects were sustained at age 5 for this group.

A second and related point has to do with the services received after an intervention ends. It has been argued that preschool education program effects are reduced over time because poor children typically go to lower quality schools than do middle-income children; therefore, children targeted for programs such as HS or EHS go on to receive less stimulating classroom instruction (Brooks-Gunn, 2003; Lee et al., 1998; Magnuson, Ruhm, & Waldfogel, 2007). This argument is not directly relevant for our findings here, however, in that children were followed through age 5, prior to the beginning of school, and the intervention ended at age 3. However, it does lead to a possible explanation of the follow-up findings. A large proportion of children in both the treatment and the control group did go on to enroll in formal preschool programs through the 3- to 5-year age period. Therefore, it is possible that the control group was catching up to the treatment group at age 5 in academic skills (given that so many of the control group children were in programs at age 4 or 5). In fact, when examining control and program group means over time, it seems that the control children were catching up to the treatment group children, rather than the EHS children losing ground.

Similar findings (i.e., control group children catching up) are reported in evaluations of preschool education when children are assessed in elementary school, which tempers the arguments about low quality schools accounting for diminished preschool education effects over time. These findings lead to the question of whether early services make a difference in outcomes, above and beyond those received at years 4 and 5. Although the EHS evaluation cannot address this possibility directly, it was able to look (nonexperimentally) at children who received services in the first three and the fourth and fifth years of life versus those who received services in one or the other, or neither. Vocabulary scores were higher for children who received services at both time periods, although achievement test scores seemed to be more influenced by preschool formal education. Perhaps direct instruction is more likely to occur in preschool than in programs for younger children, particularly for reading and math (Camilli et al., 2010; Clements & Sarema, 2011; Dickinson, 2011). At the same time, aggressive behavior was reduced by EHS even though it was increased slightly by preschool formal education, as others have reported (Magnusson, Ruhm, & Waldfogel, 2007; NICHD ECCRN, 2003a). Perhaps, as we stated earlier, EHS acts as a protective factor against the slight rises in aggression associated with preschool group programming.

A third possibility for the modest effect sizes at the end of the program has to do with the intensity of services received by the EHS children, bearing in mind that EHS is a nationally implemented program with potentially greater variation in intensity then the smaller scale intervention programs that have been evaluated. Several analyses of the IHDP, which also served children from birth to 3, report links between number of days at the center and child outcomes, both in the short-term and in the long-term (i.e., at age 8; Hill et al., 2003; Liaw, Meisels, & Brooks-Gunn, 1995; Ramey et al., 1997). The most sophisticated of the three analyses involved propensity score matching. These nonexperimental analyses suggest that children with more days in the center are more likely to show benefits from the program, both at the end of the program and 2–5 years later. Effects were present at ages 3–8 on cognitive and achievement outcomes for children who received over 300 days in the center (about 150–175 days per year). We speculate that the large impacts in the Abecedarian project and IHDP at the end of their respective programs (over three-quarters of a standard deviation) are probably due to the fact that so many of the children went to the centers for at least 150 days per year. Cognitive effects were seen in the entire Early Head Start sample at ages 2 and 3, although effects might have been greater at age 3, and sustained at age 5, with more-intense services.

A fourth explanation has to do with the content of the services received. Although formal preschool programs may use well-developed curricula, programs for younger children often develop their own, or adopt components of several curricula. EHS programs participating in the national evaluation implemented a variety of curricula and had varied theories that determined the content of the services provided, as documented in the evaluation's implementation study (ACF, 1999; 2002b). Although curricula used and services provided met broad criteria specified in the Head Start Program Performance Standards, there was considerable variability in their specific elements and in the quality of their implementation.

In general, early childhood education curricula for preschool children have been developed with more emphasis on learning theory and fidelity of curriculum implementation for young children (Clements & Sarema, 2011; Dickinson, 2011). Also, since preschool education is almost exclusively delivered in centers by teachers, rather than with a mix of staff in a variety of settings (home, parent group, center), variability in implementation is likely. This is probably true in many birth-to 3-programs, not just EHS.

Some of the most persistent impacts were in domains considered important for later success. For example, aggressive behavior problems, which EHS programs reduced at all three age points, are predictive of later behavior problems and low school engagement, although perhaps not of academic test scores (Moffitt et al.,2002; Duncan et al., 2007). Attention, which EHS also influenced positively, is even more consistently linked to school achievement than behavior problems (Duncan et al., 2007). Parent reading to children (and learning stimulation) is also linked to positive outcomes later on (Magnuson et al., 2009; Phillips et al., 1998; Raikes et al., 2006). Although we need to understand the lack of direct impacts on measures of achievement-related outcomes at age 5, we believe that ignoring other outcomes (which themselves are also important predictors of later school success) to the exclusion of the others that EHS had a positive impact on would be short-sighted.

IMPLICATIONS FOR POLICY

Three broad sets of implications can be drawn from these findings: (1) about the lasting benefits of early childhood interventions that begin before birth or in infancy; (2) about the nature and timing of programmatic experiences for children throughout the first 5 years of life; and (3) about how data from program evaluations can be more useful to social policy when analyses extend beyond basic evaluation questions about a program's effectiveness and attempt to understand more about the many contributions that cumulative experiences make to children's developmental trajectories. After discussing these broad implications, we suggest more specific implications for practice and conclude with implications for future program evaluations.

Investigating the experiences children had between ages 3 and 5 (and not simply assessing impacts in isolation 2 years after the program ended) provides context for poor children's development. Although having been in an EHS program conferred some advantage to the treatment group in terms of enrolling in formal early care and education programs between ages 3 and 5, substantial proportions of the control group children also enrolled in these programs.

We also learned that, from a developmental perspective, children's age 3 outcomes are important as mediators of later prekindergarten performance. This set of findings supports the hypothesis that early experiences are important: Both the sustained impacts of EHS experience 2 years later and the role of early (age 3) impacts as mediators of later outcomes point to the enduring value of experiences provided to low-income children during the first 3 years of life. That the direct sustained impacts were in the realm of social, emotional, and attentional development may relate to the importance of the first 3 years of life for formation of parent–child relationships and children's social regulatory processes. However, it is important to note that more nuanced mediated analyses point to the indirect effects of impacts on cognitive development at 3 years of age as well as in the social realm (observed child engagement of parent) on age 5 social, emotional, and attentional outcomes.

The research reported in this monograph contributes to the scant literature on the effects of differential timing of program experiences children have up to age 5. As one would expect, the experiences children have between ages 3 and 5 also influence their prekindergarten performance, but the nature of this influence differs by developmental domain and according to children's demographic characteristics. One possible interpretation of these nonexperimental results is that children's development and parent behaviors may be optimized when formal program services that begin prenatally or in the first year of life and extend to age 3 are followed by formal programs between ages 3 and 5. An actual experimental test of this proposition would be a welcome addition to the field (i.e., assigning children and families to receive services at various ages in the first 5 years of life).

Program experiences in the preschool years following EHS appear to augment the benefits of the birth to age 3 experience, but primarily in areas of "academic" learning, but to negate the earlier benefits in the area of aggressive behavior problems. The finding that formal program participation at ages 3–5 is associated with greater parental support for children's learning may suggest an interesting interaction process such that having one's child enrolled in prekindergarten may spur parents on to more reading and in-home support for their child's program-based learning experiences. It is useful to reflect on these analyses in light of the covariance analyses reported in Chapter VI. There we saw that aggressive behavior patterns at age 5 were greatest for the children who enrolled in formal programs between ages 3 and 5 and who had *not* been in EHS (i.e., the control group members who went on to enroll in Head Start and other prekindergarten programs). But, as we have also seen, there are tradeoffs. Being in EHS without going on to Head Start or other preschool programs was not as advantageous in terms of the school-related achievement outcomes measured at age 5. The analyses suggested that advantages are conferred on children who enroll in age 3–5 formal programs in development of the "academic" letter-word identification outcome, which may be thought to represent a skill set that seems to respond to contemporaneous intervention and most likely to specific instruction.

However, as interesting as the story is that tends to point to a primacy effect for social–emotional outcomes from birth to age 3 programs, and a contemporaneous effect for achievement-related outcomes related to ages 3–5 programs, it may be more complex than that. The analyses in Chapter VI suggest that program effects do accumulate, although the "cumulation" may occur in various ways with benefits accruing differently for different outcomes, such that children who experienced both EHS and formal programs tended to be faring best at age 5. This finding is consistent with the conceptual models postulated previously (Heckman & Masterov, 2004; Ramey & Ramey, 1998).

Two developmental domains at age 3 appear to be particularly important in influencing later developmental outcomes. Policy makers can take note of the importance of designing programs that support children's cognitive abilities but also their relationship with their primary caregiver in the first 3 years of life. When children displayed higher cognitive skills and were rated higher in engaging their parents during a play task, development in a number of domains at age 5 was enhanced.

IMPLICATIONS FOR PRACTICE

The Role of Parenting

The birth to age 3 period is an opportune time to intervene to support parenting and changes in parenting. Although, clearly, later interventions can target parenting, parents are believed to be more open to modifying their parenting styles when children are young, and earlier interventions are believed to prevent the establishment of patterns that might be resistant to change (little evidence exists on either point, however).

In terms of implications specifically for EHS programs, several findings, including the overall findings showing lasting effects in social, emotional, and approaches to learning outcomes, the mediating role of parenting impacts, and enduring effects in home-based programs with their emphasis on parenting, reinforces and supports the emphasis that programs place on working with parents and focusing on the parent–child relationship and children's social and emotional functioning. This suggests that programs should continue to place an emphasis on supporting parents in whatever program options they offer, either home-based or center-based services. Further innovation is needed to help EHS and other programs develop precision in targeting the parenting behaviors that matter for children's development.

Continuity and Transitions

That children who received EHS followed by formal preschool experiences seemed to be faring best suggests that continuity in treatments could be enhanced. Lack of preschool programs for 3-year-olds is a special problem. It appears to us that following a parental-to-3 program like EHS with formal preschool programs in the age 3–5 period creates the greatest opportunity for ensuring that children from low-income families will start formal schooling on a more positive footing. This finding is important because few programs have attempted a full birth-to-age-5 intervention within a single program—the notable exceptions are the Abecedarian Project (Campbell & Ramey, 1995) and the CCDP (St. Pierre et al., 1997). It would be useful to be able to document where children go when they leave EHS—and/ or create plans (much like an IEP) for the services they should receive after graduating from EHS. Perhaps various models for providing continuity could be tested.

Meeting the Needs of Higher Risk Families

An important finding is that children in families at the highest levels of demographic risk do best when the comprehensive services of EHS are continued birth through 5. These highest risk families are ones that programs often struggle to keep engaged, and it may take the entire 0–5 period to see benefits for these families. HS has long emphasized serving the highest risk families and the current study underscores the value of 5 years of HS (EHS + 3–5 HS) for these families. The findings also suggest that innovation is needed to better meet the needs of these highest risk families.

Enhancing Impacts for Hispanic Children and Families

At age 5, Early Head Start had an impact on receptive vocabulary for Spanish-speaking children, yet impacts overall for the Hispanic subgroup (including both English- and Spanish-speaking children) were not notable. Much more needs to be done to understand why impacts are smaller for this group of families. We recommend experimentation with different intervention models, curricula, and various instructional strategies for English language learners (or dual language learners) to identify best practices (Hernandez, Takanishi, & Marutz, 2009; Kuhn & Greenberg, 2010; Magnusson, Lahaie, & Waldfogel, 2006).

IMPLICATIONS FOR PROGRAM EVALUATIONS

Taken together, the chapters of this monograph illustrate how data from program evaluations can be more useful to social policy when analyses extend beyond basic evaluation questions about a program's effectiveness and attempt to understand more about the many contributions that cumulative experiences make to children's developmental trajectories. We encourage the funders of program evaluations, and the groups who carry out the studies, to consider the added value of analyses that delve into the factors responsible for the program effects and the nuances in the data that may help explain particular patterns of evaluation findings. This monograph is an example of such an approach. Two points summarize this implication:

1. Go beneath the surface of overall, full-group analyses and examine impacts within subgroups that are particularly policy relevant.
2. Consider supplementing the main experimental analyses with careful nonexperimental analyses for investigating policy questions that fall outside the impact analyses. Even as the less-definitive, exploratory analyses such as those reported in this

monograph do, such analytic approaches in the context of experimental studies can guide the considerations of policy makers.

Conducting such additional analysis results in information about the possible influences of cumulative experiences in the first 5 years of life. A clear inference is that services for poor children will be most beneficial if they begin in the early years and either continue until the children enter kindergarten or provide for continuity of program services across programs throughout this 5-year period.

NOTES

17. In fact, we know a lot. See ACF (2002a, Chapter IV) for analyses of the impact of EHS on services received.

18. For example, several sites developed their own "models." One used the CELEBRATE model as a guide, and home visitors attended to and addressed with parents the importance of cues, eye contact/expression, etc. Home visitors constructed an individualized curriculum for each family, drawing from published curricula such as Portage, Small Wonder, and various other resources. Another site used methods "based on" Parents as Teachers (PAT), and carried over the home visiting strategies they had developed when a CCDP site. Another site simply called its approach a mental health home visiting model. Two others used the PAT curriculum. Yet another reported "Activities are drawn from a variety of sources, including published curricula such as Partners in Parenting Education (PIPE)—parent activities to facilitate attachment; Hawaii Early Learning Profile (HELP)—age-appropriate assessment activities that sensitize parents to children's evolving developmental capacities; With Love and Wisdom; WestEd's Program for Infant/Toddler Caregivers; Creative Curriculum; Small Wonder; Teaching Strategies; Baby Your Baby; and First Steps," etc.

REFERENCES

Achenbach, T. M., & Rescorla, L. A. (2000). *Manual of ASEBA preschool forms and profiles.* Burlington, VT: University of Vermont, Research Center for Children, Youth, and Families.

Administration for Children and Families. (1999, December). *Leading the way: Characteristics and early experiences of selected Early Head Start programs; Volume II: Program profiles.* Washington, DC: U.S. Department of Health and Human Services.

Administration for Children and Families. (2002a, June). *Making a difference in the lives of infants and toddlers and their families: The impacts of Early Head Start.* Washington, DC: U.S. Department of Health and Human Services.

Administration for Children and Families. (2002b, December). *Pathways to quality and full implementation in Early Head Start programs.* Washington, DC: U.S. Department of Health and Human Services.

Administration for Children and Families. (2003, May). *Head Start FACES 2000: A whole-child perspective on program performance; fourth progress report.* Washington, DC: U.S. Department of Health and Human Services.

Administration for Children and Families. (2004, February). *The role of Early Head Start in addressing the child care needs of low-income families with infants and toddlers.* Washington, DC: U.S. Department of Health and Human Services.

Administration for Children and Families. (2007a). Early Head Start Research and Evaluation Project (EHSREP) 1996-Current. <http://www.acf.hhs.gov/programs/opre/ehs/ehs_resrch/ehs_overview.html#overview> [Accessed September 14, 2007].

Administration for Children and Families. (2007b). Early Head Start Research and Evaluation Project (EHSRE) 1996-Current, Instruments. <http://www.acf.hhs.gov/programs/opre/ehs/ehs_resrch/index.html#instru> [Accessed September 14, 2007].

Administration for Children and Families. (2010, January). *Head Start impact study final report.* Washington, DC: U.S. Department of Health and Human Services.

Administration on Children, Youth and Families. (2001). *Building their futures: How Early Head Start programs are enhancing the lives of infants and toddlers in low-income families.* Vol. I. Technical Report. Washington, DC: U.S. Department of Health and Human Services.

Administration on Children, Youth and Families. (2006). Head Start Performance Measures Center Family and Child Experiences Survey (FACES 2000): Technical Report. Washington, DC: U.S. Department of Health and Human Services.

Anderson, M. L. (2008). Multiple inference and gender differences in the effects of early intervention: A reevaluation of the Abecedarian, Perry Preschool, and Early Training Projects. *Journal of the American Statistical Association*, **103**, 1481–1495.

Barnet, B., Liu, J., DeVoe, M., Alperovitz-Bichell, K., & Duggan, A. K. (2007). Home visiting for adolescent mothers: Effects on parenting, maternal life course, and primary care linkages. *Annals of Family Medicine*, **5**(3), 224–232.

Barnett, W. S. (1995). Long-term effects of early childhood programs on cognitive and school outcomes. *The Future of Children*, **5**(3), 25–50.

Barnett, W. S. (2011). Effective ness of Educational Intervention. *Science*, **333**(6045), 975–978.

Barnett, W. S., Carolan, M. E., Fitzgerald, J., & Squires, J. H. (2011). *The state of preschool 2011: State preschool yearbook*. New Brunswick, NJ: National Institute for Early Education Research.

Barnett, W. S., Lamy, C., Jung, K. (2005, December). *The effects of state prekindergarten programs on young children's school readiness in five states*. New Brunswick, NJ: National Institute for Early Education Research, Rutgers University.

Barnett, W. S., Robin, K. B., Hustedt, J. T., & Schulman, K. L. (2003). *The state of preschool: 2003 state preschool yearbook*.

Bassok, D. (2010). Do Black and Hispanic children benefit more from preschool? Understanding differences in preschool effects across racial groups. *Child Development*, **81**, 1828–1845.

Bayley, N. (1993). *Bayley scales of infant development* (2nd ed.): Manual. New York: The Psychological Corporation.

Berlin, L. J., Brooks-Gunn, J., & Aber, J. L. (2001). Promoting early childhood development through comprehensive community initiatives. *Children's Services: Social Policy, Research and Practice*, **4**, 1–24.

Bradley, R., & Caldwell, B. (1988). Using the HOME Inventory to assess the family environment. *Pediatric Nursing*, **14**, 97–102.

Bradley, R. H., Caldwell, B. M., Rock, S. L., Ramey, C. T., Barnard, K. E., Gray, C., et al. (1989). Home environment and cognitive development in the first 3 years of life: A collaborative study involving six sites and three ethnic groups in North America. *Developmental Psychology*, **25**, 217–235.

Bradley, R. H. (1994). The HOME Inventory: Review and reflections. In H. W. Reese (Ed.), *Advances in child development and behavior* (Vol. 25, pp. 241–288). San Diego, CA: Academic Press.

Brady-Smith, C., Brooks-Gunn, J., Tamis-LeMonda, C. S., Ispa, J. M., Fuligni, A. S., … Fine, M. (2013). Mothers' interactions with infants: A person-oriented, within ethnic group approach. *Parenting: Science and Practice*.

Bronson, M. B. Pierson, D. E., & Tivnan, T. (1984). The effects of early education on children's competence in elementary school. *Evaluation Review*, **8**, 615–629.

Brooks-Gunn, J. (2003). Do you believe in magic? What we can expect from early childhood intervention programs. Social Policy Report, 17.

Brooks-Gunn, J. (2004). Intervention and policy as change agents for young children. In P. L. Chase-Lansdale, K. Kiernan, & R. J. Friedman (Eds.), *Human development across lives and generations: The potential for change* (pp. 293–340). New York, NY: Cambridge University.

Brooks-Gunn, J. (2011). Early childhood education: The likelihood of sustained effects. In E. Zigler, W. Gilliam, & S. Barnett (Eds.), *The preschool education debates* (pp. 200–205). Baltimore, MD: Brookes Publishing.

145

Brooks-Gunn, J., Berlin, L. J., & Fuligni, A. S. (2000). Early childhood intervention programs: What about the family? In J. P. Shonkoff & S. J. Meisels (Eds.), *Handbook on early childhood intervention* (2nd ed., pp. 549–588). New York: Cambridge University Press.

Brooks-Gunn, J., & Duncan, G. J. (1997). The effects of poverty on children. *The Future of Children, 7*, 55–71.

Brooks-Gunn, J., Fuligni, A. S., & Berlin, L. J. (2003). *Early child development in the 21st Century: Profiles of current research initiatives.* New York: Teachers College Press.

Brooks-Gunn, J., Gross, R. T., Kraemer, H. C., Spiker, D., & Shapiro, (1992). Enhancing the cognitive outcomes of low-birth-weight, premature infants: For whom is the intervention most effective. *Pediatrics, 89*, 1209–1215.

Brooks-Gunn, J., Klebanov, P., Liaw, F., & Spiker, D. (1993). Enhancing the development of low-birthweight premature infants: Changes in cognition and behavior over the first three years. *Child Development, 64*, 736–753.

Brooks-Gunn, J., & Markman, L. (2005). The contribution of parenting to ethnic and racial gaps in school readiness. *The Future of Children, 15*(1), 138–167.

Brooks-Gunn, J., McCarton, C., Casey, P., McCormick, M., Bauer, C., Bernbaum, J., et al. (1994). Early intervention in low birth weight, premature infants: Results through age 5 years from the Infant Health and Development Program. *Journal of the American Medical Association, 272*, 1257–1262.

Burchinal, M. R., Campbell, F. A., Bryant, D. M., Wasik, B. H., & Ramey, C. T. (1997). Early intervention and mediating processes in cognitive performance of children of low-income African American families. *Child Development, 68*, 935–954.

Caldwell, B. M., & Bradley, R. H. (1984). *Administration manual: Home observation for measurement of the environment.* Little Rock: University of Arkansas at Little Rock.

Camilli, G., Vargas, S., Ryan, S., & Barnett, W. S. (2010). Meta-analysis of the effects of early education interventions on cognitive and social development. *Teachers College Record, 112*.

Campbell, F. A., & Ramey, C. T. (1994). Effects of early intervention on intellectual and academic achievement: A follow-up study of children from low-income families. *Child Development, 65*, 684–698.

Campbell, F. A., Pungello, E. P., Miller-Johnson, S., Burchinal, M., & Ramey, C. T. (2001). The development of cognitive and academic abilities: Growth curves from an early childhood educational experiment. *Developmental Psychology, 37*, 231–242.

Campbell, F. A., & Ramey, C. T. (1995). Cognitive and school outcomes for high risk African-American students at middle adolescence: Positive effects of early intervention. *American Educational Research Journal, 32*, 743–772.

Capizzano, J., & Adams, G. (2003). *Children in low-income families are less likely to be in center-based child care. Snapshot of America's Families III (No. 16).* Washington, DC: Urban Institute.

Capizzano, J., Adams, G., & Ost, J. (2007). *Caring for children of color: The child care patterns of White, Black and Hispanic children under 5. Executive Summary.* Washington, DC: The Urban Institute. Retrieved from <www.urban.org> [Accessed May 21, 2007].

Child Care Bureau. (2006a). Fiscal year 2005 Child Care and Development Fund summary of expenditure by categorical items. Retrieved December 8, 2006, from <http://www.acf.hhs.gov/programs/ccb/data/expenditures/05acf696/table1.htm>

Child Care Bureau. (2006b). Child Care and Development Fund: Average monthly adjusted number of families and children served (FY 2005). Retrieved December 8, 2006, from <http://www.acf.hhs.gov/programs/ccb/data/ccdf_data/05acf800/table1.htm>

146

Clements, D. H., & Sarema, J. (2011). Early childhood mathematics intervention. *Science* **333** (6045), 968–970.

Cohen, J. (1988). *Statistical power analysis for the behavioral sciences* (2nd ed.). Hillsdale, NJ: Lawrence Earlbaum.

Connell, J. P., & Kubisch, A. C. (2001). Community approaches to improving outcomes for urban children, youth and families: Current trends and future directions. In A. Booth & A. C. Crouter (Eds.), *Does It Take A Village?* Mahwah, NJ: Lawrence Erlbaum.

Cook, T. D., & Campbell, D. T. (1979). *Quasi-experimentation: Design and analysis issues for field settings.* Chicago: Rand-McNally.

Cunha, F., Heckman, J. J., Lochner, L. J., & Masterov, D. V. (2006). Interpreting the evidence on life cycle skill formation. In E. A. Hanushek & F. Welch (Eds.), *Handbook of the economics of education* (pp. 697–812). Amsterdam: North Holland.

Currie, J. (2001). Early childhood education programs. *The Journal of Economic Perspectives,* **15,** 213–238.

Daro, D., & Harding, K. (1999). Healthy Families America: Using research to enhance practice. *Future of Children,* **9,** 152–176.

Degnan, K. A. (2006). *Developmental profiles of aggression across early childhood: Contributions of emotion regulation and maternal behavior.* (Unpublished doctoral dissertation). University of North Carolina, Greensboro.

Dickinson, D. K. (2011). Teachers' language practices and academic outcomes of preschool children. *Science* **333**(6045), 964–967.

Duncan, G. J., Brooks-Gunn, J., & Klebanov, P. K. (1994). Economic deprivation and early-childhood development. *Child Development,* **65,** 296–318.

Duncan, G. J., Dowsett, C. J., Claessens, A., Magnuson, K., Huston, A. C., Klebanov, P., et al. (2007). School readiness and later achievement. *Developmental Psychology,* **43,** 1428–1446.

Duncan, G. J., & Magnuson, K. A. (2005). Can family socioeconomic resources account for racial and ethnic test score gaps? *The Future of Children,* **15,** 35–54.

Duncan, G. J., & Magnuson, K. (2006). Costs and benefits from early investments to promote human capital and positive behavior. In N. F. Watt, C. Ayoub, R. H. Bradley, J. E. Puma, & W. A. LeBoeuf (Eds.), *The crisis in youth mental health* (pp. 27–51). Westport, CT: Praeger.

Dunn, L. M., & Dunn, L. M. (1997). *Peabody Picture Vocabulary Test* (3rd ed.). Circle Pines, MN: American Guidance Service.

Dunn, L. M., Padilla, E. R., Lugo, D. E., & Dunn, L. M. (1986). *Examiner's manual for the Test de Vocabulario en Imagenes Peabody (Peabody Picture Vocabulary Test) Adaptación Hispanoamericana (Hispanic-American adaptation).* Circle Pines, MN: American Guidance Service.

Early Childhood Learning and Knowledge Center. (2004). *Head Start Program fact sheet fiscal year 2004.* Washington, DC: Administration for Children and Families. http://eclkc.ohs.acf.hhs.gov/hslc/mr/factsheets/HeadStartPrograms.htm.

Fenson, L., Pethick, S., Renda, C., Cox, J. L., Dale, P. S., & Reznick, S. J. (2000). Short-form versions of the MacArthur Communicative Development Inventories. *Applied Psycholinguistics,* **21,** 95–115.

Field, T., Wigmaker, S., Stringer, S., & Ignatoff, E. (1980). Teenage, lower-class, Black mothers and their preterm infants: An intervention and developmental follow-up. *Child Development,* **51,** 426–436.

Fleiss, J. L., & Cohen, J. (1973). The Equivalence of Weighted Kappa and the Intraclass Correlation Coefficient as Measures of Reliability. *Educational and Psychological Measurement*, **33**, 613–619.

Fuligni, A., & Brooks-Gunn, J. (2013). Mother-child interactions in Early Head Start: Age and ethnic differences in low-income dyads. *Parenting: Science and Practice*, **13**, 1–26.

Fuligni, A. S., Han, W., & Brooks-Gunn, J. (2004). The Infant–Toddler HOME in the 2nd and 3rd years of life. *Parenting: Science and Practice*, **4**, 139–159.

Fuligni, A., Brady-Smith, C., Tamis-LeMonda, C., Bradley, R. H., Chazan-Cohen, R., Boyce, L., & Brooks-Gunn, J. (2013). Patterns of supportive parenting in the first 3 years of life: Correlates and consequences in low-income White, Black, and Latino families. *Parenting: Science and Practice*, **13**, 44–57.

Garber, H. L., & Heber, R. (1981). The efficacy of early intervention with family rehabilitation. In M. J. Begab (Ed.), *Psychological influences in regarded performance* (pp. 71–87). Baltimore, MD: University Park Press.

Garces, E., Thomas, D., & Currie, J. (2002). Longer-term effects of Head Start. *The American Economic Review*, **92**, 999–1012.

Gelfand, D., Teti, D., Seiner, S., & Jameson, P. (1996). Helping mothers fight depression: Evaluation of a home-based intervention program for depressed mothers and their infants. *Journal of Clinical Child Psychology*, **25**, 406–422.

Gomby, D. (2005). Home visitation in 2005: Outcomes for children and parents. Working Paper No. 7. Washington, DC: Invest in Kids Working Group, Committee for Economic Development.

Gormley, W. T., Jr. (2011). From science to policy in early childhood education. *Science*, **333** (6045), 978–981.

Gormley, W. T., Jr., Gayer, T., Phillips, D., & Dawson, B. (2005). The effects of universal pre-k on cognitive development. *Developmental Psychology*, **41**, 872–884.

Grace, C., Shores, E. F., Zaslow, M., Brown, B., Anfseerer, D., & Bell, L. (2006). *Rural disparities in baseline data of the Early Childhood Longitudinal Study: A chartbook*. National Center for Rural Early Childhood Learning Initiatives: Mississippi State University.

Gray, S. W., & Klaus, R. A. (1970). The Early Training Project: A seventh-year report. *Child Development*, **41**, 909–924.

Hart, B., & Risley, T. (1995). *Meaningful differences in the everyday experiences of young American children*. Baltimore, MD: Paul H. Brookes.

Heckman, J. J. (2006). A broader view of what education policy should be. In N. F. Watt, C. Ayoub, R. H. Bradley, J. E. Puma & W. A. LeBoeuf (Eds.), *The crisis in youth mental health* (pp. 3–26). Westport, CT: Praeger.

Heckman, J. J., & Masterov, D. V. (2004). The productivity argument for investing in young children. Working Paper No. 5. Washington, DC: Invest in Kids Working Group.

Heinicke, C., Fineman, N., Rodning, C., Ruth, G., Recchia, S., & Guthrie, D. (2001). Relationship-based intervention with at-risk mothers: Outcome in first year of life. *Infant Mental Health Journal*, **20**(4), 349–374.

Hernandez, D. J., Takanishi, R., & Marotz, K. G. (2009). Life circumstances and public policies for young children in immigrant families. *Early Childhood Research Quarterly*, **24**(4), 487–501.

Hill, J. L., Brooks-Gunn, J., & Waldfogel, J. (2003). Sustained effects of high participation in an early intervention for low-birth-weight premature infants. *Developmental Psychology*, **39**, 730–744.

148

Hill, J. L., Waldfogel, J., & Brooks-Gunn, J. (2002). Differential effects of high-quality child care. *Journal of Policy Analysis and Management*, **21**, 601–627.

Howard, K. S., & Brooks-Gunn, J. (2009). The role of home-visiting programs in preventing child abuse and neglect. *Future of Children*, **19**(2), 119–146.

Infant Health and Development Program. (1990). Enhancing the outcomes of low-birthweight, premature infants: A multisite, randomized trial. *Journal of the American Medical Association*, **263**, 3035–3042.

Iruka, I. U., & Carver, P. R. (2006). *Initial: Results from the 2005 NHES Early Childhood Program Participation Survey (NCES 2006-075)*. U.S. Department of Education. Washington, DC: National Center for Education Statistics.

Jacobson, S., & Frye, K. (1991). Effect of maternal social support on attachment: Experimental evidence. *Child Development*, **62**, 572–582.

Johnson, D. L., & Blumenthal, J. B. (1985). A ten year follow-up. *Child Development*, **56**, 376–391.

Johnson, Z., Howell, F., & Molloy, B. (1993). Community mothers' programme: Randomised controlled trial on non-professional intervention in parenting. *British Medical Journal*, **306**, 1449–1452.

Karoly, L. A., Kilburn, M. R., & Cannon, J. S. (2005). *Early childhood interventions: Proven results future promise*. Santa Monica, CA: Rand Corporation.

Kenny, D. A., Kashy, D. A., & Bolger, N. (1998). Data analysis in social psychology. In D. T. Gilbert, S. T. Fiske, & G. Lindzey, (Eds.) *Handbook of social psychology* (4th ed. Vol. 1, pp. 233–265). New York: Oxford University Press.

Kitzman, H., Cole, R., Yoos, H., & Olds, D. (1997). Challenges experienced by home visitors: A qualitative study of program implementation. *Journal of Community Psychology*, **25**, 95–109.

Klebanov, P., & Brooks-Gunn, J. (2006). Cumulative, human capital, and psychological risk in the context of early intervention: Links with IQ at ages 3, 5 and 8. *Annals of the New York Academy of Sciences*, **1094**, 63–82.

Klebanov, P. K., Brooks-Gunn, J., & McCormick, M. C. (2001). Maternal coping strategies and emotional distress: Results of an early intervention program for low birth weight young children. *Developmental Psychology*, **37**, 654–667.

Klebanov, P. K., Brooks-Gunn, J., McCarton, C., & McCormick, M. C. (1998). The contribution of neighborhood and family income to developmental test scores over the first three years of life. *Child Development*, **69**, 1420–1436.

Knudsen, E. I., Heckman, J. J., Cameron, J. L., & Shonkoff, J. P. (2006). Economic, neurobiological, and behavioral perspectives on building America's future workforce. *Proceedings of the National Academy of Sciences*, **103**, 10155–10162.

Kuhn, J. M., & Greenberg, J. P. (2010). Factors predicting early childhood education and care use by immigrant families. *Social Science Research*, **39**, 642–651.

Lee, V. E., Brooks-Gunn, J., Schnur, E., & Liaw, F.-R. (1990). Are Head Start effects sustained? A longitudinal follow-up comparison of disadvantaged children attending Head Start, no preschool, and other preschool programs. *Child Development*, **61**, 495–507.

Lee, V. E., & Loeb, S. (1995). Where do Head Start attendees end up? One reason why preschool effects fade out. *Educational Evaluation and Policy Analysis*, **17**, 62–82.

Lee, V. E., Loeb, S., & Lubeck, S. (1998). Contextual effects of prekindergarten classrooms for disadvantaged children on cognitive development: The case of Chapter 1. *Child Development*, **69**, 479–494.

Leventhal, T., Brooks-Gunn, J., McCormick, M. C., & McCarton, C. M. (2000). Patterns of service use in preschool children: Correlates, consequences, and the role of early intervention. *Child Development*, **71**, 802–819.

Liaw, F., & Brooks-Gunn, J. (1994). Cumulative familial risks and low birth weight children's cognitive and behavioral development. *Journal of Clinical Child Psychology*, **23**, 360–372.

Liaw, F. R., & Brooks-Gunn, J. (1993). Patterns of low birth weight children's cognitive development. *Developmental Psychology*, **29**, 1024–1035.

Liaw, F., Meisels, S. J., & Brooks-Gunn, J. (1995). The effects of experience of early intervention on low birth weight, premature children: The infant health & development program. *Early Childhood Research Quarterly*, **10**, 405–431.

Linver, M., Brooks-Gunn, J., & Kohen, D. (1999). Parenting behavior and emotional health as mediators of family poverty effects upon young low birth-weight children's cognitive ability. *Annals of the New York Academy of Sciences*, **896**, 376–378.

Love, J. M., Kisker, E. E., Ross, C., Raikes, H., Constantine, J., Boller, K., et al. (2005). The effectiveness of Early Head Start for 3-year-old children and their parents: Lessons for policy and programs. *Developmental Psychology*, **41**, 885–901.

Ludwig, J., & Miller, D. L. (2006). *Does Head Start improve children's life chances? Evidence from a regression discontinuity design.* Bonn, Germany: Institute for the Study of Labor IZA DP #2111.

Lyons-Ruth, K., & Easterbrooks, M. A. (2006). Assessing mediated models of family change in response to infant home-visiting: A two-phase longitudinal analysis. *Infant Mental Health Journal*, **27**, 55–69.

Magnuson, K. A., Ruhm, C., & Waldfogel, J. (2007). Does prekindergarten improve school preparation and performance? *Economics of Education Review*, **26**, 33–51.

Magnuson, K. A., & Waldfogel, J. (2005). Early childhood care and education: Effects on ethnic and racial gaps in school readiness. *The Future of Children*, **15**, 169–196.

Martin, A., Brooks-Gunn, J., Klebanov, P., Buka, S. L., & McCormick, M. C. (2008). Long-term maternal effects of early childhood intervention: Findings from the Infant Health and Development Program. *Journal of Applied Developmental Psychology*, **29**, 101–117.

McCarton, C., Brooks-Gunn, J., Wallace, I., Bauer, C., Bennett, F., Bernbaum, J., et al. (1997). Results at 8 years of intervention for low birth weight premature infants: The Infant Health Development Program. *Journal of the American Medical Association*, **227**, 126–132.

McCormick, M. C., Brooks-Gunn, J., Buka, S. L., Goldman, J., Yu, M., Salganik, S., et al. (2006). Early intervention in low birth weight premature infants: Results at 18 years of age for the Infant Health and Development Program. *Pediatrics*, **117**(3), 771–780.

McLaughlin, A. E., Campbell, F. A., Pungello, E. P., & Skinner, M. (2007). Depressive symptoms in young adults: The influences of the early home environment and early educational care. *Child Development*, **78**(3), 746–756.

Moffitt, T. E., Caspi, A., Rutter, M., & Silva, P. A., (2001). *Sex differences in antisocial behavior: Conduct disorder, delinquency, and violence in the Dunedin Longitudinal Study.* Cambridge, UK: Cambridge University Press.

Moos, R. H., & Moos, B. S. (1976). A typology of family social environments. *Family Process*, **15**, 357–372.

Mott, F. L. (2004). The utility of the HOME-SF scale for child development research in a large national longitudinal survey: The National Longitudinal Survey of Youth 1979 cohort. *Parenting: Science & Practice*, **4**, 259–270.

Mulligan, G. M., Brinhall, D., & West, J. (2005). *Child care and early education of infants, toddlers, and preschoolers: 2001 (NCES 2006-039). U.S. Department of Education.* Washington, DC: U.S. Government Printing Office.

National Center for Education Statistics. (n.d.). Early Childhood Longitudinal Study—Birth Cohort (ECLS-B): Instruments & Assessments. <http://nces.ed.gov/ecls/birthinstruments.asp> [Accessed September 14, 2007].

National Institute of Child Health and Human Development [NICHD] Early Child Care Research Network. (2000). The relation of child care to cognitive and language development. *Child Development,* **71**, 960–980.

National Institute of Child Health and Human Development [NICHD] Early Child Care Research Network. (2001). Nonmaternal care and family factors in early development: An overview of the NICHD study of early child care. *Journal of Applied Developmental Psychology,* **22**, 454–457.

National Institute of Child Health & Human Development (NICHD) Early Child Care Research Network. (2003a). Does amount of time spent in child care predict socioemotional adjustment during the transition to kindergarten? *Child Development,* **74**, 976–1005.

National Institute of Child Health & Human Development (NICHD) Early Child Care Research Network. (2003b). Social functioning in first grade: Associations with earlier home and child care predictors and with current classroom experiences. *Child Development,* **74**, 1639–1662.

National Institute of Child Health and Human Development [NICHD] Early Child Care Resource Network. (2003c). Does quality of child care affect child outcomes at age 4½? *Developmental Psychology,* **39**, 451–469.

National Institute of Child Health and Human Development [NICHD] Early Child Care Research Network. (2005a). Early child care and children's development in the primary grades: Follow-up results from the NICHD study of early child care. *American Educational Research Journal,* **43**, 537–570.

National Institute of Child Health and Human Development [NICHD] Early Child Care Research Network. (2005b). *Child care and child development.* New York: Guilford Press.

Olds, D. L. (1999). Long-term effects of nurse home visitation on children's criminal and antisocial behavior: 15-year follow-up of a randomized controlled trial. *Journal of the American Medical Association,* **281**, 1377.

Olds, D. (2006). Nurse family partnership. In N. F. Watt, C. Ayoub, R. H. Bradley, J. Puma, & W. LeBoeuf (Eds.), *The crisis in youth mental health: Early intervention programs and policies* (pp. 147–180). Westport, CT: Praeger.

Olds, D. L., Eckenrode, J., Henderson, C. R., Kitzman, H., Powers, J., Cole, R., et al. (1997). Long term effects of home visitation on maternal life course and child abuse and neglect: Fifteen year follow-up of a randomized trial. *Journal of the American Medical Association,* **278**, 637–643.

Olds, D. L., Henderson, C. R., Jr., & Kitzman, H., (1994). Does prenatal and infancy nurse home visitation have enduring effects on qualities of parental caregiving and child health at 25 to 50 months of life? *Pediatrics,* **93**, 89–98.

Olds, D., Henderson, C., Kitzman, H., & Cole, R. (1995). Effects of prenatal and infancy nurse home visitation on surveillance of child maltreatment. *Pediatrics,* **95**, 365–372.

Olds, D., Kitzman, H., Cole, R., Robinson, J., Sidora, K., Luckey, D. W., et al. (2004). Effects of nurse home visiting on maternal life course development: Age 6 follow up results of a randomized trial. *Pediatrics*, **114**, 1550–1559.

Olds, D., Robinson, J., O'Brien, R., Luckey, D., Pettitt, L., Henderson, C., Talmi, A., et al. (2002). Home visiting by paraprofessionals and by nurses: A randomized controlled trial. *Pediatrics*, **110**, 486–496.

Owen, M. T., Barefoot, B., Vaughn, A., Dominguez, G., & Ware, A. M. (1996). 54-Month Parent-Child Structured Interaction Qualitative Rating Scales. NICHD Study of Early Child Care Research Consortium.

Phillips, M., Brooks-Gunn, J., Duncan, G. J., Klebanov, P. K., & Jencks, C. (1998). Family background, parenting practices, and the black-white test score gap. In C. Jencks, & M. Phillips, (Eds.) *The black-white test score gap* (pp. 103–143). Washington, DC: Brookings Institution Press.

Pierson, D. E., Bronson, M. B., Dromey, E., Swartz, J. P., Tivnan, T., & Walker, D. K. (1983). The impact of early education: Measured by classroom observations and teacher ratings of children in kindergarten. *Evaluation Review*, **7**, 191–216.

Pierson, D. E., Walker, D. K., & Tivnan, T. (1984). A school based program from infancy to kindergarten for children and their parents. *Personnel and Guidance Journal*, **62**, 448–455.

Radloff, L. S. (1977). The CES-D Scale: A self-report depression scale for research in the general population. *Applied Psychological Measurement*, **1**, 385–401.

Rae, G. (1988). The equivalence of multiple rater kappa statistics and intraclass correlation coefficients. *Educational and Psychological Measurement*, **48**, 367–374.

Raikes, H., Pan, B. A., Luze, G., Tamis-LeMonda, C. S., Brooks-Gunn, J., Constantine, J., et al. (2006). Mother-child book reading in low-income families: Correlations and outcomes during the first three years of life. *Child Development*, **77**, 924–953.

Ramey, C. T., Bryant, D. M., Sparling, J. J., & Wasick, B. H. (1985). Project CARE: A comparison of two early intervention strategies to prevent retarded development. *Topics in Early Childhood Special Education*, **5**, 12–25.

Ramey, C. T., Bryant, D. M., Wasik, B. H., Sparling, J. J., Fendt, K. H., & LaVange, L. M. (1997). Participation in the intervention and its effect on the cognitive outcome. In R.T. Gross, D. Spiker, & C.W. Haynes, (Eds.), *Helping low birth weight, premature babies: The Infant Health and Development Program* (pp. 190–202). Stanford, CA: Stanford University Press.

Ramey, C. T., & Campbell, F. A., (1984). Preventive education for high-risk children: Cognitive consequences of the Carolina Abecedarian Project. *American Journal of Mental Deficiency*, **88**, 515–523.

Ramey, C. T., & Ramey, S. L. (1998). Early intervention and early experience. *American Psychologist*, **53**, 109–120.

Ramey, C. T., & Ramey, S. L. (2006). Early learning and school readiness: Can early intervention make a difference? In N. F. Watt, C. Ayoub, R. H. Bradley, J. E. Puma & A. LeBoeuf (Eds.), *The crisis in youth mental health* (pp. 291–318). Westport, CT: Praeger.

Raudenbush, S. W., Byrk, A. S., Cheong, Y. F., & Congdon, R. T. (2004). *HLM 6: Hierarchical linear and nonlinear modeling*. Lincolnwood, IL: Scientific Software International.

Reardon, S., & Galindo, C. (2009). The Hispanic-White achievement gap in math and reading in the elementary grades. *American Education Research Journal*, **46**(3), 853–891.

Reynolds, A., Magnuson, K., & Ou, S.-R. (2006, January). PK-3 programs and practices that work in children's first decade (FDC Working Paper: Advancing PK-3, No. 6). New York: Foundation for Child Development.

Reynolds, A. J., Ou, S., & Topitzes, J. W. (2004). Paths of effects of early childhood intervention on educational attainment and delinquency: A confirmatory analysis of the Chicago Child-Parent Centers. *Child Development*, **75**, 1299–1328.

Reynolds, A., & Temple, J. A. (2006). Impacts of the Chicago Child-Parent Centers on child and family development. In N. F. Watt, C. Ayoub, R. H. Bradley, J. E. Puma, & W. A. LeBoeuf (Eds.), *The crisis in youth mental health* (pp. 229–250). Westport, CT: Praeger.

Reynolds, A. J., Temple, J. A., Ou, S-r., Arteaga, I. A., & White, B. A. B. (2011). School-based early childhood education and age-28 well-being: Effects by timing, dosage, and subgroups. *Science*, **333**(6040), 360–364.

Reynolds, A. J., Wang, M. C., & Walberg, I. J. (Eds.). (2003). *Early childhood programs for a new century*. Washington, DC: Child Welfare League of America.

Roid, G. H., & Miller, L. J. (1997). *Examiners manual: Leiter International Performance Scale-Revised*. Chicago: Stoelting Co.

Rosenthal, E., Rathbun, A., & West, J. (2005). Regional differences in kindergartners' early education experiences. *Education Statistics Quarterly*, **7**(12), 15–24.

Ross, C. E., Mirowsky, J., & Huber, J. (1983). Dividing work, sharing work, and in between: Marriage patterns and depression. *American Sociological Review*, **48**, 809–823.

Rouse, C., Brooks-Gunn, J., & McLanahan, S. (2005). Introducing the issue, "School readiness: Closing racial and ethnic gaps," *The Future of Children*, **15**(1), 5–14.

Sameroff, A. J., & Fiese, B. H. (2000). Models of development and developmental risk. In C. Zeanah (Ed.), *Handbook of infant mental health* (pp. 3–19). New York: Guilford Press.

Schmit, S., (2012a, November). *Early Head Start participants, programs, families and staff in 2011*. Washington, DC: CLASP.

Schmit, S., (2012b, November). *Head Start participants, programs, families and staff in 2011*. Washington, DC: CLASP.

Schweinhart, L. J. (2006). The High/Scope approach: Evidence that participatory learning in early childhood contributes to human development. In N. F. Watt, C. Ayoub, R. H. Bradley, J. E. Puma & W. A. LeBoeuf (Eds.), *The crisis in youth mental health* (pp. 207–227). Westport, CT: Praeger.

Schweinhart, L. J., Weikart, D. P., & Larner, M. B. (1986). Consequences of three preschool curriculum models through age 15. *Early Childhood Research Quarterly*, **1**, 15–45.

Seitz, V., & Provence, S. (1990). Caregiver focused models of early intervention. In J. Shonkoff & S. Meisels (Eds.), *Handbook of early childhood intervention* (pp. 400–427). New York: Cambridge University Press.

Seitz, V., Rosenbaum, L. K., & Apfel, N. H. (1985). Effects of family support intervention: A ten-year follow up. *Child Development*, **56**, 376–391.

Shadish, W. R., Cook, T. D., & Campbell, D. T. (2002). *Experimental and quasi-experimental designs for generalized causal inference*. New York: Houghton-Mifflin Co.

Shonkoff, J. P. (2011). Protecting brains, not simply stimulating minds. *Science*, **333**(6045), 982–983.

Shrout, P. E., & Fleiss, J. L. (1979). Intraclass correlations: Uses in assessing rater reliability. *Psychological Bulletin*, **86**, 420–428.

St. Pierre, R. G., Goodson, B., Layzer, J., & Bernstein, L. (1994). *National evaluation of the Comprehensive Child Development Program: Report to Congress.* Cambridge, MA: Abt Associates.

St. Pierre, R. G., Goodson, B., Layzer, J., & Bernstein, L. (1997). *National impact evaluation of the Comprehensive Child Development Program: Final report.* Cambridge, MA: Abt Associates.

Stipek, D. J., & Ryan, R. H. (1997). Economically disadvantaged preschoolers: Ready to learn but further to go. *Developmental Psychology, 33,* 711–723.

Sweet, M., & Appelbaum, M. (2004). Is home visiting an effective strategy? A meta-analytic review of home visiting programs for families with young children. *Child Development, 75,* 1436–1456.

Thoits, P. A. (2006). Personal agency in the stress process. *Journal of Health and Social Behavior, 47,* 309–323.

U.S. Department of Health and Human Services, Office of Human Development Services. (1990, September). *Head Start research and evaluation: A blueprint for the Future; recommendations of the Advisory Panel for the Head Start Evaluation Design Project.* Washington, DC: U.S. Department of Health and Human Services.

U.S. Department of Health and Human Services. (1994, September). *The statement of the Advisory Committee on Services for Families with Infants and Toddlers.* Washington, DC: U.S. Department of Health and Human Services.

U.S. Department of Health and Human Services, ACF. (2005, May). *Head Start Impact Study: First year findings.* Washington, DC: U.S. Department of Health and Human Services.

Wagner, M. M., & Clayton, S. L. (1999). The Parents as Teachers Program: Results from two demonstrations. *The Future of Children, 9*(1), 91–115.

Wen, X., Leow, C., Hahs-Vaughn, D. B., Korfmacher, J., & Marcus, S. M. (2011). Are two years better than one year? A propensity score analyses of the impact of Head Start program duration on children's school performance in kindergarten. *Early Childhood Research Quarterly, 27,* 684–694.

Williams, K. T., & Wang, J. J. (1997). *Technical References to the Peabody Picture Vocabulary Test-Third Edition (PPVT-III).* Bloomington, MN: Pearson Assessments.

Wong, V. C., Cook, T. D., Barnett, S., & Jung, K. (2008). An effectiveness-based evaluation of five state pre-kindergarten programs. *Journal of Policy Analysis and Management, 27,* 122–154.

Woodcock, R. W., & Johnson, M. B. (1990). *Woodcock-Johnson Revised Tests of Achievement.* Itasca, IL: Riverside Publishing.

Woodcock, R. W., & Munoz-Sandoval, A. F. (1996). *Batería Woodcock-Munoz: Pruebas de Aprovechamiento-Revisada.* Itasca, IL: Riverside Publishing.

Zhai, F., Brooks-Gunn, J., & Waldfogel, J. (2011). Head Start and urban children's school readiness: A birth cohort study in 18 cities. *Developmental Psychology, 47,* 134–152.

Zigler, E., Taussig, C., & Black, K. (1992). Early childhood intervention: A promising preventative for juvenile delinquency. *American Psychologist, 47,* 997–1006.

Zigler, E., Gilliam, W. S., & Barnett, W. S. (2011). *The Pre-K Debates: Current controversies and issues.* Baltimore, MD: Paul H. Brookes Publishing.

Zill, N. (1999). The role of kindergarten in promoting educational quality and excellence. In R. Pianta & M. Cox (Eds.), *The transition to kindergarten.* Baltimore, MD: Brookes Publishing Company.

ACKNOWLEDGMENTS

The The findings reported here are based on research conducted as part of the national Early Head Start Research and Evaluation Project funded by the Administration for Children and Families (ACF), U.S. Department of Health and Human Services under Contract DHHS-105-95-1936, Task Order No. 32, and Contract 282-98-0021, to Mathematica Policy Research, Inc., Princeton, NJ, and grants for data collection with 15 university research partners. The EHS Research Consortium consists of representatives from 17 programs participating in the evaluation, 15 local research teams, the evaluation contractors, and ACF. Research institutions in the Consortium (and principal researchers) include: ACF (Rachel Chazan-Cohen, Judith Jerald, Esther Kresh, and Helen Raikes); Catholic University of America (Michaela Farber, Harriet Liebow, Nancy Taylor, Elizabeth Timberlake, and Shavaun Wall); Columbia University (Lisa Berlin, Christy Brady-Smith, Pia Rebello-Britta, Coleen O'Neal, Magdelina Hernandez, Jeanne Brooks-Gunn, Rebecca C. Fauth, Alison Fuligni, Anne Martin, and Rebecca Ryan); Harvard University (Catherine Ayoub, Barbara Alexander Pan, and Catherine Snow); Iowa State University (Gayle Luze and Carla Peterson); Mathematica Policy Research (Kimberly Boller, Cheryl DeSaw, Ellen Eliason Kisker, John M. Love, Welmoet van Kammen, Susan Sprachman, and Cheri Vogel); Medical University of South Carolina (Richard A. Faldowski and Gui-Young Hong); Michigan State University (Holly Brophy-Herb, Hiram Fitzgerald, and Rachel Schiffman); New York University (Mark Spellmann and Catherine Tamis-LeMonda); NPC Research (Beth Green); University of Arkansas (Robert Bradley, Andrea Hart, Mark Swanson, Leanne Whiteside-Mansell); University of California at Los Angeles (Carollee Howes and Alison Wishard Guerra); University of Colorado Health Sciences Center (Robert Emde, Kevin Everhart, Mary Maguire Klute, Jon Korfmacher, Jini Puma, JoAnn Robinson, Jeffrey Shears, and Norman Watt); University of Kansas (Jane Atwater, Judith

Correspondence concerning this monograph should be addressed to John M. Love, 1016 Canyon Park Drive, Ashland, OR 97520, email: jlove@mind.net

155

Carta; and Jean Ann Summers); University of Missouri-Columbia (Mark Fine, Jean Ispa, and Kathy Thornburg); University of Pittsburgh (Carol McAllister); University of Washington School of Education (Eduardo Armijo and Joseph Stowitschek); University of Washington School of Nursing (Kathryn Barnard and Susan Spieker); Utah State University (Gina Cook and Lori Roggman).

The authors thank staff members at the 17 Early Head Start programs involved in the study as well as all the children and families who agreed to participate over time. We are also grateful to Mariel Quinones Braun, Joanna DeWolfe, Jessica Mills and Sherri Lundell O'Shea of Xtria, and Anna Keleman of Columbia University for their editorial assistance; and to Anne Bloomenthal, Emily Moiduddin, Xiaofan Sun, and Yange Xue of Mathematica for their extensive analytic support.

The content of this publication does not necessarily reflect the views or policies of the Department of Health and Human Services, nor does mention of trade names, commercial products, or organizations imply endorsement by the U.S. Government.

CONTRIBUTORS

Jeanne Brooks-Gunn, Ph.D. is the Virginia and Leonard Marx Professor of Child Development and Education at Teachers College and the College of Physicians and Surgeons at Columbia University, and she directs the National Center for Children and Families (www.policyforchildren.org). She is interested in environmental, biological, and psychological factors that contribute to children's well-being. She is a member of the Institute of Medicine of the National Academies and the National Academy of Education. She has received the policy award from SRCD and was co-editor of their *Social Policy Report.*

Rachel Chazan-Cohen, Ph.D., is Associate Professor of Applied Developmental Psychology at George Mason University. Previously, she was the coordinator of infant and toddler research in the Office of Planning, Research, and Evaluation in the Administration for Children and Families, U.S. Department of Health and Human Services. She is particularly interested in the biological, relational, and environmental factors influencing the development of at-risk children, and most especially, on the creation, evaluation, and refinement of intervention programs for families with infants and toddlers.

Richard A. Faldowski, Ph.D., is Associate Professor, Human Development and Family Studies, University of North Carolina at Greensboro. His work includes dual emphases on research design and quantitative analysis of longitudinal evaluations of intervention programs, as well as the use of empirical findings to improve treatment and prevention program practice. Of particular importance, within these interests, are programs and services for children and families placed at risk by health, poverty, abuse, and other psychosocial circumstances.

Ellen Eliason Kisker, Ph.D., is President and Managing Partner of Twin Peaks Partners, LLC. She provides research and technical support for rigorous evaluations of education and human services programs, particularly those serving young children and their families. She played a key role in designing and conducting the national evaluation of Early Head Start, has served as a principal investigator leading the review of the effectiveness of early childhood education interventions and the review of early childhood education interventions for children with disabilities for the What Works Clearinghouse, and is currently providing analytical and technical support for research being conducted by several Regional Educational Labs.

Mary Maguire Klute, Ph.D., is the Director of Research and Evaluation at the Buechner Institute for Governance in the School of Public Affairs, University of Colorado, Denver. Her research interests include the examination of preventive interventions to support children's social and emotional development and school readiness, with a focus on children living in poverty. Much of her current work also focuses on how early childhood education programs can use data for quality improvement.

John M. Love, Ph.D., retired as senior fellow at Mathematica Policy Research in 2010 and now provides consultation on program evaluation and early childhood policy issues to state and county agencies. He is president of the Ashland Institute for Early Childhood Science and Policy. In addition to directing the Early Head Start national evaluation contract from his inception, he has studied Head Start, preschool, and child care programs since the early 1970s.

Anne Martin, Dr.P.H., is Senior Research Scientist at the National Center for Children and Families at Teachers College, Columbia University. Her research focuses on disadvantaged young children and their home and child care environments.

Helen Raikes, Ph.D., is Willa Cather Professor and Professor, Child, Youth and Family Studies, University of Nebraska-Lincoln. Her research has focused on infants, toddlers and preschool age children at greatest risk, early language and social emotional development, and on parenting with an emphasis on understanding influences on the developmental trajectories of vulnerable children that are amenable to intervention. Another strand of research focuses on state and federal programs and policies that affect young children's developmental outcomes. She was a SRCD Social Policy Fellow at the Administration on Children, Youth and Families when the Early Head Start Research and Evaluation Study began.

Cheri A. Vogel, Ph.D., is a Senior Researcher at Mathematica Policy Research. Her work focuses on early childhood education and programs that serve young children and their families. She has been involved in many aspects of research in Early Head Start and currently leads the Early Head Start Family and Child Experiences Survey (Baby FACES). Her interests include evaluation of early childhood education programs and developing and adapting infant/toddler measures for use in large-scale research projects.

STATEMENT OF EDITORIAL POLICY

The SRCD *Monographs* series aims to publish major reports of developmental research that generates authoritative new findings and that foster a fresh perspective and/or integration of data/research on conceptually significant issues. Submissions may consist of individually or group-authored reports of findings from some single large-scale investigation or from a series of experiments centering on a particular question. Multiauthored sets of independent studies concerning the same underlying question also may be appropriate. A critical requirement in such instances is that the individual authors address common issues and that the contribution arising from the set as a whole be unique, substantial, and well integrated. Manuscripts reporting interdisciplinary or multidisciplinary research on significant developmental questions and those including evidence from diverse cultural, racial, and ethnic groups are of particular interest. Also of special interest are manuscripts that bridge basic and applied developmental science, and that reflect the international perspective of the Society. Because the aim of the *Monographs* series is to enhance cross-fertilization among disciplines or subfields as well as advance knowledge on specialized topics, the links between the specific issues under study and larger questions relating to developmental processes should emerge clearly and be apparent for both general readers and specialists on the topic. In short, irrespective of how it may be framed, work that contributes significant data and/or extends a developmental perspective will be considered.

Potential authors who may be unsure whether the manuscript they are planning wouldmake an appropriate submission to the SRCD *Monographs* are invited to draft an outline or prospectus of what they propose and send it to the incoming editor for review and comment.

Potential authors are not required to be members of the Society for Research in Child Development nor affiliated with the academic discipline of psychology to submit a manuscript for consideration by the *Monographs*. The significance of the work in extending developmental theory and in contributing new empirical information is the crucial consideration.

Submissions should contain a minimum of 80 manuscript pages (including tables and references). The upper boundary of 150–175 pages is more flexible, but authors should try to keep within this limit. If color artwork is submitted, and the authors believe color art is necessary to the presentation of their work, the submissions letter should indicate that one or more authors or their institutions are prepared to pay the substantial costs associated with color art reproduction. Please submit manuscripts electronically to the SRCD *Monographs* Online Submissions and Review Site (Scholar One) at http://mc.manuscriptcentral. com/mono. Please contact the *Monographs* office with any questions at monographs@srcd.org.

The corresponding author for any manuscript must, in the submission letter, warrant that all coauthors are in agreement with the content of the manuscript. The corresponding author also is responsible for informing all coauthors, in a timely manner, of manuscript submission, editorial decisions, reviews received, and any revisions recommended. Before publication, the corresponding author must warrant in the submissions letter that the study has been conducted according to the ethical guidelines of the Society for Research in Child Development.

A more detailed description of all editorial policies, evaluation processes, and format requirements, is given in the "Guidelines for the Preparation of Publication Submissions," which can be found at the SRCD website by clicking on *Monographs*, or by contacting the editor.

Monographs Editorial Office
e-mail: monographs@srcd.org

Editor, Patricia J. Bauer
Department of Psychology, Emory University
36 Eagle Row
Atlanta, GA 30322
e-mail: pjbauer@emory.edu

Note to NIH Grantees

Pursuant to NIH mandate, Society through Wiley-Blackwell will post the accepted version of Contributions authored by NIH grantholders to PubMed Central upon acceptance. This accepted version will be made publicly available 12 months after publication. For further information, see http://www.wiley.com/go/nihmandate.

SUBJECT INDEX

parenting and home environment, *69*
parent support during play, 71, 90
prekindergarten programs, 13
risk factors, 17
social-emotional development, 67, *68*, 71
spanking, 71, 90
speech problems, 71, 90
trial participants, vii, 3, 136
aggression. *See* behavior problems
attention
    African Americans, 71, 90
    EHS and HS impacts, vii, 90, 138, 139
    lower-risk subgroup, 82

bedtime, regular. *See* parenting characteristics
behavior problems
    African Americans, 71, 90
    center-based programs, 104
    criminal adolescent behavior, 12, 13
    EHS and HS impacts, vii, viii, 27, 51, 90, 114, 120, 133, 134, 137
    formal programs, vii, 114, 135–136, 140
    highest-risk subgroup, 124, 126, 128
    home-based programs, 103
    mixed-approach programs, 105
    parent-child semistructured play, 27–29
    prenatal to age 3 intervention programs, 11–12
    Whites, 71, 90
birth to school entry programs, literature review, 1, 13–15
books in home. *See* parenting characteristics

center-based programs
    academic skills, *99*, 135
    African Americans, 10, 71, 103
    age differences, 106–107, 109
    aggressive behavior, 104, 135
    attendance figures, vii, 8–9
    bedtime, regular, 105
    behavior problems, *99*, 104
    birth to school entry programs, 13–14
    child health and safety, 95, *99*, 105, 107
    cognitive development, 15, 39, 94, *99*, 104–105, 107, 108, 135
    education (parent), 94
    EHS and HS outcomes, 134, 135, 136
    emotional regulation, 95
    family well-being and mental health, *99*, 103
    Hispanics, 10, 65

impact analyses at ages and parents, 36–40, *41–43*
literature review, 1–18, 131–133
measures, 22, *23–26*, 27–32
mediators of impacts, 56–59
participants, vii, 132. *See also* African Americans; Hispanics; Whites
patterns of impacts for programs, 93–109
racial/ethnic diversity, 64–65
research questions, 37–40
response rates/response bias, 32–35
results, 136–138
summarized, vii
education (parent), 10, 16, 19n 4, 32, 34, 48, *50, 53–54,* 65, 71, 94, 129n 16, 135
emergency room visits. *See* child health and safety
emotional development. *See* social–emotional development
employment/job training/self-sufficiency, vii, 3, 16, *26,* 32, 34, *42,* 45–46, 65, *68, 69, 73, 75, 77, 80, 84, 88,* 91, 94, *97, 99,* 103, 104, 105, 106, 107, 108, 129n 16

family well-being and mental health. *See* parenting characteristics
formal programs
    academic skills, 114–116, *115, 119,* 120, *123,* 127
    African Americans, 71, 134
    age differences, 110–129
    attendance figures, vii, 7
    behavior problems, vii, 114, 135–136, 140
    child health, *115*
    defined, 3, 112
    depressive/mental health symptoms, *115,* 116, 118, *119,* 120, *123*
    disability services, 116
    EHS and HS outcomes, 18, 110–129
    family demographic risks, 116–118
    family well-being and mental health, 116, 118 *119,* 120, *123*
    forms of, 8
    highest-risk group, 91–92, 122, *123,* 124, 127
    home environment, *115 119,* 120, *123*
    language development, 118
    learning approaches, *115,* 118 *119, 123*
    literacy skills, 118
    parenting and home environment, *115,* 118, *119,* 120, *123*
    parent-reported aggression, vii
    participation, literature review, 7–10
    prevalence, 7–10
    school readiness, vii, 3
    social-emotional development, 114, *115, 119,* 120, *123,* 124
    special education services, 116

CURRENT

.